MW00700499

Best Wishes
Dec 20 /2017

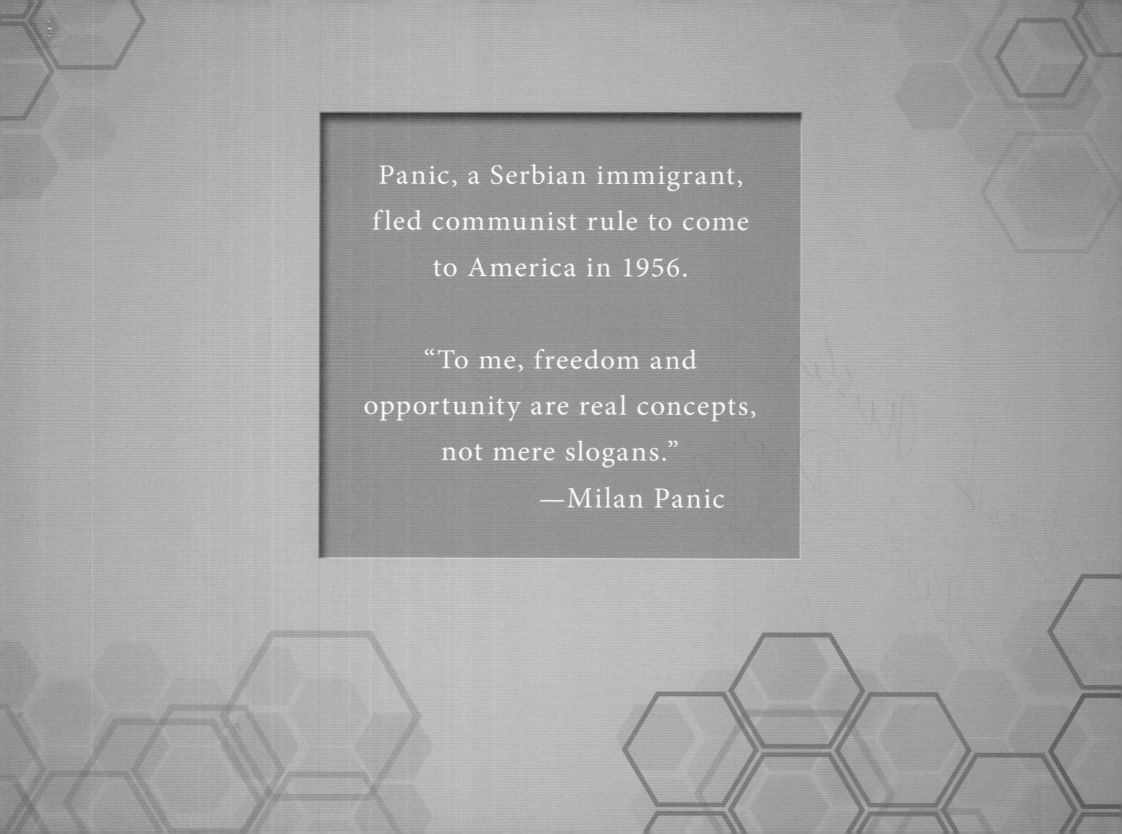

Panic, a Serbian immigrant,
fled communist rule to come
to America in 1956.

"To me, freedom and
opportunity are real concepts,
not mere slogans."

—Milan Panic

WARRIOR CEO

THE REMARKABLE JOURNEY OF MILAN PANIC AND ICN PHARMACEUTICALS

MARK TAYLOR

TAYLOR PUBLISHING LLC
NEWPORT COAST, CA

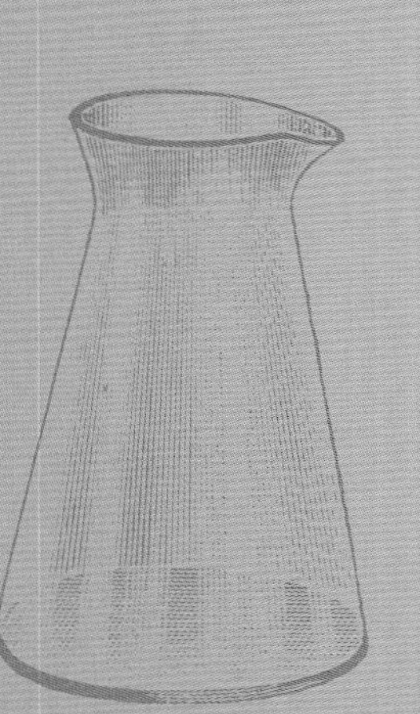

Published by
TAYLOR PUBLISHING LLC
Newport Coast, CA

Publisher's Cataloging-in-Publication Data
Taylor, Mark

Warrior CEO : the remarkable journey of Milan Panic and ICN Pharmaceuticals / Mark Taylor. – Newport Coast, CA : Taylor Pub. LLC, 2019.

p. ; cm.

ISBN13: 978-0-9980219-0-4

1. Panic, Milan, 1929- 2. ICN Pharmaceuticals, Inc.--History. 3. Businessmen--United States--Biography. 4. Pharmaceutical industry--United States--Biography. I. Title.

HD9666.95.P36 T39 2019
338.761615092—dc23 2018904309

Project coordination by Jenkins Group Inc.
www.bookpublishing.com

Design by Yvonne Fetig Roehler

Printed in Malaysia
23 22 21 20 19 • 5 4 3 2 1

CONTENTS

Milan Panic arriving in America from Germany, 1956

INTRODUCTION

My dad's friend Gil Haakh predicted early on that Milan Panic would leave a lasting legacy in the pharmaceutical industry and influence thousands of lives along the way. Mr. Haakh was right. Milan was unique, a larger-than-life force. He was one of those special strangers who comes along and changes your life.

He and my dad were buddies in the '60s. Milan wanted to soak up American life, and Dad was the perfect conduit. As a kid, I remember family BBQs, USC football games, boxing, even the Indianapolis 500. Milan loved to compete. I'd watch him and Dad do battle at tennis, ping-pong, even betting on horses at the track. Dad trained thoroughbreds before becoming a stockbroker and kept his box at Santa Anita Park in Arcadia. I recall tagging along with them a few times when they went to the races. Amazingly, Milan won every race he bet. After the horse crossed the finish line, he would smile, reach into his pocket, and display the winning ticket. Years later, I asked Dad how Milan won all the time. He laughed and told me Milan bet every single horse in the race. Winning was everything to him.

After college, Milan invited me into the company. ICN sponsored an internship program for foreign graduate students, and I was part of it. He loved having smart young people around him. We marveled at his command of the business. In management meetings, he was always five line items ahead of the presenter on every aspect of the business, especially cash flow. He knew the divisions better than the general managers. You better know your numbers or Milan would crush you. He was inspiring. Once he took me to Geneva. I remember joining him at a meeting with lawyers and bankers, mostly all Swiss. I had a tape recorder concealed in my jacket. I wanted to learn, and because all the discussion topics were foreign to me, I would play the tapes later in my hotel room to better understand. But one of the guys saw me turn it on and yelled. Milan just smiled. He was not embarrassed. He quietly told me to put it away and then explained to his guests that I was just a kid trying to learn a few things. The Swiss were not amused. Milan didn't care; he was more proud of my real yearning for his business.

In the mid-'90s, I worked for an investment bank in downtown Los Angeles. A stockbroker named Rafi Khan was plotting to take over ICN. He gathered a large number of institutional votes and was threatening a proxy fight. Milan had always disposed of these adversaries before, but this time he was away, in Yugoslavia as prime minister. I felt the company was vulnerable in his absence. One day I called his office in Belgrade and got right through to him. He was always so happy to hear from me. I tried to warn him that there was this broker named Rafi Khan who I thought possessed the votes to take over ICN. Milan laughed and waved me off. "Mark, thank you for worrying about me, but don't," he said. "I am trying to achieve peace here. Do you think I'm worried for one minute about some stock salesman in Beverly Hills?" I should have known better. Milan came back to ICN a few months later and brazenly ran the advertisement "Don't Be Conned by Khan" in the *Wall Street Journal*. Rafi was toast. ICN then went on to double sales and profits the next three years.

Later that decade, I was running business development for Allen Chao of Watson Pharmaceuticals. Watson was growing at double digits like ICN, and Chao was a Wall Street favorite. In 1999, I encountered Milan at a heath care conference in New York just after his annual meeting at Carnegie Hall. We talked in the hallway, and he asked me whether I had learned enough from Chao to come back to ICN and finally do something for him. I said, "Sure, make me an offer." He said, "If you do well, you can run North America, but you better perform. There's another catch. You must quit Watson tomorrow and be on a plane Friday for Montenegro. We have our five-year planning meeting." He said if I could get to Budapest by mid-Friday, I could fly with him the rest of the way. I made it.

En route, as the ICN plane flew over Belgrade, I wondered for a second whether Yugoslavia's strongman Milosevic, a bitter enemy of Milan's, might push a button below and blow us out of the sky. Crazy as it sounds, it was 1999, and Serbia was a war zone. I looked over at Bill MacDonald, who seemed to be thinking the same thing. Then Milan entered the cabin smiling, and it was all OK. We landed in Montenegro 30 minutes later and joined 200 ICN executives from around the world who had made similar treks. The meeting was held at an old spa and wellness resort in Igalo, near Dubrovnik on the Adriatic. I asked why Igalo, of all places and was told it used to be Marshall Tito's summer home. Well, that explained it. Life was never dull at ICN Pharmaceuticals!

In 2001, I was running the company's North American business, and we acquired a business in Wales. Not much was going on in Swansea those days, so the acquisition made big news. Months later, Prince Charles invited Milan and me to join other business leaders who had also made investments in Wales. We were to have dinner at his Highgrove Estate. I was beside myself. Milan, however, could care less. He didn't like princes. On the day of the event, he was in London closing a deal, and I practically begged him to get in the car to make the four-hour drive. He complained the whole way. Finally, he looked at the seating chart and noticed he was next to Camilla. "Who's she?" he asked. I laughed to myself and thought, *vintage MP*. I answered him and told him not to worry: "She's supposed to be funny. You'll both be a hit." They were.

In 2002, Milan was back in a proxy contest, but this time the odds were stacked against him. He was 72. I remember going to see ICN's largest institutional shareholder, ironically another good friend of my dad's. I figured I could talk him into voting for management and finally give Milan something back for all that he had done for me over the years. Unfortunately, there would be no proxy card for MP this time. My heart sank. I felt I had failed him. This was really the end of the Panic era at ICN, and I of all people was the bearer of bad news. I went back to the Waldorf with my head down. He was in the Bull and Bear with a bunch of people. I slipped in and tried to quietly take a seat. Within seconds Milan bellowed out, "Mark did you bring back the votes?" I apologized and shook my head no. But rather than get mad, he smiled. He held up his glass of wine and uttered his trademark statement: "Well, it could be worse." Then he said, "Let's toast." We all laughed while crying inside. He then asked who at the table could help him prepare a résumé. In all his life, he had never written one. We laughed again. That was the Milan we all knew and loved. Our Warrior CEO!

> Rather than get mad, he smiled.
> He held up his glass of wine and uttered his
> trademark statement: "Well, it could be worse."

Milan Panic, Warrior CEO

1960–1969

- December 7, 1960—International Chemical & Nuclear (ICN) incorporated under the laws of California. Roberts A. Smith, PhD, professor of chemistry at UCLA, elected to serve alongside Milan Panic as director.
- July 15, 1961—Operations begin after the receipt of $110K in contributed capital from private investors led by Donat R. Richards, MD, who purchased 110K common shares at $1 per share.
- November 1961—ICN begins manufacturing products. First-year sales $8K with operating loss of $34K.
- August 2, 1962—ICN issues shares to acquire Bio-Nuclear Inc. and Bio-Zyme Inc. Company conducts first equity sale of common stock to public via Registration A offering, led by First Citizens Bank. ICN raises $180K.
- August 2, 1962—Key executives Weldon Jolley, PhD; Velimar Cubrilovic; and Richard Fallis join the company. Jolley elected to board of directors.
- October 26, 1963—Space Ventures issues ICN a $150K note at 8.5% interest, convertible into 37,500 shares. ICN's first debt financing.
- 1963—ICN achieves first annual profits of $21K on sales of $248K, or $0.05/share.
- 1963—Dan H. Campbell, PhD, professor of immunochemistry at Caltech, elected to ICN Board of Directors.
- November 24, 1964—ICN grants a one-for-four reverse stock split.
- 1966—ICN creates the Nucleic Acid Research Institute (NARI) under the direction of Dr. Alvin Glasky and Dr. Lionel Simon.
- 1966—ICN buys 84% of US Nuclear.
- 1967—ICN exceeds $1M in annual sales for the first time.
- July 18, 1967—Eastman Dillon closes private placement of 25K ICN shares at $40. Proceeds $1M.
- September 1967—ICN enters pharma business via purchase of United Laboratories.
- January 17, 1968—Eastman Dillon sells 175K shares at $40. ICN buys all shares of Strong Cobb Arner and Strong Cobb Arner Canada from Foremost-McKesson for cash of $5.9M.
- 1968—Herbert S. Lightstone joins ICN from Syntex. Assumes new post of VP Corporate Development.
- 1968—Stock price range $46–$121. ICN's earnings continue to double year-on-year.
- October 1968—ICN moves headquarters to 171 Lake Street, Pasadena, California.
- December 8, 1968—ICN buys Laboratorios Servet S.A., Mexico City, renamed ICN Mexico. First international subsidiary.
- 1968—ICN buys Rawson Drug and Sundry from Foremost Mckesson.
- 1968—Sales $41.2M, EPS $0.65. Declares a two-for-one split.
- 1969—ICN buys Comptoir de la Parfumerie in Geneva.
- 1969—Sales increased to $83.1M, up 101%. EPS doubled to $1.30 from $0.65. Fifth consecutive year that ICN doubled EPS over preceding year.
- 1969—ICN buys Nutritional Biochemicals, gets L-DOPA.
- 1969—ICN appoints Dr. Roland K. Robins as director of research.
- 1969—ICN lists common stock on the American Stock Exchange.
- 1969—ICN sells 255K shares of International Chemical & Nuclear common stock at $37.50 per share. ICN's first SEC registered common share offering.

THE SIXTIES

ONLY IN AMERICA

Above: Max S. Dunn

ICN®

Left: ICN logo

Right: First management team:
Milan Panic,
Milan Ubavich,
Wilson L. Orr,
Roberts A. Smith,
Harding J. Frindt, and
Stephen P. Wukelich

December 7, 1960—International Chemical & Nuclear (ICN) incorporated under the laws of California.

MILAN PANIC,
President and Chairman
of the Board of Directors

MILAN UBAVICH,
Director, Secretary and Treasurer

WILSON L. ORR, Ph. D.,
Director, Vice President

ROBERT A. SMITH, Ph. D.,
Director

HARDING J. FRINDT,
Director-Marketing

STEPHEN P. WUKELICH,
Director-Sales

GETTING STARTED

In early 1961, Milan Panic convened the first board meeting of International Chemical & Nuclear (ICN) at his home on Orange Grove Boulevard in Pasadena, California. The company had been incorporated in December, and the young biochemist wanted to get operations started. Panic's goal was to build a pharmaceutical company, but first he needed cash flow. He planned to begin by producing radiolabeled research chemicals used in life sciences, a small but growing market. This would generate sales and later provide access to pharmaceutical think tanks for leads on new drugs to develop. First on the agenda that day was the appointment of an R&D committee to advise on product strategy and manufacturing. Producing isotopic compounds was highly specialized. Panic needed the best technical expertise he could find.

Fortunately, ICN's board already included some of the area's top minds in biochemistry. Panic, a Serbian immigrant who fled communist rule to come to America in 1956, had been recruiting candidates for two years while pursuing an advanced degree in chemistry at the University of Southern California (USC).

First on board was his professor, Dr. Norman Kharash. Joining soon after was Roberts A. Smith, PhD, professor of biochemistry at neighboring UCLA. Max S. Dunn, PhD, an expert in amino acid chemistry and dean of UCLA's graduate school, was added a few months later. From Caltech, Panic landed radioisotope experts Peter H. Lowry and Kenneth H. Shaw and a very prestigious board member in Dan H. Campbell, PhD, a professor of immunochemistry and a close collaborator of Nobel Prize winner Linus Pauling. Rounding out the team was Weldon Jolley, PhD, an associate professor of biochemistry at Loma Linda University, who joined the board in 1962 after ICN merged with his company, BIO-ZYME Chemical Corp.

With key advisors in place and the initial business plan approved, Panic went looking for seed money. He presented ICN to an investment club in Glendale, hosted by Donat R. Richards, MD, a local ob-gyn who also taught at USC. In July 1961, the group purchased $110,000 worth of ICN stock at $1 per share. Over the next few years, Dr. Richards would buy more shares at prices up to $1.50 per share, becoming ICN's largest shareholder next to Panic.

Between 1961 and 1966, Panic raised $500,000 in debt and equity at prices between $0.62 and $1.80 per share. In 1962, the company merged with BIO-ZYME . Coinciding with the BIO-ZYME deal was a Reg A stock offering led by First Citizens Bank that raised $180,000. In 1963, ICN issued $150,000 of 8.5% convertible notes to a San Diego–based investment group named Space Ventures. Three years later these notes converted to 187,000 ICN shares. Space Ventures then sold the shares back to Panic, Richards, and other board members.

ICN stock, listed in the OTC pink sheets, traded between $0.62 and $4 per share the first four years. In late 1964, the board granted shareholders a one-for-four stock split, which trimmed total shares outstanding to just 102,000. It would be the first of four stock splits granted that decade. By mid-1966, the share count grew to 165,243 as the company began using common stock as currency to fund acquisitions.

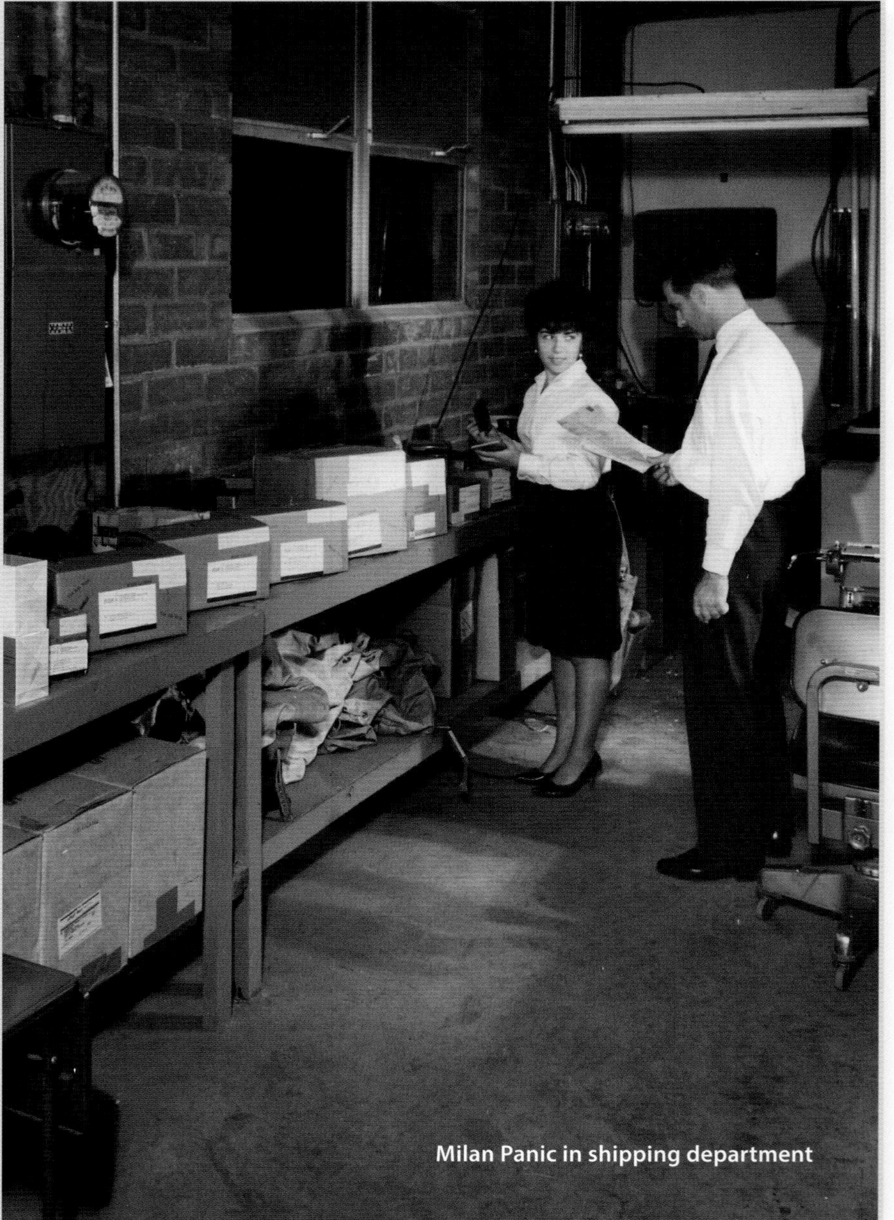

Milan Panic in shipping department

EARLY YEARS

In late 1961, production started at ICN's facility in the City of Industry, California. The company reported a mere $8,000 in revenue its first fiscal year. In 1962, BIO-ZYME added working capital, raw material, a centrifuge to extract DNA, and a small line of radio chemicals. Importantly, the management team expanded, with the addition of Richard Fallis, Velimar Cubrilovic, Joe Fontana, and Fred Andrea. These men were vital to the company's early success and became indispensable to Panic during their many years together.

The product catalog quickly grew. ICN offered a reliable source of more than 5,000 radioactive compounds, tracers, biochemicals, special diets for animals used in research, enzymes, carbohydrates, nucleic acid derivatives, and equipment for radiation detection. By the company's second year, its mailing list exceeded 20,000 customers at leading universities, hospitals, biomedical research facilities, and pharmaceutical discovery labs. Soon, ICN became one of the leading suppliers of deoxyribonucleic acid isolated from salmon sperm. It also added its first pharmaceutical line, IDU, an antiviral agent synthesized in ICN labs and sold directly to physicians for the treatment of herpes simplex keratitis, a virus-induced eye disorder.

As the market for radioactive chemicals grew and more applications evolved in the diagnostic and nuclear medicine fields, ICN found itself besieged with customer requests to synthesize new compounds. Not all were completely legitimate. There was the strange case of the young Berkley chemist Augustus Stanley, of *Electric Kool-Aid Acid Test* fame, who reportedly acquired from ICN a few hundred grams of lysergic acid (LSD), which he claimed was strictly for research purposes. What the famous book describing the counterculture of the '60s doesn't say is that Panic, immediately suspicious of Stanley, alerted the local narcotics bureau and cut him off as a customer.

New England Nuclear and Sigma Chemical were just forming, so ICN had a slight head start in the market. By 1965, the company was manufacturing as many as 500 organic chemicals labeled with carbon-14 and more than 100 labeled with hydrogen-3 (tritium). The radiochemical line included compounds labeled with sulfur-35, phosphorous-32, chlorine-36, nitrogen-15, carbon-113, oxygen-18, and deuterium. Additional isotope capacity needed to be secured by leasing a reactor at the State University of New York at Buffalo on a time-sharing basis.

Panic micromanaged every aspect of company operations. Working six days a week and 18 hours a day, he could be found in the lab or shipping department, on the phone to customers, or representing the company at trade shows. At night, he would review every order and bill of material to ensure that each compound was produced profitably. Making money was about cost and yield, and Panic proved to be a shrewd operator with a keen sense of business. In 1963, he reported to shareholders ICN's first profit of $21,191, on sales of $248,053. By 1965, sales grew to $413,000 and profits to $40,659.

BIO-ZYME CHEMICAL CORP.
(a California Corporation)
100,000 Shares
COMMON STOCK
$2.00 Par Value

First ICN company photo

Earnings per share doubled to $0.08. ICN's thinly traded stock started to react, although it was subject to huge price swings given the tiny float. By the end of 1966, ICN traded at $19 per share.

Success only drove Panic harder. He figured research chemicals were, at best, a $30-million-a-year market, but with Sigma and New England Nuclear on the rise, the most share ICN could hope for was 20%. That business wasn't big enough. ICN's future required blockbuster new drugs, the lifeblood of the pharmaceutical industry. This was Panic's founding mission, the reason the scientists and advisors joined him in the first place. Everyone believed modified nucleic acids and their derivatives would unleash the next frontier of medicine. It was time to execute part two of the plan and develop patented prescription drugs. Syntex had its niche in steroids and birth control. ICN would find its niche in antiviral and anticancer compounds, all derived from the constituents of DNA and RNA.

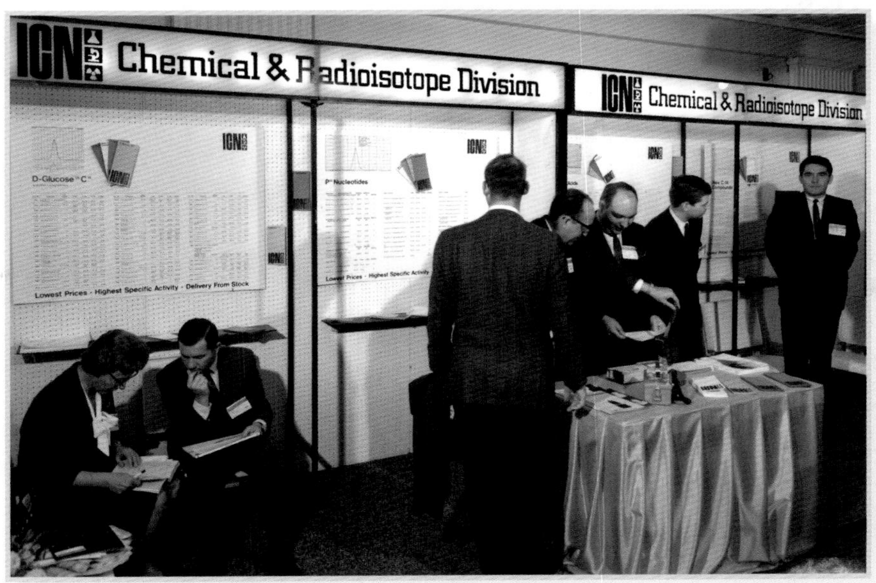

> ICN would find its niche in antivirals and anticancers, all derived from the constituents of DNA and RNA.

Above and right: ICN at trade shows

SUNDAY TRIBUNE for Dec. 31, 1961

Valley Profiles

Milan Panic

By Tony Potter

With the coming of the New Year, thoughts of the international struggle loom before us . . .and of the Berlin wall and the prison of tyranny it symbolizes. But there is also hope — hope for freedom, peace and opportunity.

Milan Panic (pronounced "pon-each") is a particularly significant figure as we start off the new year. He is a symbol of hope — and of opportunity fulfilled.

Five years ago he was trapped in a Communist state. He is from Belgrade, Yugoslavia. Today, at 32, he is president of the International Chemical and Nuclear Corporation in the City of Industry.

★

HIS METEORIC rise is no accident. It is the result of aggressiveness, brains, and the will to never let up short of his goal.

Hard work and hard sports molded his character (or, rather, were an outgrowth of it).

He became an expert cross-country skier and cyclist. Cycling is one of the most popular sports in Europe. National teams travel all over the world to compete. This gave Panic his chance to escape. He was the top cyclist in Yugoslavia and traveled with the Yugoslav team.

★

"I WAS very well known and was on my way to race in Holland when I escaped. I received political asylum in Neuremburg."

Cross-out the picture of the spectacular ecsape. . .the chase in the murky night. . .a figure, jumping over a wall. That's not how Panic escaped.

"I took a taxi and left," he said calmly.

"I thought I was in great danger, but fortunately I was too little a bird. Also I think the Yugoslavian government kept it quiet because I was well known and it would have been bad publicity for them."

★

PANIC SAYS Yugoslavia is "just as bad as other Communist countries." He is also violently against any kind of aid to Communist bloc countries (and made a brusque, disapproving reference to U.S. jet planes going to Yugoslavia).

"I do not think Tito's regime will change," Panic said. "An example of the harassed and restricted life there is the opening of mail. All letters going in and out of the country are censored."

In Germany, Panic won a scholarship to Heidelburg where he earned his Ph.D. He came directly from Heidelburg to Fontana, Calif., where he had distant relatives and got a job at Kaiser Steel. He worked there from midnight to 8 a.m., in the daytime traveled 60 miles each way to study chemistry at USC. He then won a fellowship to study as the assistant to Dr. Norman Kirasch (a top man in the biochemical field) and there gained the knowledge and contacts needed to start the company.

"Twenty five scientists now work with me," Panic said. "Many were my professors."

★

THE COMPANY (International Chemical and Nuclear Corp.) specializes in producing radioactive biochemicals for medical and chemical research.

"We believed we had enough technical know-how to start the company. It was just a matter of finding the business to back it," he said.

Referring to his success, Panic said, "It's simply a matter of work and not giving up . . . and then just a matter of time."

The phone rang interrupting his conversation . . . a call from St. Louis. Panic completed an expensive order.

"I'm no salesman," he said after hanging up, "but, you know, you can always sell the better cheese if the people know it's better."

Of his newly adopted country the young scientist says, "Everything is here . . . the opportunity is here. No other country can offer such opportunity to the man who is willing to work."

Milan Panic is willing to work. He has taken advantage of his opportunities — and at times made them.

Left:
First article about Milan Panic, 1961

Top middle:
George Renne

Top right:
Bernard Segal

Bottom right:
ICN's first R&D committe:
Dan H. Campbell, Weldon B. Jolley, Roberts A. Smith, Kenneth Shaw, and Roland K. Robins

research and development committee

A Special Research and Development Committee is the governing body for all development carried on by the ICN staff.

These eminent scientists bring to ICN a wealth of knowledge and experience in biochemistry, immunochemistry, experimental medicine and organic chemistry.

Some of the research projects under consideration by this group are antimetabolities, antiradiation therapy and standardization of tissue culture media. The Research and Development group is available for staff consultation at all times.

CHAIRMAN
DAN H. CAMPBELL, Ph.D.
Professor of Immunochemistry, California Institute of Technology, Pasadena

THEODORE GEISSMAN Ph.D.
Professor of Chemistry, University of California, Los Angeles

WELDON B. JOLLEY, Ph.D.
Associate Professor of Biochemistry, Loma Linda University, Loma Linda

ROBERTS A. SMITH Ph.D.
Associate Professor of Chemistry, University of California, Los Angeles

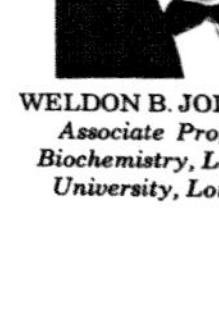

KENNETH SHAW, Ph.D.
Director of Clinical Research Laboratory, Children's Hospital, Los Angeles

ROLAND K. ROBINS Ph.D.
Professor of Chemistry, Arizona State University, Tempe, Arizona

RIBAMINOL

The board authorized a three-step plan. First, the company would create a nucleic acid chemistry unit to screen for new drug targets. Second, based on the potential of those candidates, it would raise institutional capital on Wall Street to fund clinical development. And third, once funding was committed, the company would make acquisitions in the drug sector to grow revenue, provide cash flow for R&D, and add marketing and distribution for the new products. All Panic needed now was experienced management, a profitable base business, and at least one exciting new compound in the pipeline. With that, he figured, the stock would take care of itself.

Building a functional corporate team was the easy part. Lured by Panic's magnetism and sensing an exciting opportunity, executives came knocking. George Renne, a financial VP at Beckman Instruments, joined the board to advise on finance and accounting. William Rhame, former president of Texstar, headed up corporate strategy and became the principal deal finder. Panic's personal lawyer Bernard Segal functioned as general counsel, and Gilbert Haakh, a top Los Angeles–based SEC attorney, was engaged to advise on securities law. Panic moved headquarters to a sleek one-story building on Lake Avenue in Pasadena, right across from United California Bank.

In May 1966, the transformation began with the opening of the Nucleic Acid Research Institute (NARI). Its charter was to discover new drug targets that could become effective agents in treating cancer, viruses, and neurological disorders. Advancements in biotechnology had armed researchers with a much deeper understanding of how DNA and RNA regulate and control cell function. NARI would provide its scientists the infrastructure, staffing, and tools to effectively screen thousands of pharmacologically active substances for biological activity. Only the most promising would be selected for clinical development.

The institute's first director was the renowned biochemist Alvin J. Glasky, PhD, who gained his fame at Abbott Laboratories by developing the memory-enhancing pill Cylert. Starting in a trailer outside ICN's manufacturing facility, Glasky and Dr. Lionel Simon synthesized ribaminol, a diethylaminoethanol derivative of RNA that was more potent than Cylert in stimulating protein synthesis in the brain. Dubbed "the smart pill," its discovery was big news to local business writers, OTC traders, and speculators. ICN's quarterly earnings were advancing at the same time. Investors suddenly had both an earnings play and the dazzle of a wonder drug to keep them excited. Shares rallied even higher.

Alvin J. Glasky

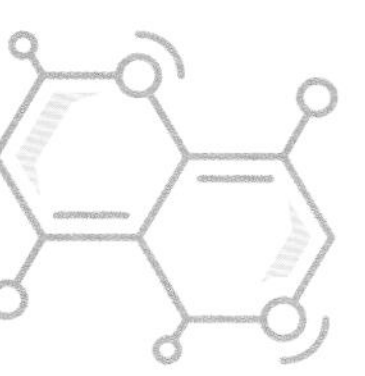

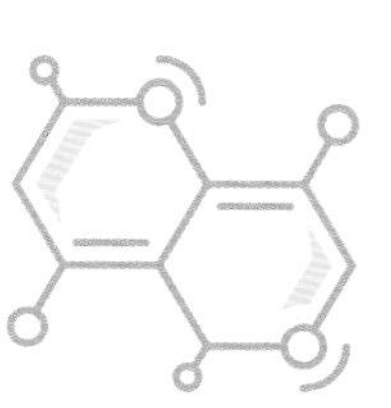

Top left: Milan Panic holding first checks from Eastman Dillon

Top right: Milan Panic using stock in lieu of cash to buy a company

Left: Milan Panic with Dwight C. Baum

EASTMAN DILLON

ICN's breakout year came in 1967. The stock was in the 40s largely on ribaminol hype, and new acquisitions were being announced once a month. Sales, barely $1 million at the start of the year, would rise to $3.5 million by year's end, with earnings advancing even faster to $0.16 per share. Five deals inked back-to-back made this happen.

First was Chem-Trac, a division of Baird-Atomic. Immediately following were Volk Radiochemical Corporation, a division of U.S. Nuclear Corporation, the Applied Nucleonics Corporation, the Nuclear Science & Engineering Corporation, and Environmental Sciences Inc. While small, each was profitable and contributed to a growing research chemical division. And because ICN's stock price was so high, Panic could exchange fewer shares for the business and gain incremental earnings per share through consolidation, a concept known as accretion. He would become a master at this.

But Panic was far from satisfied. He and Rhame failed to close their first pharma deal. Opportunities existed, but prices were out of reach. ICN needed Wall Street. Finding an investment banker who could raise serious institutional money became imperative.

Two Los Angeles–based stockbrokers from Eastman Dillon, Union Securities & Co. made this happen. Tom Taylor and Dominic Liuzzi had been positioning ICN stock for clients since 1965 and were close to Panic. In early 1967, they set him up with Eastman's New York–based pharmaceutical analyst Arthur Rausch, who reluctantly took a quick breakfast meeting at a Denny's restaurant in Covina, California, to hear the story. Panic arrived ready to sell. Soon after, an enthusiastic Rausch was on the phone with senior banker Dwight C. Baum to arrange a follow-up. In July, Eastman underwrote ICN's first private placement, a 25,000 share offering to a small group of institutions at $40 per share. Gerald "Jerry" Tsai Jr., the famed mutual fund manager at Fidelity Management, was in for an allocation, as was Seth H. Baker, a partner in the respected New York brokerage firm DeCoppet and Doremus. Baker and Baum would join ICN's board, with Baker chairing the newly created finance committee. Analysts published research reports, and institutional investors such as Tsai began monitoring the company's every move. ICN was on the map.

Eastman Dillon's Tom Taylor

Top left: 10 years after arriving in the United States, Milan Panic buys Pasadena Estate in forclosure for under $200k

Bottom left: Milan Panic speaks at Pasadena Bond Club, October 2, 1967

Bottom middle: ICN buys Strong Cobb Arner from Foremost-McKesson

Right: Financial writer Alex Campbell writes about ICN

PASADENA BOND CLUB
Oldest Bond Club on the Pacific Coast
Organized 1921

1000 EAST GREEN STREET
PASADENA, CALIFORNIA 91101

MONDAY, OCTOBER 2, 1967

HUNTINGTON-SHERATON

LUNCHEON - 12:30 SHARP

GUEST SPEAKER - MILAN PANIC

PRESIDENT & DIRECTOR

INTERNATIONAL CHEMICAL & NUCLEAR

Through the efforts of Tom Taylor, we are very fortunate to have as our guest speaker, MILAN PANIC, President of International Chemical & Nuclear, one of the outstanding young companies in the field of radioactive chemicals, radiation instruments, and pharmaceuticals.

Mr. Panic was born in Belgrade, Yugoslavia, on December 20, 1929. He attended the University of Belgrade from 1949 to 1955, where he received his B. A. degree. In 1955 he went to the University of Heidelberg, Germany, for post graduate study.

Arriving in U. S. A. in 1956, and Los Angeles in particular, he started work as a chemist for Cyclo-Chem Corp. From 1957 to 1958 he was Research Assistant in the Department of Chemistry at the University of California. From 1958 to 1960 Mr. Panic was involved in research work including studies in cancer therapy.

Since 1960 he has been president and director of International Chemical & Nuclear Corp., located at City of Industry in California. Sales and earnings, which last year were in excess of $670,000 and 80 cents per share respectively, have continued to climb this year. If you have missed the market action of this issue in recent months, now is your chance to become "abreast of the action" and learn the underlying reasons for this movement and the outlook for the Company.

Mr. Panic is married, has four children, and resides in Pasadena.

Make reservations early.

GEORGE R. FROST
Program Chairman

ICN Buys Pharmaceutical Unit of Foremost-M'Kesson

International Chemical & Nuclear Corp. became the largest company of its type in the West this week with the acquisition of Strong-Cobb-Arner, Inc., a Cleveland based pharmaceutical division of Foremost-McKesson Inc.

The acquisition, for an undisclosed amount of cash approximating Foremost-McKesson's investment, is the fourth acquisition by ICN this year and a major step in the company's program to diversify further into the pharmaceutical field.

In making the announcement, ICN president Milan Panic revealed that Strong-Cobb-Arner has plants in Cleveland; Murray Hills, N.J.; Sun Valley, Calif.; and Fort Erie, Canada. SCA is a major manufacturer of custom pharmaceutical products.

Consummation of the sale is subject to ICN's making the necessary financial arrangements and the approval of the Federal Trade Commission.

Foremost Dairies, predecessor to Foremost-McKesson, originally acquired Strong-Cobb-Arner in 1956 for approximately $15 million in cash and debentures and agreed to dispose of it under terms of an FTC consent order prior to Foremost's merger with McKesson & Robbins in July of this year.

Sales of Strong-Cobb-Arner have not been released since 1965 when they stood at $11 million. Strong-Cobb-Arner has 600 employes and ICN has 250. ICN will operate Strong-Cobb-Arner as an independent subsidiary.

International Chemical & Nuclear within the last 11 months has acquired: Nuclear Science & Engineering of Pittsburgh, Pa. and U. S. Nuclear Corp., United Laboratories and Technical Associates, all here in California.

MARKET Comment

ALEX N. CAMPBELL, Financial Editor

'Memory Pill' Makes ICN Stock Volatile

INTERNATIONAL Chemical and Nuclear (over-the-counter) has been jumping all over the board during the past few sessions. In fact, in one session the price jumped from $22 to $27½ and back down to $22. At the moment we hesitate to quote a price because of the action.

For those of you who follow this column you will remember that we wrote about this company last May. The story was unusual, we thought, because of the potential of developing a "smart pill."

The "smart pill" or "memory pill," whichever you prefer, is a drug that increases a person's ability to remember things and also increases ones ability to learn. It has shown a remarkable ability to sharpen the memory of old people who were loosing their ability to remember.

Anyway, yesterday the company announced that the drug in presently undergoing toxicity laboratory testing and it is expected to become "available for clinical testing by the end of March" here in the United States.

We talked with Milan Panic, president of ICN, and asked if there were any plans for marketing the memory pill this year?

Plan Marketing Pill in Europe

He answered that they were projecting marketing plans for the "pill" in Europe this year. He said that was all he could say at this time.

Panic did add, however, that the company had applied for a patent on a new "shock treatment" drug. He believes this drug has quite a future but, of course, nothing like the memory drug.

It was probably the announcement the memory drug was ready for clinical testing that moved the stock but the real purpose of the press release was to announce that the company had acquired U.S. Nuclear Corp. It is in the business of marketing radioactive materials and related radiation detection, mechanical shielding and delivery equipment.

Panic said that U.S. Nuclear product lines complements ICN's own products and will open new industrial and medical markets.

The president also announced that earnings for 1966 reached 80 cents per share or just double the 40 cents reported in 1965.

We asked Panic if he thought the company could keep up this rate of growth during 1967?

Potential Demand 'Just Tremendous'

He answered that he thought they could on their present product line. On the other hand, if and when the memory pill comes to the market then all estimates are off because the potential demand for this drug is "just tremendous."

International Chemical and Nuclear stock is quoted in our over-the-counter list but we would warn again that the market is relatively thin and the market jumps around like a "super ball."

ADDING PHARMA

United Laboratories, a local Pasadena-based maker of injectable antibiotics, veterinary products, and ethical drugs, was for sale. In September 1967, ICN snapped it up for cash and stock. Annual revenue was under $1 million, but at last ICN had a small footprint in pharmaceuticals and was soon on the hunt for bigger prey. The wait was short. Within a month, Rhame and Panic found a big catch, and this one was 10 times ICN's size.

Earlier that year, Foremost Dairies announced it was merging with McKesson & Robbins to form the nation's largest distributor of pharmaceuticals, alcoholic beverages, and chemicals. As a condition to close, however, the Federal Trade Commission insisted Foremost divest its Strong Cobb Arner unit (SCA). SCA was a 135-year old custom pharmaceutical and formulation manufacturer with operations in the United States and Canada. It sold to more than 500 customers and had manufacturing capability in tablets, capsules, liquids, syrups, creams, and sustained-release dosage forms. Its product line included minerals, vitamins, antacids, analgesics, steroids, hormonals, antibiotics, cardiovasculars, thyroid preparations, and dermatologics. ICN had drug discovery and experience in injectables but no capability in either the formulation or GMP production of broad-based pharmaceuticals. SCA was perfect. Panic and Rhame flew to San Francisco to make the pitch.

Rudolph "Rudy" Drews, the parochial CEO of Foremost, put SCA on auction and was negotiating with several interested parties. Bids were due by mid-December. ICN joined the process late and at first was viewed as a long shot. Panic had no record in drugs; the company was still essentially a start-up. And, worse, it was devoid of cash. But Drews liked him. This guy is special, he would tell colleagues. He was willing to bet that Panic would make Foremost money. A bond between the two men quickly developed. ICN's deadline was extended to January.

Back in the office, the team huddled. A secondary offering was out of the question. There wasn't enough time, and ICN had never been through a formal SEC review before. Eastman was engaged again to do a private placement, but this one needed to be four times the size to raise the required $7 million. Fortunately, Blythe's investors made money on the first deal and wanted more stock. It would come down to price.

Luck was on ICN's side. In early November, Panic and the team met with New York investors, including Jerry Tsai, and commitments were

ICN board meeting

reached at $100 per share. However, after factoring in the discount, the stock needed to trade above $120, and it was only $87. Fortunately, Glasky just happened to be in the city at the same time to present ribaminol results to key opinion leaders at the American Psychiatric Association conference at the Roosevelt Hotel. The data showed that rats treated with the drug improved performance by 100% in learning tests. The release drew significant press the next day, including the *Wall Street Journal*. ICN stock flew past $120, and Eastman had its deal.

Prior to close, the board split the stock two-and-a-half-to-one, making the official placement 175,000 shares at $40. ICN took receipt of the $7 million and on the same day purchased all the shares of SCA and its Canadian affiliate for $5.9 million in cash. The new additions contributed annual revenue of $11 million and were profitable. Panic had scored big, and the street responded. Within a week, ICN was back to $60.

Drews and Panic would do a second deal together 12 months later. This time, Foremost took $8 million in ICN stock for Rawson Drug and Sundry, a $25-million-per-year rack jobber that sold and displayed

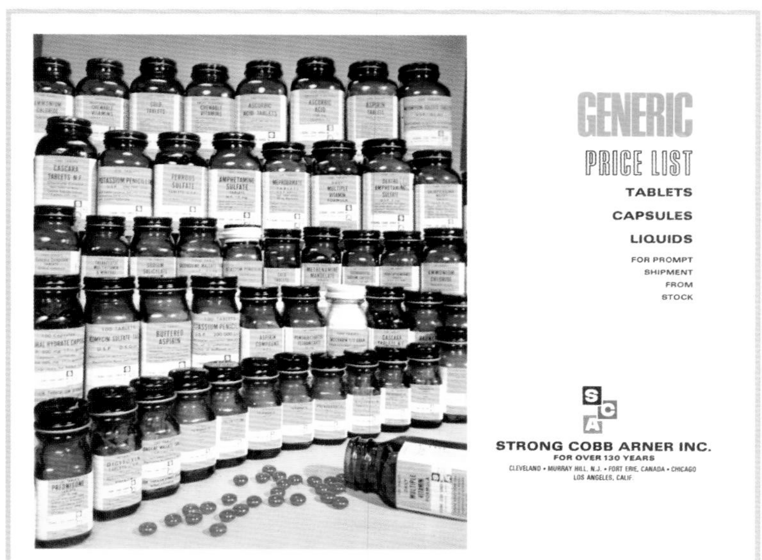

Left: Strong Cobb Arner Inc. generic price list

Above: Milan Panic speaks at Rawson Drug & Sundry Co. sales meeting, Oakland, California

Opposite page, left: Laboratorios Servet women's soccer team

Opposite page, right: Milan Panic in the news

December 8, 1968—ICN acquired its first international company, Laboratorios Servet S.A. in Mexico City, renamed ICN Mexico.

proprietary drugs, generics, and health and beauty aids in supermarkets and drug stores across the United States. While merchandising to retail outlets was not exactly a fit with the company's plans in pharmaceuticals, it provided solid cash flow for research and immediately boosted earnings. Foremost became ICN's largest stockholder, later selling a majority of those shares for a hefty profit in ICN's first SEC-registered offering in 1969.

In 1968, ICN reported $41 million in sales and earnings of $1.1 million. The pharmaceutical division, firmly established with United and SCA, would later add Bentex Pharmaceuticals, a Texas-based direct-mail marketer of branded generics and medical equipment; W.H. King Drug, a Raleigh, North Carolina–based drug and hospital supplier selling to hospitals, drug stores, nursing homes, and office-based physicians in the Carolinas and southern Virginia; and SIG, a direct-to-physician drug detailer acquired from Revlon. All were stock deals. Even Wall Street got to play. Jerry Tsai, eager to add to his ICN position, would negotiate a side deal with Revlon to buy its ICN shares privately.

Later that year, ICN acquired its first international company, Laboratorios Servet S.A. based in Mexico City, for $3.5 million in cash. To finance this deal, ICN borrowed from a foreign subsidiary of United California Bank, issuing a three-year unsecured note payable. Servet was a highly profitable $4-million-per-year domestic manufacturer and marketer of branded pharmaceuticals throughout Mexico and Central America. The deal was strategic inasmuch as the pharma market in Latin America was growing faster than the United States and Servet was a leading company. But there was another reason. Regulators in Mexico and South America approved new drugs faster than the FDA. ICN needed foreign markets to launch NARI products in a timely manner. Ribaminol was the first candidate. Many others would follow.

Yugoslavian Refugee Strikes It Rich Here

By CLAUDIA BIKE
Review Staff Writer

About 12 years ago a 27-year-old student from Yugoslavia who decided he didn't like communism was selected by Vice President Richard Nixon to enter the United States under a prisoners' escape program.

The serious chemistry student continued his studies at the University of Southern California until he spotted an opportunity in private industry. He saw no reliable source for development of nuclear chemicals, so he created one.

Today International Chemical and Nuclear Corporation, founded by president Milan Panic in 1961, has surged forward with multi-million dollar sales and has swallowed up a competitor over three times its size.

In the past three months Panic's company has sold a record $1,308,724 worth of pharmaceutical and radiant chemical products [illegible]

Panic (rhymes with Spanish) who expects as much from his employees as he gives to a job himself.

Panic looks forward to the day when he can press buttons on his desk to control his expanding business. He wants to know when cash is changing hands, who is absent from work and which employees were late.

The tan, blonde-haired president grew up in Yugoslavia, the son of an attorney who by necessity worked for the government. He finds it hard to tell in one sentence why he left the Iron Curtain country.

The company specializes in the area of nucleic acids and is conducting its own research at the new ICN Nucleic Acid Research Institute.

ICN is also developing a line of pharmaceuticals.

Panic started his business with one room and a secretary in Glendale and now has about 10 plants covering over 500,000 square feet. "I want to build a big pharmaceutical and nuclear company," said Panic.

"I must select the right people and the right system," he declared.

Panic, his wife Jelica and their four children, Nicholas,

Profile

When Panic arrived in the United States, he could not speak English. He said he still has some difficulty. Dr. Max S. Dunn, a close friend and vice president at ICN, said, [illegible]

Milan Jr., Dawn and Vivian, ages 6-16, live in Pasadena. Will the children follow in their father's footsteps?

"The company is publicly owned," said Panic. [illegible]

His subsidiaries and [illegible] are organized into four divisions, chemical and radioisotope, instrumental, pharmaceutical and research and development.

In the company's rosy future is a product that can become more earthshaking than "the pill." It is another pill which the corporation is developing which may increase memory abilities.

Ribaminol, a [illegible]

Success brings a smile.

MAINTAINING THE PACE

By 1969, just nine years after reporting $8,000 in first-year sales, ICN had grown to $83 million in annual revenue, $2.8 million in profits, and $0.65 in earnings per share. Profits essentially doubled each year for five consecutive years. The stock, now trading on the American Stock Exchange, reached $200 per share pre-split, with a price earnings multiple ranging between 100 and 200 times earnings. Pooling of interest accounting was still popular, providing ICN plenty of additional firepower. But before the decade could officially wrap, Panic needed to further strengthen the management team and adequately fund R&D to ensure the company's agressive growth ambitions could be met.

Lester Korn, of the executive search firm bearing his name, was hired to recruit executives capable of running a $250-million-a-year global company. Joe Davis from Litton Industries joined as CFO. Herbert Lightstone from Syntex became VP corporate development. John C. Hancock from Cravath, Swaine, and Moore served as general counsel, and Jim Greenwald was hired from the company's auditor Peat Marwick Mitchell to fill the new post of corporate controller.

ICN's JetStar

Bankers were lining up with deals, and Panic kept the company's new 10-seat Lockheed JetStar fueled at Burbank Airport, ready to chase down and close the next acquisition.

CALIFORNIA BUSINESS — March 6, 1968—Page 11

100% rise in earnings seen by ICN

By a Staff Writer

The fast growth pattern followed by International Chemical & Nuclear Corp. since 1964 will continue through 1968, and most likely well beyond, stockholders were told at the company's annual meeting last week.

President Milan Panic first told the stockholders "I'm almost afraid to tell you what to expect this year," but then later in the meeting in response to a question from the floor said ICN would earn about $1.28 a share. That would double last year's 64 cents a share (adjusted for a 5-2 stock split Jan. 15, 1968).

In 1964, the Burbank-based manufacturer of pharmaceutical and radioactive chemical products, lost 57 cents a share. It turned around in 1965, posting earnings of 16 cents a share. In 1966, it earned 32 cents and then, in 1967, 64 cents.

* * *

OVER THE SAME period, sales advanced from $264,614 to $3,557,440. Panic told shareholders sales would exceed $15 million in 1968. Bulk of the new sales and earnings will stem from Strong-Cobb-Arner Co., acquired on Jan. 17, this year from Foremost-McKesson, Inc. in an all-cash transaction.

In response to a stockholder's question, Panic said it was ICN's intention to list its shares on the American Stock Exchange before the end of the year. Currently traded over the counter, ICN stock has moved from $10 a share to its current levels in the low-to-middle $50s between stockholder meetings.

The company's glamour product, a memory-jogging drug, came in for very little discussion at the meeting. In response to a shareholder's question about its progress, Panic said it is "Out of the research stages and in the testing stages." He did not say when test results would be announced.

* * *

PANIC CHARACTERIZED ICN as a "profit-oriented company" whose growth would come from the development of new products, a greater return on existing products and acquisitions.

Asked whether he would consider acquiring companies in non-related fields, Panic said "for the time being we will stay in the pharmaceutical and nuclear field. We have no intention of becoming a conglomerate."

In the perfunctory voting, stockholders elected an 11-man board and adopted management's Qualified Stock Option Plan which sets aside 68,000 shares of stock for officers and key employes.

PIPELINE

Now that ICN had the capital to invest in research, it needed a pipeline—and fast. Roland K. Robins was hired to run NARI, replacing Glasky, who left to start his own venture. Robins was one of the top medicinal chemists in the world, creator of the gout drug allopurinol, and an expert in nucleic acids. In 1969, he moved the operation to a 10-acre, four-building campus in Irvine, California, that Panic and Renne had purchased for $320,000. Within time, NARI's staff grew to 100 scientists, 35 with doctoral degrees. All the key disciplines were represented, including medicinal chemistry, biophysical chemistry, microbiology, organic chemistry, virology, and molecular pharmacology. Robins wanted the largest discovery operation dedicated to nucleic acids and virology in the world. The markets were enormous: viral infections were thought to be responsible for more than 60% of all episodes of human illness. He promised Panic and the board that he would deliver the science and eventually the drugs, but they had to keep the budgets funded.

Panic wanted more. He insisted that NARI advance at least one blockbuster to market by 1975, followed by one new drug per year thereafter. NARI's research expenses would be capitalized on a straight-line basis over a five-year period to minimize the impact on earnings per share. He then promised shareholders that by 1975 ICN would become a $500-million-a-year pharmaceutical company. Future acquisitions would not only be accretive but also add commercial power in the top 15 international markets. Once the United States, Canada, Latin America, and Europe were resourced, he would move to the Far East. As far as Milan Panic was concerned, nothing was out of reach.

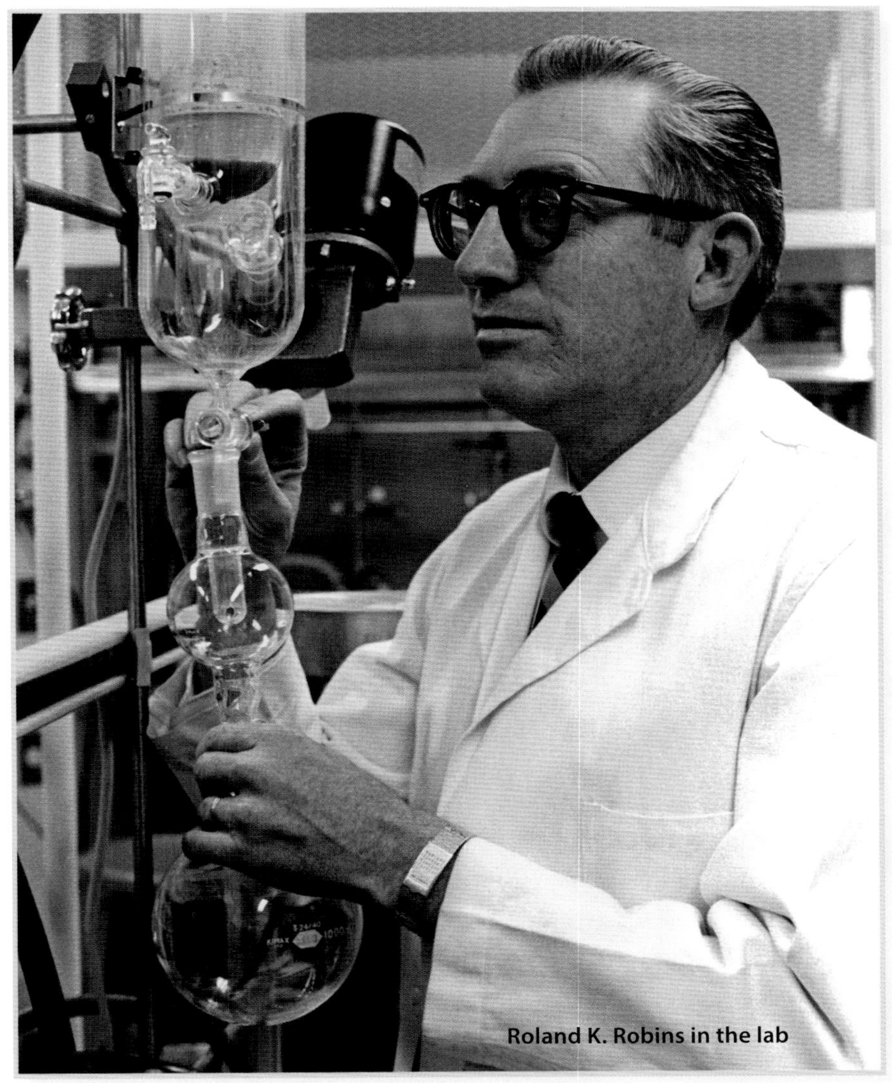
Roland K. Robins in the lab

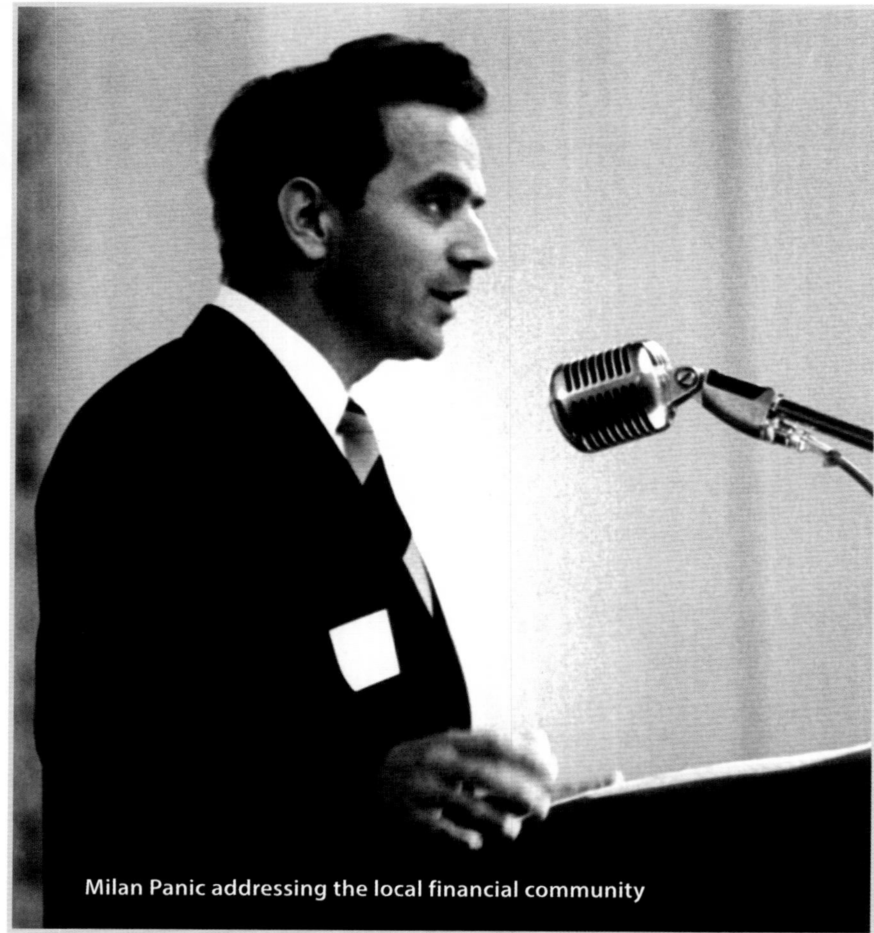

Milan Panic addressing the local financial community

Internally, the board was more cautious. Those who had lived through boom and bust business cycles before knew that the so-called "go-go" years characterizing the '60s would eventually end, stock multiples would drop and with that the company's ability to do accretive deals. The new issue market, which priced a record 1,000 IPOs in 1969, would dry up. Wall Street would then demand organic growth, quality of earnings, and increasing amounts of each sales dollar invested in R&D. It was a difficult balancing act for any young company, with little room for error.

A few critics emerged and began challenging Panic's projections, citing the company's small US sales force, lack of near-term product opportunities, and lack of FDA approvals. There was no doubt that ICN could buy companies. But the question nagging investors was whether ICN could get a new drug application through the FDA and then successfully market the product against tough competition. That was the mark of a top pharmaceutical company. ICN wasn't there yet. It needed to buy something with a near-term drug to launch.

Roland K. Robins discussing DNA at shareholders meeting

Breaking ground on the Irvine research facility

ICN Chemical & Nuclear Corporation Reseach Center, Irvine, California

L-DOPA

In 1969, ICN got its chance. Nutritional Biochemicals Corporation (NBC) was for sale. The Cleveland-based company, a rather mundane provider of biochemicals and reagents, had suddenly found itself in an enviable position. Because of an old distribution license with Japan's Sankyo Chemicals, NBC had become the largest US supplier of L-DOPA, a naturally occurring amino acid that had recently shown in clinical studies could slow the progression to Parkinson's disease. Quickly, neurologists around the country and in Canada began establishing investigator-sponsored clinical studies so they could treat their patients. Drug giants F. Hoffmann–La Roche and Norwich-Eaton were readying NDAs in response to public pressure on the FDA to approve L-DOPA for prescription use. And NBC was supplying the entire market, including Roche. Analysts began projecting a $150-million market.

Panic jumped on the opportunity, paying $13 million in cash and stock for NBC. The plan was to have SCA immediately formulate finished capsules so ICN could file an NDA around the same time as Roche and Norwich. The Roche product was essentially NBC's, and ICN management believed that all it would have to do to satisfy the FDA would be to demonstrate bioequivalence. A new regulatory affairs group was formed at ICN led by Dr. Matthew Ellenhorn, a former FDA reviewer. Confidant of a quick approval, management prepared to launch the compound Levodopa.

As an insurance policy, Lightstone signed a co-marketing deal with Smith, Kline & French (SKF). SKF would sell to primary care using its detail force of 500 reps, leaving ICN to market to neurologists. Time was of the essence. Roche was rumored to win approval early in 1970. ICN had to catch up. It was OK to be third—but not a distant third. Plus, ICN had the advantage of control over supply and a direct relationship with 200 neurologists who were buying investigational L-DOPA for their trials. Panic reasoned that the FDA would be sympathetic, especially if he told the agency that he was prepared to sell at a lower price. The race was on!

October 1968—ICN moves headquarters to 171 Lake Street, Pasadena, California.

Above: Milan Panic, Ray Doupe, and Coke Reeves walking down Lake Avenue in Pasadena, California

Left: Purchase of Nutritional Biochemicals Corporation (NBC)

Opposite page, top left: Milan Panic speaking at the shareholders meeting held at the Hungtington-Sheraton Hotel in Pasadena

Opposite page, bottom left: NBC acquisition tombstone

Opposite page, right: ICN's first SEC registered placement

ICN

International Chemical & Nuclear Corporation

has acquired

Nutritional Biochemicals Corporation

The undersigned assisted ICN in this transaction.

Smith, Barney & Co.
Incorporated

December 30, 1969

255,000 Shares

INTERNATIONAL CHEMICAL & NUCLEAR CORPORATION

Common Stock

(Par Value $1.00 per share)

Of the 255,000 shares offered hereby, 100,000 shares will be issued and sold by the Company and the remaining 155,000 shares are issued and outstanding and are being sold by the stockholders named under "Principal and Selling Stockholders".

The common stock is traded in the over-the-counter market. The reported bid and ask prices on February 25, 1969 were $40 and $45, respectively. The Company intends to apply for listing of the common stock on the American Stock Exchange.

THESE SECURITIES HAVE NOT BEEN APPROVED OR DISAPPROVED BY THE SECURITIES AND EXCHANGE COMMISSION NOR HAS THE COMMISSION PASSED UPON THE ACCURACY OR ADEQUACY OF THIS PROSPECTUS. ANY REPRESENTATION TO THE CONTRARY IS A CRIMINAL OFFENSE.

	Price to Public	Underwriting Discounts and Commissions	Proceeds to Company (1)	Proceeds to Selling Stockholders (1) (2)
Per Share	$........	$........	$........	$........
Total	$........	$........	$........	$........

(1) Before deducting expenses estimated at $...... payable by the Company and $...... payable by the Selling Stockholders.

(2) The Selling Stockholders have agreed not to dispose of any shares of common stock of the Company, without the consent of the Underwriters, for a period of 90 days after the commencement of the public offering of the common stock offered hereby. See "Underwriting" herein.

The common stock is offered subject to prior sale, when, as and if delivered to and accepted by the Underwriters, and subject to approval of certain legal matters by Messrs. O'Melveny & Myers, counsel for the Underwriters, and Messrs. Donnelly, Clark, Chase & Haakh, counsel for the Company and for the Selling Stockholders, and to certain other conditions. It is expected that delivery of the common stock and payment therefor will be made on or about , 1969.

EASTMAN DILLON, UNION SECURITIES & CO.

1970–1979

- March 1970—NARI moves to four-building research campus in Irvine, California; 229 PhDs eventually on payroll, all searching for new antiviral and anticancer discoveries.
- June 2, 1970—ICN files NDA on L-DOPA.
- June 18, 1970—ICN begins trading on NYSE. Stock opens at $45.75.
- June 11, 1970—Dr. J. T. Witkowski of NARI synthesizes an unnatural nucleoside assigned the number 1229, later named ribavirin.
- April 6, 1970—Swiss franc offering closes a 7.5% convertible note due 1975. Dow Banking Corp. underwrites. Total $33.5M.
- 1970—ICN acquires ARCO group of companies based in Lugano, Switzerland.
- March 1971—ICN buys Winley-Morris in Montreal.
- June 25, 1971—Stock splits two-for-one.
- September 1, 1971—ICN acquires Usafarma S.A. and Inquibras S.A. of São Paulo, Brazil. Inquibras API plant set up to produce bulk ribavirin for worldwide market.
- October 29, 1971—ICN borrows $20.3M from First National City Bank, NY (unsecured, in Swiss francs, for $15.5M for 5 years at 4.75%), and United California Bank, LA (unsecured, $4.8M for 1 year at 4.3125%). Proceeds to acquire M. Woelm KG, a major West German pharmaceutical company, for approximately $16M cash.
- December 1972—ICN moves corporate to 2727 Campus Drive, Irvine.
- April 16, 1973—ICN board approves name change to ICN Pharmaceuticals Inc.
- November 5, 1973—ICN and Sanko Pharmaceutical Industry Co. LTD, Tokyo, enter a joint venture. Sanko issues 300K shares, giving ICN 20%. First involvement for ICN in Japan.
- March 1973—US operations move to 90,000-square-foot plant in Covina, California, one of the largest production facilities on the West Coast.
- November 30, 1973—ICN Pharmaceuticals grants worldwide rights to all forms of ribavirin to Lederle Division of American Cyanamid. Ribavirin IND approved.
- 1973—ICN begins human clinical studies in Brazil and Mexico for hepatitis, herpes, and general viral diseases.
- September 1975—ICN Brazil launches Virazole (Viramid) in Brazil. Posts first-year sales of $1.5M, one of the top products introduced in Brazil.
- 1975—Lederle returns ribavirin rights to ICN.
- 1976—Robert H. Finch, Esq., former Secretary of Health, Education, and Welfare, elected to board of directors.
- February 1976—ICN sells German subsidiary to Revlon for cash of $25M.
- 1977—Viramid is the leading antiviral in Brazil and the fifth-leading product launched in Brazil last 10 years. Vilona is number one antiviral in Mexico.

THE SEVENTIES

WE WILL NOT FAIL

Milan Panic in 1970

PHARMACEUTICAL STOCKS

Pharmaceutical companies were considered good investments. Drug makers were profitable, fast growing, and usually had exciting new product stories to drive their stock prices. Historically, the sector's revenue and earnings grew at better than 10% per year. In the '50s, these gains were fueled by a steady flow of FDA-approved new chemical entities (NCEs). In the '60s, however, NCEs declined sharply after the Kefauver-Harris amendments became law. Still, the better companies found ways to outperform, either by diversifying into other areas of health care or by accelerating foreign expansion. This ability to deliver, irrespective of the business or regulatory cycle, earned pharma companies their reputation as solid defensive plays.

Wall Street favored drug stocks that consistently beat earnings projections, had high internal growth rates, and had strong and growing new product pipelines. And while Kefauver-Harris made the process for gaining FDA approval of new drugs much tougher, each competitor was affected equally. Investors saw this as survival of the fittest and tended to rely on the institutional drug analysts to recommend which companies were the most attractive.

Board of Directors

Milan Panic · *Harvey Andrews* · *Dwight C. Baum* · *Dan H. Campbell,* PH.D. · *Manuel F. Cohen* · *Max S. Dunn,* PH.D.

Weldon B. Jolley, PH.D. · *William T. Rhame,* D.C.S. · *Donat R. Richard,* M.D. · *Roberts A. Smith,* PH.D. · *Harold M. Williams,* PH.D.

Corporate and Division Management

Jose Perez Carballo · *Fred Damlos* · *Joe E. Davis* · *Richard Fallis* · *Camillo Ferrari* · *Louis E. Genoud*

John C. Hancock · *Philip Kane* · *Ben Knulst* · *James R. Lewis* · *Herbert S. Lightstone* · *Harry Mann*

Harry Montgomery · *M. C. Reeves* · *Dr. Roland Robins* · *Dean L. Stubblefield* · *Kamen Troller* · *James R. Greenwald*

ICN Board of Directors and Corporate and Division Management

ENTER INTERNATIONAL CHEMICAL & NUCLEAR (ICN)

Seen initially as a go-go stock, ICN began to attract veteran pharmaceutical analysts by consistently reporting record results. Entering the '70s, six brokerage firms rated the company a strong buy, suitable for aggressive, risk-oriented investors. ICN was a hyper-growth stock, expected to grow at 30% per year to maintain its lofty price and multiple. The company, led by its dynamic young CEO, was a proven acquirer but also appeared to have found the right formula to balance that external growth with cutting-edge R&D.

ICN shareholders, most of whom had made a lot of money, viewed Milan Panic almost as a celebrity. He could do no wrong. But Panic knew all could be lost with one strategic slip. The key was keeping Wall Street informed. He instructed ICN's PR staff to keep the press releases flowing on deals, L-DOPA, NARI discoveries, and new executive hires and appointments to the board. Accordingly, an acquisition was announced monthly. Shareholder letters and quarterly reports highlighted ICN's $1-million-a-month sales of investigational L-DOPA to neurologists. The NDA would soon be filed. And steady NARI updates were released regularly indicating that ICN scientists were close to announcing the blockbuster that would unleash a new growth phase for the company. The biotechnology revolution was just getting started, and Panic wanted to solidify ICN's reputation as an emerging leader in antiviral chemotherapy, a market potentially bigger than antibiotics.

> Steady NARI updates indicated that ICN's scientists were close to announcing the blockbuster that would unleash a new growth phase for the company.

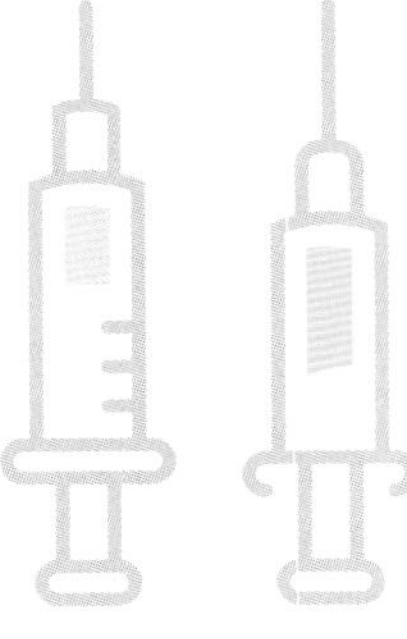

First day of trading on the New York Stock Exchange

NYSE: ICN

In June 1970, ICN was invited to list on the New York Stock Exchange, under the symbol ICN. Shares opened at $46, a multiple of 40 times expected 1970 earnings. ICN had become a "Big Board" stock, trading alongside the likes of Merck, Warner Lambert, Squibb, Pfizer, Syntex, G.D. Searle, and Schering-Plough. It capped a remarkable run for the young company and even more for its founder, Panic, the former Yugoslav bicycle champ who had only become a naturalized US citizen in 1963. The business press ran multiple features of his rags-to-riches rise, culminating in a *Fortune* magazine story entitled "A Serbian Boy Builds His Dream Castle in the Drug Business." ICN was hot, and investors kept buying.

But alongside the bulls remained those few persistent bears. They insisted ICN was inflating its earnings by capitalizing R&D expenses and deferring acquisition costs, a practice out of sync with industry peers. They pointed to unamortized deferred costs on ICN's balance sheet, which had risen to $1.6 million, or $0.47 per share. They warned this was a potential write-off that could slash earnings if growth were to slow. Investors paid scant attention. Panic had promised $500 million in sales by 1975, and few were doubting him.

June 18, 1970—ICN begins trading on the New York Stock Exchange. Shares began trading at $46. ICN had become a "Big Board" stock, trading alongside the likes of Merck, Warner, Lambert, Squibb, Pfizer, Syntex, G.D. Searle, and Schering-Plough.

Left top: ICN PARIS-LABO

Left bottom: ICN Arco

Above: Quality control, ICN Arco

Right top: Weighing station, ICN Spain

Right bottom: ICN Italy soccer team

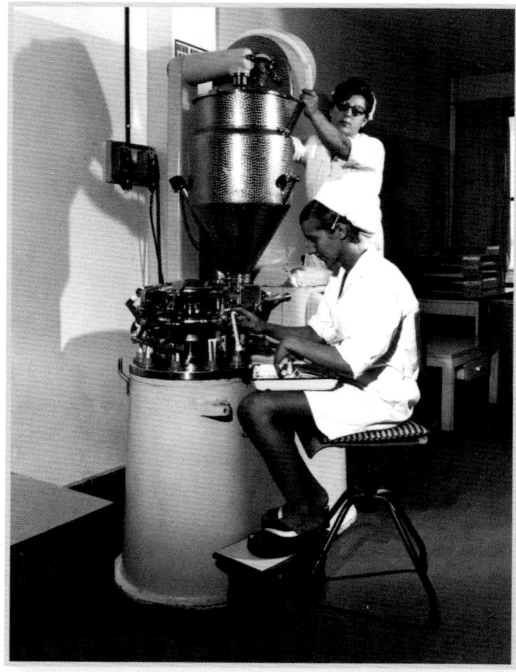

BUILDING PHARMA

Acquisitions were sought in the top 15 international pharmaceutical markets. Lightstone and Haakh worked tirelessly on a dozen transactions at a time. Bankers proposed new deals almost every week. Lehman Brothers health care banker Frederick Frank identified an acquisition in Switzerland that would lead off a series of strategic moves throughout Europe. Panic put himself in charge of European expansion. The JetStar crossed the Atlantic 35 times in the first six months of 1970. Panic figured he had a little more than a year to secure $50 million in European sales. He moved his family from Pasadena to Switzerland, putting the kids in Swiss schools while taking up residence in a modest home on Lake Leman. ICN Europe headquarters were established in Geneva, at 9 rue boissonnas, and Panic was there every two weeks.

Anticipating rapid growth, ICN tapped the Eurodollar debt markets for the first time, borrowing $7.5 million in Swiss francs by issuing a five-year 5% bank note, convertible into ICN at $53 per share. More financings followed. The board wanted access to new sources of capital, and investing in foreign currencies seemed like a good idea—and cheaper. The Swiss capital market was particularly attractive, becaming practically a second home for ICN. Panic's exploits there would later become legendary, leading him into the boardrooms of the country's largest and most secretive pharmaceutical companies—and not always with open arms.

Fred Frank's idea, Arco Group, was a manufacturer of bulk antibiotics and finished dosage forms that operated out of an FDA-approved plant in Lugano. Arco products were sold throughout Europe and exported to 70 countries abroad. The company had subsidiaries in Greece, Italy, Pakistan, and Mexico. Annual sales were $14 million, with tetracycline and ampicillin accounting for 25% of the business. In early '70, Arco became a wholly owned subsidiary of ICN.

More deals followed. ICN snapped up Geneva-based Comptoir de la Parfumerie S.A. and Bicidi S.A., formulators and distributors of medicated cosmetics and toiletries in Switzerland and France. The Italian market opened its doors via the purchase of Sparko S.p.A., a bulk raw materials and antibiotics producer based in Milan. Brands were quickly repackaged under the ICN label. Within the first year, the group launched Levodopa and introduced a new sustained-release tetracycline called Tetrarco.

Improfarm S.A., a Madrid-based manufacturer of gamma globulin, antibiotics, and antihelmentics, was acquired, providing access to Spain. A Netherlands holding company comprising four entities, Etablissementen R. Barberot N.V., Farmabo N.V., Euromedica N.V., and Bergerac N.V., was acquired for stock. This provided ICN a leading presence in hard and soft contact lenses, sleep aids, and antipsychotics.

By the end of 1970, Panic had established pharmaceutical subsidiaries in Switzerland, Holland, Italy, and Spain. All combined, the new additions contributed $22.7 million in revenue that year, $2 million to the bottom line, and $0.22 in earnings per share.

Herb Lightstone, on target to achieve the European objective, did not want to neglect the United States and Canada. Dartell Laboratories,

a $2-million-per-year maker of nutritionals, vitamins, and supplements based in Los Angeles, was acquired for stock. Dartell fit with Rawson's distribution into the growing health foods sections of supermarkets. It also added to the United Labs and Bentex physician-dispensed units because of its business with chiropractors, who relied on its line of mega vitamins and phosphorous-free calcium to treat bone disorders. Strong Cobb's business grew organically as well. The company launched a new sustained-release formulation of vitamin C called Ascorbicap and a male hormone called Testred. SCA also performed custom-manufacturing and private-label services for Lederle, Merck, Pfizer, and Parke-Davis. ICN's generics business was gaining traction too, largely due to new government pressure on pricing and a much easier approval pathway at the FDA.

Above: Improfarm S.A. management team

Left: ICN Geneva team

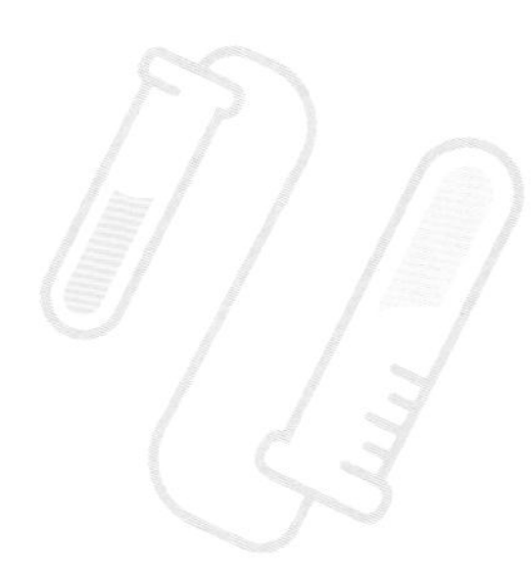

A CALL FROM CANADA

Purchase of Empire Labs

Early in 1970, Panic was summoned from a meeting in his Pasadena office to answer a call from Morris Goodman, an ex-pharmacist based in Montreal who owned a Canadian pharmaceutical company called Winley-Morris Limited. He wanted the Canadian distribution rights to L-DOPA. Goodman was aware of L-DOPA's utility in Parkinson's because one of the early pioneers of L-DOPA research had been Dr. Andre Barbeau, director of neurobiology at the Montreal Clinical Research Institute. Part of Goodman's business was securing Canadian licenses. He had a knack for finding opportunities—and L-DOPA could be big. Goodman had never heard of ICN but was told it was the biggest supplier and he was confident he could make a deal.

Panic had a different idea. He flew to Montreal to meet Goodman and extend an offer to buy Winley-Morris. Reluctant at first, Goodman eventually gave in. ICN was not big pharma, but it was growing fast, had a huge stock price, and had ambitious plans for Canada. Morris, like others, was taken with Panic and figured the two could do big things together. Plus, ICN had L-DOPA and some soon-to-be announced discoveries at NARI that Goodman believed would make ICN into a major world player. He wanted to be in on the ground floor.

But ICN benefitted too. Morris was exceptionally bright and had a lot to offer. He was an accomplished business builder at the forefront of a revolution in Canadian generics, a movement he had a lot to do with creating. The Canadian government had passed Bill C-102, mandating compulsory licensing—meaning that Canadian companies could launch their own versions of patented products simply by paying a small royalty to the innovator. This protected the Canadian market from foreign dominance. And Morris was working on a bunch of new product ideas. He told Panic that within 10 years ICN could be a powerhouse generics provider, both in the United States and in Canada. And SCA had the formulation capability to knock off practically every dosage form.

Generics were coming of age. They had risen to 10% of all US pharmacy-dispensed prescriptions. They were also easier to get approved based on bioequivalence than were NCEs, which required extensive clinical studies. Patents on big drugs were beginning to expire, and a large market opportunity was emerging. Goodman would lead the effort. He had three able colleagues in Ted Wise, Richard MacKay, and Jack Kay. A year later, a renamed ICN Canada would acquire Barry Sherman's Sherman and Ulster Limited, a small manufacturer of ethical products and generics based in Toronto.

Levodopa was launched in 1972. Goodman finally had his license and would soon be marketing 150 other products, including ethical brands, OTCs, generics, even the medicated cosmetic and toiletry line from Switzerland. Within a few years, Goodman acquired a modern FDA-approved plant in Montreal from Roche and consolidated all the various companies into one fully integrated unit.

NARI scientists with model of ribavirin molecule
Left to right: Roland K. Robins, J.T. Witkowski, and Robert Sidwell

Morris Goodman's concern is building a leading health-care company in Canada

Morris Goodman, President, ICN Canada

A balance between cooperation and autonomy helps make ICN's divisions in Canada and around the world more profitable every year. As a worldwide health-care company with 16 divisions and 34 facilities in 11 countries, ICN has many opportunities to grow and profit by an interchange of ideas between its operating executives. It takes advantage of these opportunities by fostering a constant exchange of information between its managers.

ICN is a major producer and distributor of pharmaceuticals, a distributor of non-prescription drugs and non-drug items, and a manufacturer of biochemicals and radio-active materials. In the Western Hemisphere, ICN is active in the United States, Brazil, Mexico and, of course, Canada.

In Europe, we have operations in Belgium, France, Germany, Holland, Italy, Spain and Switzerland. In the Pacific Basin, we have a division in Indonesia and have opened a Tokyo office as a further step into that important market.

What is ICN Canada?

In Canada, ICN is composed of Winley-Morris Co. Ltd.; J. M. Marsan & Co., Ltd.; Empire Laboratories, Dominion Pharmacal Company, and Strong Cobb Arner of Canada, Ltd. The company has grown and plans to continue growing by a planned combination of internal growth and acquisitions.
ICN Canada has administrative and marketing offices in Montreal and manufacturing facilities in Fort Erie and Toronto, and has 305 employees across Canada.

An incentive to produce

ICN's management policy gives local managers a great degree of autonomy. As the company expands it leaves in command the executives who have made an enterprise grow and prosper. To assure continued success, each area and division manager matches performance against an incentive plan.

18 new drug applications

Through divisions in various countries ICN filed 18 new drug applications for 11 products last year. In Canada, two new drugs have been cleared for sale by the Canadian Health Protection Branch. They are Carbolith (lithium carbonate), a drug for the treatment of the manic depressive, and Cortenema, a hydrocortisone retention enema used in the treatment of ulcerative colitis. In addition, two drugs are under clinical investigation: Levopa (L-Dopa), a drug for the treatment of Parkinson's Disease symptoms, and Etibi (ethambutol) a drug for the treatment of tuberculosis.

Directed research

ICN has an active R&D program at its Nucleic Acid Research Institute, in Irvine, California, in addition to product development work in many of the divisions. At the Institute more than 90 researchers are seeking to understand what happens in the human cell when it is invaded by a virus. By tracking the activity inside the cell, researchers can better understand how to inhibit or cure specific viral diseases. We call this directed research. Papers on new developments will be presented at 32 scientific meetings this year.

Morris Goodman, President, ICN Canada; Milan Panic, Chairman and President, ICN Corporation, and Richard J. MacKay, Executive Vice President, ICN Canada

As part of our program, ICN has developed and is now investigating a new drug called Virazole, which shows potential as a broad-spectrum anti-viral agent. In addition, this year we expect to apply to the Canadian Health Protection Branch for permission to test several other new drugs and we are currently making patent application at the rate of one every two weeks.

For more information

Send for copies of our 1971 annual report in French or English and the 1972 second quarter report to Communications Director, ICN Canada Ltd., 675 Montée de Liesse, Montreal 377, P.Q.

ICN CANADA
A Subsidiary of International Chemical & Nuclear Corporation

TIME, SEPTEMBER 11, 1972

Morris Goodman,
President, ICN Canada

Levodopa was launched in 1972. Within a few years, Goodman acquired a modern FDA-approved plant in Montreal from Roche and consolidated all the various companies into one fully integrated unit.

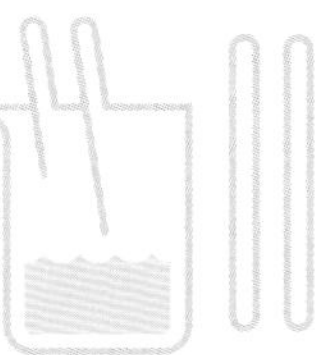

ICN 1229

Robins delivered on his promise. Starting in 1968, his group at NARI had synthesized thousands of compounds derived from or related to the components of nucleic acids. NARI scientists had published more than 200 articles in leading scientific journals including *Science*, *Proceedings of the National Academy of Sciences*, *Biochemistry*, the *Journal of Medicinal Chemistry*, and the *Journal of Organic Chemistry and Chemotherapy*. There was ICN 3952, an anti-DNA virus agent that could be developed as a topical; ICN 4684, an antibacterial agent, highly specific for gram-negative bacteria; ICN 4221, or 3-deazaguanine, a potential agent for the treatment of solid tumors; and ICN 4003, a cardiac inotropic agent that looked promising for the treatment of congestive heart failure. But none looked as exciting as ICN 1229.

The virology group at NARI had prioritized their efforts on screening antiviral candidates potentially active in respiratory disease. Primarily of viral origin, upper-tract respiratory infections were of interest because they played a role in 60% of all episodes of human illness. There were literally hundreds of virus strains that caused fever, sore throat, runny nose, bronchitis, cough, and other cold and flu symptoms. A vaccine effective against all these serotypes seemed impossible. The discovery of a nontoxic, broad-spectrum antiviral chemotherapeutic drug that stopped virus replication would constitute a major breakthrough. This was where Robins and his team wanted to make their mark.

In June 1970, Dr. J.T. Witkowski, working with Robins and the NARI virology group, synthesized a nucleoside that was assigned the code number ICN 1229. It was one of a series of triazole nucleosides he had made based on evidence that this type of molecular structure would have antiviral activity. Active in tissue culture against adenovirus, herpes virus, influenza A and B, hepatitis B, mumps and measles, and other RNA and DNA viruses, 1229 demonstrated broad-spectrum antiviral activity.

Inside the company, excitement was rising over 1229. Robins went so far as to predict at a board meeting that just as penicillin had revolutionized antimicrobials, 1229 would do the same for viruses, even the common cold.

However, before Wall Street could be informed, more testing had to be done in lab animals. The knock at the time on antivirals was that because viruses invaded the host cell, any drug that inhibited viral replication would have to act inside the cell and probably impair it in the process. But 1229 appeared to be different, at least in vitro. Its action did not damage the host cell.

Shareholders would wait 24 months before 1229's IND could be filed and clinical testing could begin. But if the drug worked, and in the right indication, it could reach the market by 1979. Suddenly, Panic's goal of $500 million didn't seem so far-fetched.

Inside, a restless Panic demanded faster time lines. Compound 1229's development became the highest company priority, outside of meeting profits. And like ribaminol and L-DOPA, Panic demanded that registration activities and clinical trials be undertaken abroad, where ICN had a growing presence and registration was faster.

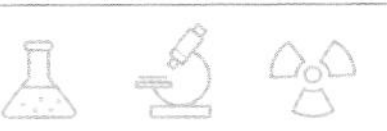

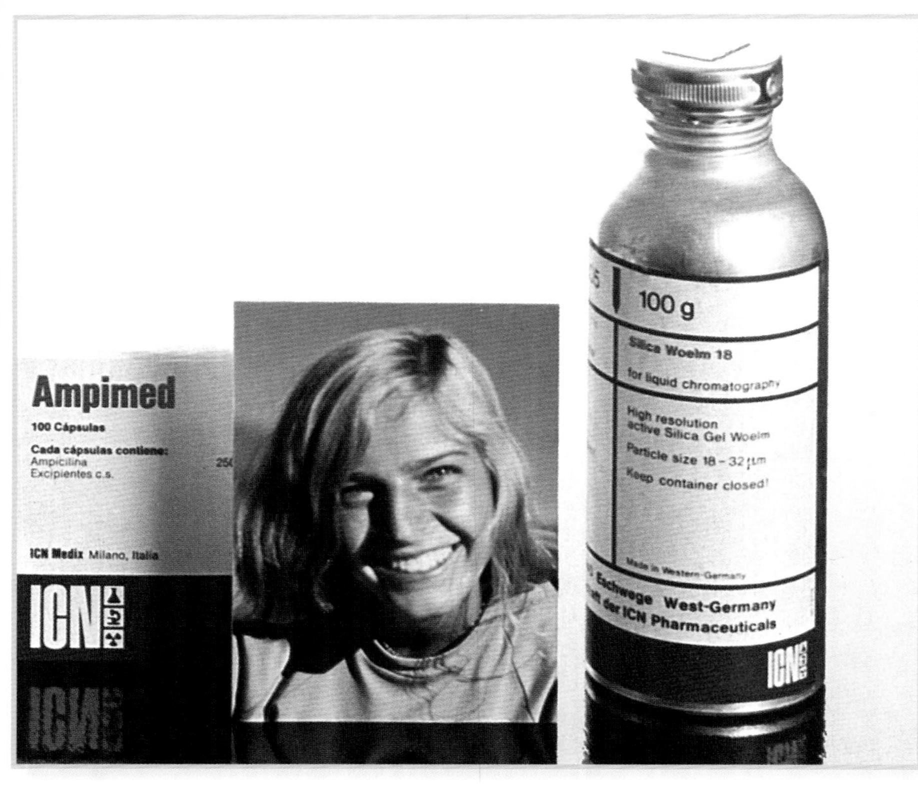

Above and right:
ICN global branding campaigns

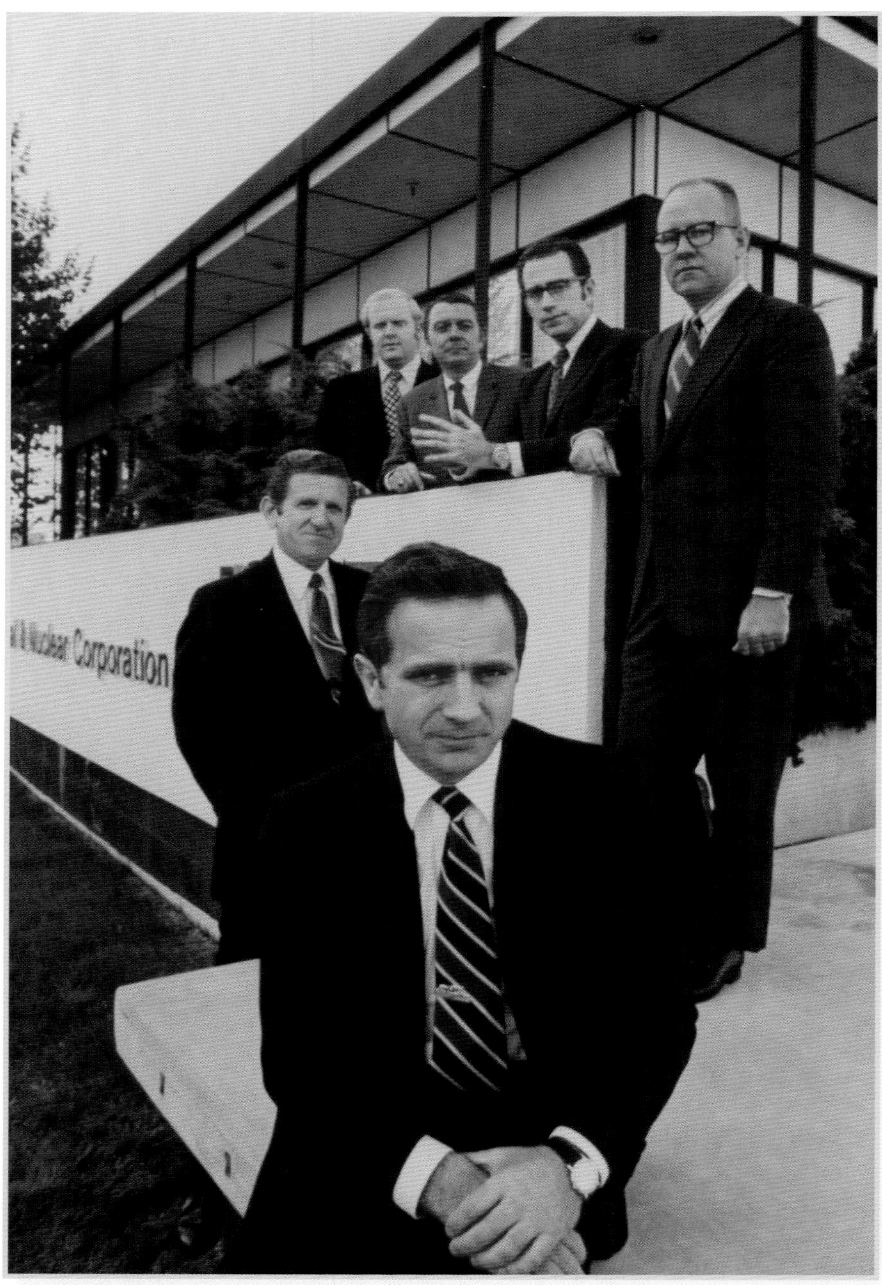

ICN's executive team pose for *Fortune* magazine

BANNER YEAR

Fiscal 1970 was ICN's seventh consecutive year of record sales and earnings. Sales topped $100 million for the first time, reaching $116 million, up 17% from the prior year. Net earnings were $5.8 million, up 44%. EPS was $1.01, up from $0.65. The balance sheet was sound, although short-term debt was creeping up as more cash was used to buy companies to limit dilution. Much of that borrowing occurred, however, in softer foreign currencies with lower interest rates. This enabled ICN to continue its strategy of buying companies with low-cost money and an inflated stock price. Fewer shares offered translated into increasing EPS after consolidation. And the debt could be paid back from increasing cash flow.

Everything seemed to be clicking. ICN stock hit a high of $58 per share. L-DOPA, sold as an investigational product to neurologists, hospitals, and clinics, booked $8 million that year at a price of $13.70 per bottle of 100 tablets. The NDA was filed in January 1971. Investors were ecstatic. Rudy Drews sold the last of his Foremost stock in yet another oversubscribed ICN offering. His bet on young Panic had paid off big. Another two-for-one stock split was granted, ICN's fifth since 1966.

ICN President Milan Panic's concern is building a worldwide health-care company.

How did ICN do last year?
International Chemical & Nuclear Corp. reported record sales and earnings for fiscal 1971. Sales were $135,800,000, an increase of 17 percent over 1970; after-tax earnings were $7,600,000, up 31 percent. Earnings per share increased 19 percent to $1.20.

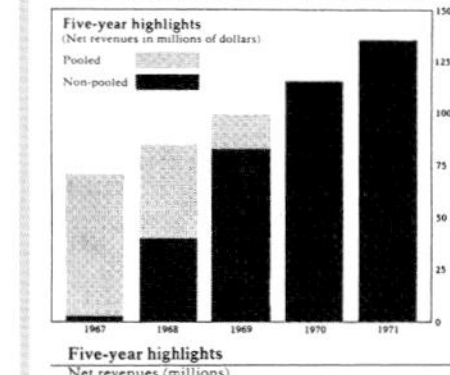

Five-year highlights

Net revenues (millions)				
1967	1968	1969	1970	1971
$ 3.6*	41.2	83.1	116.3	135.8
71.0†	86.3	99.6		
Net earnings (millions)				
1967	1968	1969	1970	1971
$ .3*	1.1	2.8	5.8	7.6
2.4†	2.1	4.0		
Earnings per share				
1967	1968	1969	1970	1971
$ .16*	.32	.65	1.01	1.20
.60†	.43	.77		

*Upper line: as originally stated
†Lower line: reflecting subsequent pooling of interests

How about long-term growth?
Fiscal 1971 was the seventh straight year of record sales and earnings. The company that started in 1961 with $8,000 in sales is now a leader in health care, listed on the New York Stock Exchange, ticker symbol: ICN. You'll find it in the stock tables right under IBM.
The stock was split two-for-one by means of a 100 percent stock dividend in 1971. A cash dividend will be given serious consideration for the future. At present cash is conserved to fund ICN's growing research program and its international expansion.

What products does ICN market?
The company is a major producer and distributor of pharmaceuticals, a distributor of nonprescription drugs and non-drug items, and a manufacturer of biochemicals and radioactive materials.

What did internal growth contribute in 1971?
Internal growth, which we identify as increases in sales and profit contributions from operating units, accounted for an 8 percent increase in sales and a 17 percent increase in earnings for the fiscal year ended November 30, 1971.

Why is it important to expand worldwide?
Because the need for health care is truly global and because multi-national marketing capability is a hedge against a bad year in any one area. In addition, the cost of marketing a drug is so high that success in only one or two markets often cannot cover development costs. ICN profits also from an exchange of ideas and products between divisions. For example, in 1972 ICN will open in Mexico an antibiotics plant that was designed by our Italian experts. We now operate 16 divisions and 34 facilities in 11 countries, and through divisions and representatives we sell in 120 countries.

What about new pharmaceuticals?
ICN's pharmaceutical divisions introduced 44 additional products during 1971, 34 branded and 10 generic.
In Europe our divisions brought a number of products to the marketplace: Inimur, a gynecological preparation; Eoden Retard, a cardiovascular product, and Tetraco L.A., a sustained-release form of tetracycline developed by ICN.
Three new products were introduced in Brazil: Trimexazol, an antibacterial; Sedazapan, an analgesic, and Ambulempax, an anti-obesity drug, and in Mexico our own line of ethical veterinary pharmaceuticals.
We recently received exclusive rights to market in the U.S. and Latin America a new kidney stone preventive developed in England. In the United States we added a line of vitamins and other nutritional products to ICN Pharmaceuticals and signed an agreement for the U.S. rights to a series of compounds, including a nucleic acid derivative that inhibits leukemia in mice. We also obtained a license in Canada to manufacture and sell a drug used in the treatment of pulmonary tuberculosis and received permission from the U.S. Food and Drug Administration to begin clinical testing of a sustained-release form of L-dopa, a drug for the relief of Parkinson's disease symptoms. Abroad, L-dopa has been registered in 59 countries, most recently in the Soviet Union.

What is ICN research doing?
At our Nucleic Acid Research Institute we are deeply involved in the study of DNA (deoxyribonucleic acid) and RNA (ribonucleic acid), the "master controllers of life." By searching into the core of the human cell, our researchers seek to understand the relationship of diseases to the cell function. ICN researchers have synthesized more than 500 DNA and RNA derivatives specifically designed to inhibit virus. About 20 percent show specific activity in cell cultures, warranting further study, as compared to about 2 percent by the industry's traditional methods.

What positive results has ICN had?
Last year our divisions made 10 patent applications covering various drugs. In 1972 we expect to apply to the FDA for permission to test several new drugs. We are continuing to investigate a unique compound called Virazole which has shown potential as a broad-spectrum antiviral agent.

Can a relatively small company like ICN market a "breakthrough" drug?
Worldwide, ICN already has over 1,000 detailmen, salesmen and field men and is steadily expanding its marketing capability. In the U.S. alone we will triple our detailmen in the next two years. Right now we only have the capability to handle any new drug in the early stages of market introduction, but we have the cadre from which to expand as needed in the future.

Where can I get more information?
Send for a copy of the 1971 annual report of International Chemical & Nuclear Corp. Just write to Communications Department, ICN, 171 S. Lake Ave., Pasadena, Calif. 91101.

ICN
International Chemical & Nuclear Corporation... A growing concern for world health care

PRESTIGIOUS BOARD

The nine-person ICN board expanded with the addition of two respected independent directors: Harold M. Williams, dean of the Graduate School of UCLA and former chairman of Norton Simon Inc., and Manuel F. Cohen, former chairman of the SEC. In a highly ceremonial event, Cohen joined Finance Committee Chairman Seth Baker, Milan Panic, and his wife, Jelica, on the floor of the NYSE to ring the opening bell.

The company, now with 5,000 employees, had operations in the United States, Canada, Mexico, Switzerland, Italy, Spain, and Holland, with total pharmaceutical sales comprising 65% of revenue. The original business, research chemicals, had been renamed ICN Nuclear. Acquisitions in this group continued with Tracerlab S.A. in Belgium and Paris Labo LTD in France. Sales for the group reached $8 million—not as grand as its sister pharma division but still respectable, given that the total business in 1966 was less than $1 million. Nuclear medicine, as the original founding board had predicted, was growing rapidly, with more of its applications devoted to cancer. The diagnostic industry was also experiencing a rapid growth phase, armed with new equipment and tools that facilitated the creation of the automated central laboratory. Accordingly, Lightstone stepped up the search for a big diagnostics provider to purchase. Panic dreamed that one day ICN-labeled assays would diagnose rare disease, followed by ICN-labeled pharmaceuticals used to treat. It all seemed so simple.

Milan Panic with Manuel F. Cohen, former chairman of the SEC

PRICE WAR

On June 3, 1970, a day before the FDA officially approved the Roche NDA for L-DOPA, FDA Commissioner Charles Edwards received a surprise visit from ICN President Milan Panic. ICN had just filed its six-volume NDA, and Panic was there to request expedited review. The FDA was about to approve Roche's product that used active pharmaceutical ingredient (API) supplied by NBC. ICN in effect would be demonstrating bioequivalence to its own product. Panic requested that the commissioner approve his application quickly because ICN had strong relationships with neurologists, could control supply, and was prepared to offer the product at a lower price per kilo than Roche. The approach, a bit unorthodox to Edwards, was typical Panic. The FDA did not yield, however. Instead, the agency required that ICN demonstrate therapeutic equivalence necessitating clinical trials, not just equivalent blood levels. ICN's approval was pushed back six months, to January 1971. Roche and Norwich-Eaton would get a lengthy head start. Inside ICN, Panic was fuming. It would not be the first time that he and the FDA crossed hairs.

Roche's Laropa was approved and offered to the public at $12.50 per bottle of 100 capsules. Eaton was approved and matched price. ICN dropped its price on investigational L-DOPA to $8.50, from $13.70. Roche stayed at $12.50. Despite the delay, ICN still felt it had a good shot. Roche was rumored to be building its own manufacturing capability at its plant in Nutley, so it remained dependent on ICN for supply. As long as new prescription demand was strong, ICN could still get its share. Post approval, ICN and SmithKline could catch up on price. No one believed that Roche would drop price to meet little ICN, especially when it had a new plant to pay for. Analysts maintained their ICN market share projections. The consensus was that ICN and SKF would garner 20%–25% of a market estimated at 1.5 million patients.

Except the demand never came. The FDA had bowed under public pressure and, in effect, jumped the gun. This was exactly what Kefauver-Harris was designed to prevent. Inadequate dose ranging studies had been undertaken forcing physicians to titrate up daily amounts from a few hundred milligrams to almost eight grams. This led to unwanted side effects and higher out-of-pocket costs to patients. The FDA made manufacturers put warning labels on each dose and conduct long-range safety studies. Doctors became increasingly reluctant to prescribe. New sustained-release formulations would eventually save the market, but for ICN, L-DOPA turned out to be a flop—and a costly one.

> You can be third to market, just not a distant third.

BARRON'S TAKES A SHOT

Veteran financial writer Alan Abelson wasted no time blasting ICN for its L-DOPA misstep in his popular weekend edition in *Barron's* "Up and Down Wall Street." Abelson's specialty was taking down Wall Street favorites, and high-priced ICN was on his radar. It was the first negative piece on Panic and ICN, but it was a doozy. The NYSE halted trading Monday morning, eventually opening the stock down five points to $25 per share. It prompted a flurry of selling. Panic and the board found their credibility severely challenged for the first time.

Fortunately, ICN's analysts responded to the article with research notes in support of the company. Abelson not only attacked L-DOPA but also criticized ICN's liberal accounting practices that seemingly inflated earnings. He took exception to ICN's deferral policy, both in booking acquisition costs and R&D expenses. He also challenged Panic's claims on internal growth, arguing that the majority of ICN's 1970 net came from acquisitions on board fewer than six months. The buy-side effectively diffused each charge, and the stock settled, even recovering slightly. Panic would get a second chance, his record deserved as much.

But lingering doubts remained. Any more slips would be catastrophic for the stock and the company's image.

„Wer ist ICN?"

ICN Pharmaceuticals, ein dynamisches, junges Unternehmen, wurde 1961 vom jetzigen Präsidenten und Aufsichtsratvorsitzenden Milan Panic, 44, gegründet.

Milan Panic ist es gelungen, in einem Jahrzehnt aus einem kleinen Spezialbetrieb ein bedeutendes, multinationales Unternehmen der Pharma-Industrie aufzubauen.

ICN Pharmaceuticals hatte 1961 gerade einen Umsatz von 8.000 $, 1972 hingegen wurde die Rekordhöhe von 162 Mio. $ erreicht.

ICN Pharmaceuticals mit einem großen Forschungszentrum in Irvine/Kalifornien, ist heute auf allen wichtigen Märkten der Welt vertreten, wobei 24 Arzneimittelbetriebe mit 5.500 Beschäftigten auf fast allen pharmazeutischen Bereichen tätig sind.

Bei einem Gespräch über die überdurchschnittlichen Erfolge der ICN Pharmaceuticals äußerte sich unlängst der Präsident Milan Panic: „Auf der Basis der bisherigen Ergebnisse erwarten wir, daß ICN ein Musterbeispiel für gesundes Wachstum eines Unternehmens dadurch wird, daß mit allen zur Verfügung stehenden Kräften der multinationale Ausbau konsequent durchgeführt wird. Es ist das langfristige Ziel der ICN, sich zu einem führenden Unternehmen für das Gesundheitswesen der ganzen Welt zu entwickeln."

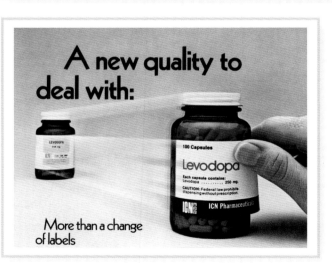

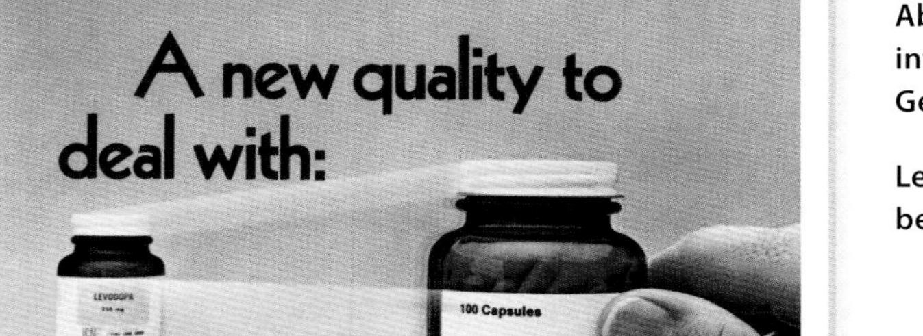

Above: ICN introduced to the German market

Left: Strong Cobb becomes ICN label

THREE BIG DEALS

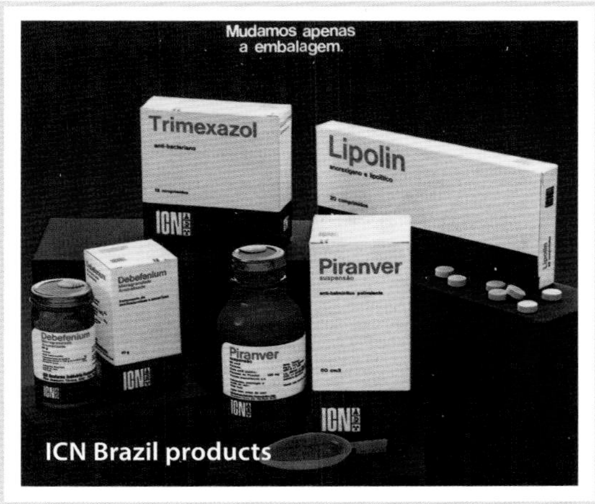

ICN Brazil products

Undeterred, Panic kept his mind on the company's goals. He was exceptionally disciplined and not easily sidetracked. Lightstone had put three big opportunities on the company's plate: one in Germany, one in Brazil, and a clinical diagnostics laboratory in Portland, Oregon. All combined, they would add $40 million in annual sales. Panic would reach his target of $50 million in Europe and in the process position ICN in three accelerating businesses. ICN's revenues would surpass $150 million. Investors would soon forget the *Barron's* story.

The big question was how to finance each purchase. Abelson's column had hurt the stock price, essentially eliminating its use as a means of currency. ICN would have to borrow to buy Usafarma and Woelm. Debt on the books would rise by $20 million, but the two pharma companies were profitable, and ICN's cash flow was strong. The deals were too good to pass up. ICN borrowed $21 million in Deutsch marks (DM) from foreign branches of United California Bank and First National City Bank in New York, at a time when the DM was 3.25 to the dollar. The unsecured 4.75% term loan notes were due in 1975. Total long-term debt rose that year to $30 million. The Brazilian cruzeiro (CR) was CR 5.63 to US $1. A currency devaluation was possible, but the country was booming, and ICN wanted a strong presence in South America.

M. Woelm K.G., based in Eschwege, Germany, closed on July 1, 1971, for 70,400 shares of ICN common, plus $13.8 million in cash. Woelm, a 65-year-old company with annual sales of $16 million, operated one of the most modern plants in Europe. Its portfolio of 60 drugs contained OTCs, analgesics, vitamins, anesthetics, sedatives, and cough/cold remedies. The company held a 58% share of the German anesthetics category and 24% of the market for appetite depressants.

Usafarma S.A. and Inquibras S.A., both of São Paulo, were purchased at the same time, for $6.6 million in cash, borrowed in Swiss francs. Usafarma was the thirty-fourth-largest company of 400 in Brazil, with a

ICN Brazil team

Woelm management meeting

sales force of 185 reps detailing more than 60 drugs. It had leading share in antiparasitics, antibacterials, and analgesics. Annual turnover was $7 million.

Inquibras, based in the São Paulo suburb of Jacarei, was a bulk API producer that supplied raw material to Usafarma for conversion into tablets, capsules, and creams. Monthly volume was two million units. The plan was to use Inquibras to manufacture bulk ICN 1229, a chemical process developed by NARI using ribose, aminoguanadine, and oxalic acid. Clinical material could then be converted in Usafarma's facility on Rua Joaquim Tavora into capsules for clinical trials in Brazil and Mexico.

Servet and Usafarma were renamed ICN LATAM. Total sales in the region now approached $12 million, with 276 reps detailing physicians in Mexico, Brazil, and parts of Central America. Brazil would serve as ICN's South America hub to neighboring Argentina, Uruguay, Chile, and Colombia. And Panic, Lightstone, and a new chief of business expansion, Phillip Seikman, were everywhere. Panic needed only four hours of sleep. He would rest at night on ICN's newly acquired BAC 1-11 jet and be at his desk in a regional ICN office by 8:00 the next morning. This might be Pasadena, Geneva, Eschwege, Montreal, Mexico City, or São Paulo, with stops in NYC between flights to visit bankers and shareholders. He was indefatigable.

United Medical Labs in Portland was the third purchase. It was one of the world's largest clinical testing labs. It offered more than 400 different confirmatory diagnostic tests to 4,500 clients. These included cardiac prenatal, drugs of abuse, hormone analysis, thyroid, biochemistry, endocrinology, hematology, infectious disease, toxicology, etc. They operated client service centers in 23 states and had a sister lab in Memphis.

Strategically, the thinking was that centralized diagnostic laboratories represented a new growth area within health care. As pharmaceutical research untapped new therapeutic areas, the tools and equipment to diagnose those new disorders would have to grow in unison. Large-batch automated tissue and blood sample testing would carry a major share of the laboratory diagnostic volume in the '70s and beyond. Because of insurance and organized medicine, these central labs would replace local mom-and-pop pathology labs. UML owners predicted that the market measured by billings would grow to 2.1 billion and share of the overall diagnostic testing market to 40%. The main driver was automated testing procedures on large high-volume analyzers, enabling fast two-day turnaround for results. In addition, UML was one of the pioneers of radioimmunoassay (RIA) testing. It had developed several new assays to offer customers. RIA was highly sensitive and specific and thus cost-effective. Panic envisioned that diagnostics represented an entirely new growth area for ICN to conquer.

ICN agreed to acquire UML for approximately $7.5 million, issuing 94,644 shares. In addition, the company guaranteed $2 million in UML loans. UML was doing $17 million annually in sales and achieving breakeven—at least that was what insiders conveyed during due diligence. The company was renamed ICN/UML. It was positioned inside ICN Nuclear, representing a new growth platform that would boost the division's prospects. Rawson would be the only unit left that needed some attention.

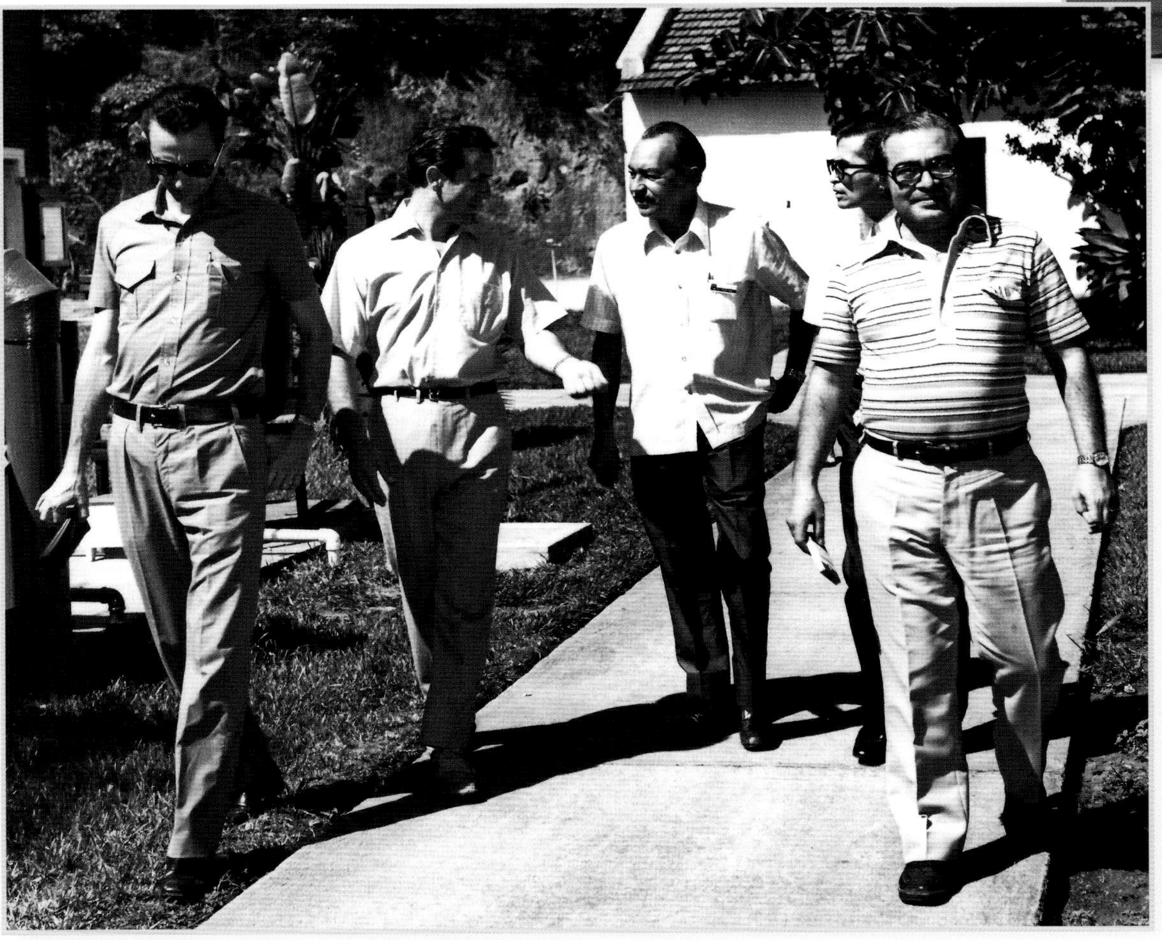

Above: Usafarma on Rua Joaquin Tavora in São Paulo

Left: Milan Panic and new ICN Usafarma team tour the API plant in Jacarei

WARNING SIGNS

1971 was ICN's tenth year of operations. Sales rose 17% to $135.7 million. Net income was $7.6 million, up 31%, and EPS was $1.20, up 19%. Foreign sales were $50.7 million, up 38%. The pharmaceutical division contributed $92 million, comprising 68% of the business. The leading category was antibiotics, at 23%. The company now had almost 1,000 employees in sales and marketing. ICN operated 34 facilities around the world, with ICN products offered in more than 100 countries. Woelm and Usafarma contributed $11 million and $0.13 in EPS.

The board, expecting another pat on the back for a job well done, was surprised when the stock fell on the news. Analysts were troubled by warning signs they saw in the results. A change in accounting practice cost the company $0.10 in EPS. It wasn't major but it surprised the street. Accounting Principles Board Opinion 16 had been adopted in the fourth quarter, requiring that all direct and indirect acquisition costs be charged against earnings. Previously, ICN included these costs in the purchase price. R&D in 1971 was $0.28, but ICN elected this time to expense the entire amount instead of deferring a portion. This left a large accrual of past NARI expenses on the balance sheet, almost $0.47. Some critics claimed foul, arguing that the only true representation of ICN's earnings power would occur if everything was expensed in the year incurred. ICN's treatment of goodwill, or excess purchase price over tangible asset value, was also criticized. ICN amortized this over 40 years, much longer than the industry standard. The balance sheet carried $23 million of this goodwill, another potential write-down risk if things went sour.

The balance sheet suddenly looked ominous. Total liabilities shot up to $62.5 million vs. $41.9 million, the increase due to the $20.3 million borrowed for Usafarma and Woelm. There seemed to be a mounting debt load and much of it in foreign currencies. The dollar was strong, so things were OK. Sensing investor concern, Panic promised to substantially reduce the debt burden in 1972.

Lastly, L-DOPA did not measure up, selling less than $1 million. The SKF deal had been terminated. Two brands, Levopa and Bendopa, were registered in 59 countries, so there was hope that this long-awaited wonder drug would finally gain some traction. Still, the annual report highlighted certain closing expenses associated with terminating Smith-Kline that might hit '73 earnings if brand sales did not materialize as promised. ICN was walking a tightrope.

ICN's BAC 1-11

MANAGEMENT

By then, the company had added significantly to its management ranks around the world. Panic was a natural leader, a man in constant motion always exhibiting high energy, exquisite european style, and fearless optimism. His control was unquestioned. He was the driving force. But ICN had grown complex, with little margin for error. Controls needed to be in place along with managerial discipline. The company was now over 50% international. Different cultures, currencies, markets, and political risks had to be effectively navigated. Time lines moved fast—very fast. The environment was exciting but challenging and extremely demanding.

In late 1971, the company's first international management meeting was held at the Huntington Sheraton Hotel in Pasadena, also the scene of the company's annual shareholder gatherings. More than 250 executives participated. Panic opened the meeting by reciting the story of F. Hoffmann–La Roche, his favorite company, suggesting that ICN's fortunes could evolve the same way as Roche's. He even predicted that someday ICN would own Roche. Nothing was out of reach, he would say. All you had to have was a plan and the confidence to succeed. At the end of the week, when the meetings ended, teams were drawn to play soccer on a field at Cal Tech, where ICN had its roots. These games became legendary and fiercely competitive—just like the company and its boss.

Several in the audience that year would rise to run ICN divisions, then transfer to corporate to help Panic, Lightstone, Hancock, Robins, and new CFO Roy Doupe run the company worldwide. Adam Jerney, a rising star who joined from Roche, would run Holland, then all of Europe. Jorge Mendonca Lima, MD, from Johnson & Johnson Brazil, headed up Usafarma and Latin America, then transferred to run the Pacific Basin as well. Hans Thierstein joined from Cheseborough Ponds to run Switzerland, advancing to corporate controller. Horst Kranz, MD, came from Woelm and eventually ran worldwide marketing. Goodman stayed in Canada, which, true to his word, had become a standout division.

Adam Jerney

Hans Thierstein

Above: Milan Panic enjoys a lighter moment with the team during a management meeting

Left: First international management meeting, held at the Huntington Sheraton Hotel in Pasadena, California

Above: NARI director Lionel Simon

Left: ICN managers playing soccer

Bottom left: Fred Andrea

Bottom middle: Horst Kranz

Bottom right: Morris Goodman

CALL IT RIBAVIRIN

The stock, battered by Abelson then pummeled over ICN's 1971 results, needed a boost. By March of 1972 it was time to tell the street about 1229.

NARI had discovered a low-molecular-weight, non-interferon-inducing broad-spectrum antiviral agent. After months of testing, the promising compound was registered under the trademark Virazole, which stood for antiviral triazole. Soon after, the USAN Council adopted the generic nonproprietary name ribavirin for the chemical.

A synthetic nucleoside, it was lauded as the first of a whole new family of antiviral compounds. It was particularly potent against the RNA virus that caused influenza and other respiratory diseases. Initial tests showed that it may be more effective against viruses than any other drug known at the time. Dr. Robert Sidwell, of NARI, was scheduled to present data from animal studies at upcoming conferences, beginning with the American Chemical Society Meeting in Boston, April 9–14. The stock rose back to the 30s in anticipation.

On the podium, Sidwell described the agent's mode of action, which was based on slowing the body's reproductive process, enabling the body's own defense mechanisms to overcome the virus invader. Ribavirin was found to possess significant antiviral activity against aerosol-induced or intranasally induced influenza A and B virus infections in mice. Three serotypes of influenza virus were cleared, and the drug was 90% effective. Few compounds were known that had this activity.

ABOVE – Dr. Roland K. Robins discusses three promising new compounds

"ICN will change the worldwide practice of medicine," Dr. Robins tells ICN managers.

1972

But the stock rise was short-lived. Analysts kept questioning whether the warning signs revealed in the 1971 report signaled a turn in direction or just a temporary setback. *Forbes* wrote a negative story called "Panic and the Street," characterizing ICN as just a hodgepodge of little pharma and biochemical companies strung together by liberal accounting.

Panic took the criticism in stride. He was learning quickly how fickle Wall Street could be. Rapid growth had its risks, and the time had come for integration. There would be more setbacks, the US economy was sputtering, interest rates were starting to rise along with inflation, and the fast growth consolidators that depended on pooling of interest accounting were rapidly losing favor. The '60s bubble had turned to bust, and stocks were dropping. But, in Panic's mind, ICN was a remarkable company. It had defied the odds and become a full-fledged pharmaceutical company. And it had ribavirin. Yes, problems were mounting, but finding solutions to them was his passion and his job.

But investor support was rapidly deteriorating. The May 1972 second quarter tested resolve. Although it was minor, per-share earnings fell to $0.26 from $0.30 a year earlier, the first earnings miss since 1964. The stock took a beating, falling from $30 to $19 in one day. And Panic was on the hot seat yet again.

The miss was due to several factors. Sparco had shut down a nonprofitable bulk chemical plant, which lowered antibiotic sales for five months while capacity was picked up at Arco. L-DOPA sold less than $1 million for the quarter, way below expectations. As a result, operating profit of ICN biochemical fell. Also, G&A was up to $2.2 million in the first six months vs. $832,000 over the same period the year before. The increase was due in part to the opening of new divisional offices in Germany and São Paulo and a new office in Tokyo.

Panic also announced plans for a $10-million plant-modernization program in the United States, financed with 7% mortgage loans. Two large pharmaceutical plants were under construction, one in Cincinnati, Ohio, and one in Covina, California. Covina would span 90,000 square feet and house SCA Sun Valley, United Labs, and Dartell. Cincinnati would consolidate the Bentex and King Drug units, SIG, and SCA Cleveland. Covina would be one of the largest pharmaceutical product facilities in the West, producing capsules, tablets, topicals, veterinary products, and its own custom and private-label services. Cincinnati's plant was 210,000 square feet, manufacturing 50 generic products in 216 package sizes and dosage forms. Cincinnati would employ 450 people and turn out 100 million tablets daily in hard capsule gelatin, tablets, powders, ointments, gels, and creams. Rawson moved into a new plant in San Leandro. And in Canada, Morris Goodman consolidated Strong Cobb, Winley-Morris, and Sherman and Ulster into a new facility in Montreal. Short sellers questioned the use of debt and cautioned shareholders that these relocations might disrupt sales.

The slip was small, causing analysts to revise downward their '72 forecasts, with the exception of the Blythe analyst, who maintained his estimate at $1.35. Still, consensus on the street was growing that the glory days of ICN reporting annual profit gains of 30% or more were over.

Fortunately, ICN rebounded in the third quarter with a 27% gain over the prior year. Through nine months, ICN was back on target at $0.86 vs. $0.79 the year before. With a huge fourth quarter, there was still the chance Blythe could be right. The stock eased back into the 20s, although many investors were concerned that ICN hadn't announced a new acquisition in nine months. ICN's filing of the ribavirin IND and the announced 20% stake in Japan's Sanko Pharmaceuticals Industries LTD temporarily eased concerns.

However, the fourth quarter and full-year report announced in March were shockers. Those feared write-offs had become reality. Sales were $164 million, up 21% from $135.7 million. But net income after accounting changes, year-end adjustments, and extraordinary and nonrecurring items was $1.3 million, a sharp decline from 1971 net of $7.6 million, or $0.21 vs. $1.20. Internally, faced with a continuing drop in antibiotics in Switzerland and the failure of meeting its own guidance, Panic and the board decided to bite the bullet in the fourth quarter and write off all that deferred R&D—essentially clean house. This change in accounting practice resulted in a nonrecurring charge of $1.6 million, or $0.25. The antibiotics drop cost $0.27, and the full cost of R&D that year, which before had been only partially expensed, was another $0.11.

But there was more. The termination of Smith-Kline's contract cost $0.06. L-DOPA for the year had sold just $542,000. ICN had to buy back inventories, even though the brands Levodopa and Bendopa were just starting to sell more. Panic promised a full recovery in '73, but this time few on the street believed him. The stock was $12, and the bloom was off the rose. Panic now had to prove he could manage, not just acquire.

Panic announced plans for a $10-million plant-modernization program in the United States, financed with 7% mortgage loans. Two large pharmaceutical plants were being built, one in Cincinnati, Ohio, and one in Covina, California.

ICN PHARMACEUTICALS INC.

In April 1973, the board changed the name of the company to ICN Pharmaceuticals Inc. Corporate moved from Pasadena into the four-building NARI campus in Irvine. Pharmaceutical, chemical, and merchandising activities were present in 15 countries worldwide. ICN had 20 divisions in the major world markets of the United States, Canada, Western Europe, Latin America, and the Far East. Six thousand employees came to work each morning.

Because of the lack of growth externally, organic growth proved much tougher, and there were shortfalls from the relocations. There was also the debt—and now more of it, given the plant expenditures. NARI's budgets were trimmed, and new discovery was essentially stopped. ICN had grown too fast; it had to retrench. To mitigate risk and stretch working capital to deal with the higher debt load, ICN partnered ribavirin with the Lederle Division of American Cyanamid. Lederle would take over funding US clinical trials in return for global marketing rights.

Panic saw it all as an exercise of failure. On the one hand, he was being criticized for growing too fast, but in the case of their prized asset ribavirin, the company had not grown fast enough. They just didn't have the marketing clout to do the potential blockbuster any justice. And he was sick about having to cut back NARI. Still, priorities had shifted. The company had to return to profitability. And most importantly, he had to do something about the debt. Interest rates were rising, and interest expense was eating profits. The stock price was $11 per share.

The 1973 report revealed these strains and challenges. Year-end sales were $170.5 million vs. $161.3 million, up 6%. Interest expense was 3.3 million, up from $1.7 million. Net income was $0.49 vs. the depressed '72 result of $0.21. The plant-modernization program necessitated an increase in mortgage debt of $3.3 million but at a staggering 7% per year. Interest rates were rising.

But there was also another surprising charge due to the company's adoption of an accounting standard called FASB 8. This required foreign loans be converted to dollars at the exchange rate prevailing at the close of the period. Previously, ICN had booked these loans at the exchange rate prevailing at the time of the loan. The dollar had turned weak against the Deutsch mark and Swiss franc. Instead of DM 3.25 to the US $1, it was now $2.5 to the dollar. ICN owed more in dollars. The difference, a translation loss, was to be charged each quarter as a nonrecurring expense. In 1973, this translation loss was $1.2 million. And like the accrued R&D, there was more on the balance sheet that may have to be written off in 1974, especially if the dollar continued to sink.

There were some bright spots. The pharmaceutical group contributed $124 million, up 8%. All divisions advanced, except the United States, which was down 3%. Just as analysts predicted, the massive US relocation had impacted the P&L. Fortunately, Germany, Brazil, and Canada were growing double-digit. Phase 2 ribavirin clinical trials were approved to start against herpes zoster, hepatitis, influenza, infectious mononucleosis, and other viral diseases in the United States, Mexico, Canada, Brazil, and England. Brazil began studies on viral hepatitis and if successful was posed to become the first country to launch the drug, expected sometime in 1975.

But the balance sheet continued to worsen. The additional mortgage debt taken on to finance the new plants resulted in higher interest expense. With that much debt, ICN would face cash flow problems. Worse, it had $25 million of debt coming due in a year.

If that wasn't enough, Panic also had to explain UML, which had turned into a nightmare acquisition, arguably ICN's biggest mistake ever. Instead of breaking even, the company was losing $2 million and had negative working capital. ICN tried to back out. It had issued 94,000 shares, which it now claimed to be a minority position. A court, however, ruled in favor of the previous owners. ICN was ordered to pay all $7.6 million, plus interest and legal costs of $2 million, but not in stock: $10 million in cash. And given a worsening of the business, the auditors insisted on a large impairment charge. The balance sheet impact was serious. ICN suddenly owed $10 million, had guaranteed additional UML loans of $2 million, and now owned a company losing money that had to be turned around.

Everyone braced for 1974—it would not be pretty. Certain directors such as Cohen and Williams jumped ship; their reputations could not weather the tough times ahead. Panic also faced personal tragedy; his wife, Jelica, died suddenly, leaving three children. He was alone, devastated by his loss. After the kids, work was his therapy, his passion. The burden of ICN was squarely on his shoulders. He built the company, and he would have to save it, no matter what the personal cost.

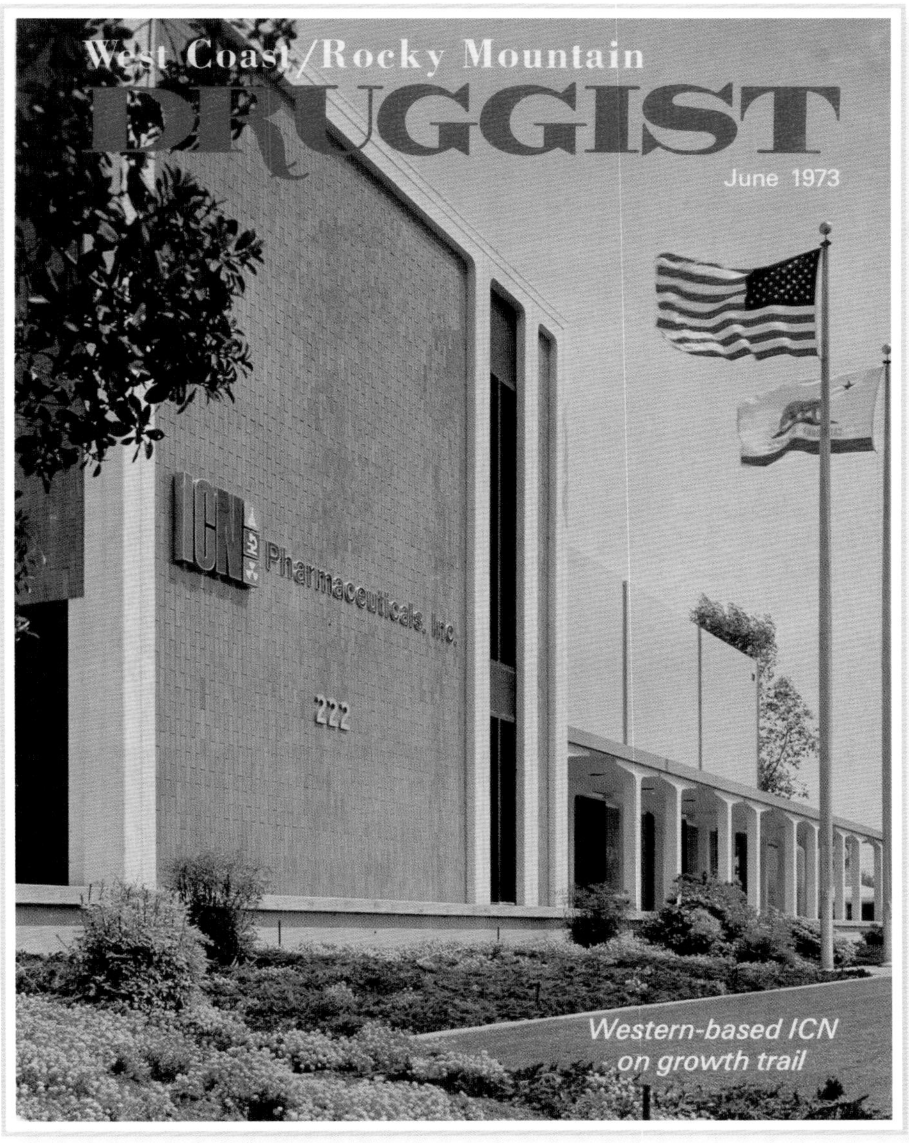

ICN's new plant in Covina, California

HITTING BOTTOM

1974 was every bit the disaster insiders had predicted. Sales were a record $178.1 million but only up 4%. The reported loss was a whopping $20.8 million, or $3.13 per share. Operating income was down 39% to $10.6 million. Currency woes hit across the board. The rise in the Swiss franc drove up European production costs. Much of the business was generic, so raising prices was not an option. On the balance sheet, the dollar's drop caused a huge translation loss of $8.1 million. The US pharmaceutical division lost $3.5 million, due entirely to lost business associated with the relocations. Interest expense was $6.1 million vs. $3.3 million the prior year and at an average rate of 12%. The US economy was was in a recession, inflation was 7%, and interest rates were rising. It was the worst time to be leveraged. And ICN lacked the required cash flow to pay its debts.

The write-off of UML goodwill was $5.5 million. There were additional losses associated with closing companies of $2.6 million. Long-term debt was $48.6 million: $35.6 million in notes payable to banks, $7.9 million owed to former owners of UML, and the rest in high-cost mortgage loans to finance the new plants. And much of this debt was tied to the prime rate, which was nearing an all-time high. Panic had to scramble. He had to renegotiate almost $30 million in debt coming due and then quickly turn around a bunch of losing operations.

The peseta in Spain was devaluing, as were the peso in Mexico and the cruzeiro in Brazil. The plane was sold, and corporate was moved to a suite of offices in the much smaller Covina plant. NARI was disbanded. Panic began driving himself to work. This was his problem to fix, and he took full responsibility. Starting in 1975, ICN's stock price was $1, and its market cap had fallen from $350 million to $10 million. Value Line publicly questioned the company's survival.

VIRAZOLE® LAUNCHED

SHEER WILL

Throught this all Panic never doubted himself. He was a problem solver and thrived when things got tough. This was make or break. He had Bob Smith, Weldon Jolley, Fred Andrea, Dick Fallis, John Hancock, Roy Doupe, and a new cadre of experienced global executives to help him turn things around. Roland had left to start a cancer unit at BYU, but he left behind ribavirin. Everyone believed ICN could be rebuilt around that drug. They also had some prized business units that were doing well. Slowly, the restructuring plan took shape.

Panic and Doupe negotiated extensions on the loans. Each division head was instructed to prune low-margin product lines. They would put every dollar possible into ribavirin, and, if necessary, sell assets to pay debt. The final action was inevitable but tough to stomach. This would mean parting with ICN's best-performing units, Woelm, Usafarma, and maybe even Canada.

Milan Panic, 1974

Panic was a problem solver and thrived when things got tough.

A BREAKTHROUGH

Fortunately, Lederle gave ribavirin back to ICN in 1975, asserting the drug was not worthy of further development. While embarrassing publicly, behind closed doors, both Panic and Smith were ecstatic. They knew otherwise. By this time, the IND had been approved, and oral ribavirin had begun US clinical trials in herpes with an NDA scheduled for filing in 1979. Herpes represented a potential $100-million market that ICN could look forward to in the '80s.

But Panic needed something more immediate. Fortunately, the '60s strategy of expanding into Mexico, and then Brazil, paid off. Ribavirin was quickly registered to begin clinical studies in hepatitis in Brazil and influenza in Mexico. By late 1975, both were on the market, trademarked as Viramid and Vilona. First-year sales in Brazil were $1.5 million, with only 25% of prescriptions written for hepatitis; the rest were split between herpes simplex and herpes zoster. In Mexico, Vilona was tested in varicella, hepatitis, measles, mumps, influenza, and herpes zoster at dosages between 300 and 600 mg per day. First-year sales were $500,000. By 1977, ribavirin was registered in 22 countries.

But a new discovery powered ICN even more. The US Army was investigating technology for the dosing of small-particle aerosols of antiviral agents administered over sustained periods of time. Their objective was to deliver better antiviral chemotherapy by depositing high drug concentrations at the site of viral replication without systemic side effects. After modest results with antivirals amantadine and rimantadine, ribavirin was tried. It worked. Ribavirin administered in small particles as an aerosol had profound effects on the upper and lower respiratory tracts.

Dr. Vernon Knight, professor of medicine and chairman of the Department of Microbiology and Immunology at Baylor College of Medicine, saw this news and got to thinking about ribavirin's potential in influenza and respiratory syncytial virus (RSV), the most important cause of respiratory tract infection in infants and young children. As a member of the National Institutes of Health's task force on immunization, he had been searching since the '60s for an effective treatment for hospitalized adult and infant cases. He contacted Smith and Jolley to sponsor trials, pledge the resources of Baylor as an investigative site and to also develop a new aerosol generator that improved the army's prototype. Smith and Jolley readily agreed. Ribavirin could be a highly effective flu agent.

By 1977, ribavirin was registered in 22 countries.

PILOT

In a small pilot study, under a new IND sponsored by ICN but run by Knight, ribavirin small-particle aerosol was shown to be effective in the treatment of influenza during an outbreak among 21 college students. This represented the first successful treatment of this virus infection. Eleven patients treated with ribavirin experienced disappearance of systemic illness and reduction of viral shedding, compared to zero effect in 10 control patients treated with placebo. The students inhaled the spray for 12-hour intervals through a hose and face mask. By the second day, their fevers were dropping, aches diminishing, and viral counts returning to zero. Treatment was well tolerated, and no toxicity was demonstrated. The estimated dose of ribavirin aerosol retained was 2 grams in 39 hours of treatment during the first 60 hours in the hospital.

The ribavirin delivery system

"Ribavirin mist, produced over a wide range of dosages by the small particle aerosol generator, is administered with the same equipment used to deliver oxygen (or mist) to the infant, such as an oxyhood."

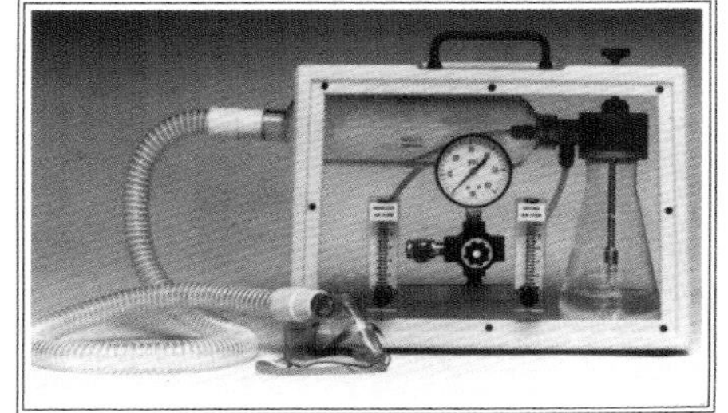

The heart of the system: The small particle aerosol generator (SPAG)

The components of SPAG are shown in the figure below.

Ribavirin aerosol may be delivered to a face mask (A), or an oxygen tent if a hood cannot be employed, making administration easy. The pneumatic flow system is operated with compressed air (B).

After passing through an external flow meter, the air enters the SPAG and is controlled at 26 psig using the SPAG pressure regulator (C).

Incoming air passes via a manifold through two flow meters equipped with control valves (D). Some of this gas is directed through a nebulizer (atomizer) (E), which generates a fine mist of hydrated ribavirin in the reservoir flask (F). This vapor then enters a drying chamber (G), which functions to dehumidify and reduce the size of the aerosol particles.

Aerosol system

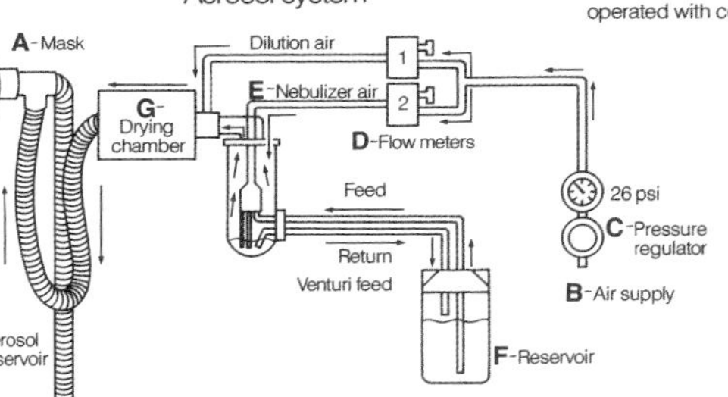

—Adapted from Knight V, Wilson SZ, Quarles JM, et al: *Lancet*, Oct 31, 1981, 945.

Small particle size: The mass median diameter of the delivered ribavirin aerosol particles ranges from 1.2 to 1.3 μm, allowing deep deposition into small respiratory tract airways.

The small-particle ribavirin delivery system

NEW LIFE

These data gave ICN new life. The team envisioned that institutional sales of ribavirin for influenza could bring $100 million in annual revenue. And because it was hospitals, they could sell the drug through their own specialized sales force. The indication seemed straightforward, and Vernon Knight and Baylor agreed to collaborate with ICN and build the aerosol generator. *Businessweek* ran a story in 1979 showcasing how a promising flu cure could reboot a struggling drug stock. All Milan Panic had to do was keep the company alive and figure out a way to raise money again.

But first, the operations. As the '70s ended, ICN was by no means out of the woods. Panic needed to continue renegotiating payment terms with the banks while he sold assets. To that end, loans due in 1975–77 were extended to 1980, and quarterly installments were implemented. Concurrently, they closed facilities, entered sale-leaseback transactions, and quickly dispersed of assets. Rawson went for $10 million; the instrument businesses Tracerlab and Paris Labo were sold. Warehouses and excess facilities were closed. The four-building NARI campus was leased. Employees dropped from 6,000 to 2,000. Inventories were reduced, and low-margin products dropped.

In the end, large pharmaceutical disposals were the only way to pay the debt. Woelm was sold to Revlon's Michel Bergerac, who had become Panic's close friend. Bergerac paid $25 million to ICN, resulting in a recorded gain of $10 million. A few years later, Bergerac would also buy Usafarma, paying $9 million cash. King Drug was sold. By 1979, Arco and all the Swiss cosmetic businesses were sold. It was painful; these were great companies that, net of non-operating charges such as translation, had performed well. Panic hung on to Mexico and Canada but closed Spain and Italy. The peseta devaluation made the business a loser.

For Panic, ending the '70s was not like ending the '60s. ICN had almost gone bankrupt. Sales had dropped to $50 million and would likely drop further. The company was still losing money, although breakeven was close and the debt had been drastically reduced. The stock was back to $5. A former friend and shareholder Lionel Steinberg turned on him and initiated a proxy fight to throw him out. Steinberg lost, but Panic's star on Wall Street had faded. He had also suffered immense personal loss. But, he had the drug. Ribavirin could save lives—in the thousands per year. By sheer will he would persevere, see this through. He had his children to care for and a payroll to meet. Failure was not an option. He was only 50 years old.

For Panic, ending the '70s was not like ending the '60s.
ICN had almost gone bankrupt.
By sheer will he would persevere, see this through.
Failure was not an option.

Inside Wall Street

A controversial cure for a recovering stock

Panic and pills: FDA approval of Virazole would mean "a new beginning."

ICN Pharmaceutical Inc., a hot stock a few years ago before it was hit by shareholders' suits, currency losses, and a proxy fight, has suddenly become a standout on the New York Stock Exchange. Since January the stock has nearly doubled, to about $8 a share. Investors, it seems, have high hopes for ICN's anti-viral drug, Virazole, which is being used or tested in myriad countries for such maladies as certain types of hepatitis and venereal disease, shingles, and the common cold.

The company says Virazole works not by killing the virus but by slowing its "replication" so that the body's own immunization system can work. While the drug is sold abroad, notably in Mexico and Brazil, it is only being clinically tested in the U. S. But on Feb. 16, ICN filed a new drug application with the Food & Drug Administration asking that Virazole be approved for the treatment of shingles, and the company has hired Dr. James L. Goddard, a former FDA commissioner, as a consultant on the drug. ICN must prove to the FDA that it is safe and effective. If granted, FDA approval could mean "a new beginning for ICN," says ICN Chairman Milan Panic, a former long-distance bicycle racer from Yugoslavia.

Side effects? To be sure, Virazole is not without its detractors. "Studies have shown the drug to have little or no efficacy against various forms of influenza," charges M. Daniel Tatkon, editor and publisher of *inforMed*, a newsletter. "Animal and human pharmacology and toxicology studies have demonstrated serious side effects associated with this medication."

Dr. Roberts A. Smith, an ICN director and professor of chemistry at the University of California at Los Angeles, who has conducted research on the drug, says: "We do not think it is toxic at all." Smith admits, however, that ICN does not recommend the drug for women of childbearing age.

Even if ICN gets FDA approval, it would still need to build a U. S. marketing organization. One approach Panic is considering is a marketing venture with another company. ICN had an agreement with American Cyanamid Co. to test Virazole, but the big chemical company canceled it in 1975.

Reduced debt. In any case, ICN, which also makes other drugs and vitamins and nutritional supplements for the chiropractic market, appears in better health than in the past. Debt has been cut to less than $30 million, down from $73 million in 1975. And Panic has

Left: Milan Panic and ICN featured in *Businessweek* magazine

Above: Tablet coating line in Covina

1980–1989

- 1980—Ribavirin in aerosol form starts clinical studies against influenza A & B conducted by Baylor College of Medicine, under direction of Dr. Vernon Knight.
- May 1980—Revlon buys Usafarma for $8M.
- August 1980—Viratek formed.
- September 30, 1981—Roberts Smith takes two-year leave from UCLA to be Viratek president.
- September 30, 1981—Viratek issues 570K shares at $8 and trades to $9.25 in aftermarket. D. H. Blair underwrites.
- November 1981—*Lancet* reports aerosolized ribavirin results on college students with influenza A at Texas A&M.
- July 15, 1982—Baylor College of Medicine and Viratek sign agreement whereby Viratek is granted exclusive rights to market a Baylor-developed aerosol generator (SPAG) to administer ribavirin in small particles to hospitalized patients with severe respiratory syncytial virus (RSV).
- September 9, 1982—Viratek files an NDA with the FDA for hospital use of Virazole (ribavirin) to treat influenza and respiratory syncytial virus.
- September 10, 1982—ICN acquires first company in 10 years, KOS Isotopes of Cambridge.
- 1983—CDC issues report that ribavirin may work in AIDS.
- 1983—Bill MacDonald joins ICN as head of tax and business development.
- September 15, 1983—E. F. Hutton underwrites 1M shares of ICN at $9.50/share.
- October 4, 1983—ICN spins out SPI Pharmaceuticals, issuing 260K shares of SPI at $12/share. Bateman Eichler and Prudential Bache underwrite.
- November 3, 1983—Viratek NDA amended to include just RSV.
- 1983—*New England Journal of Medicine* and *JAMA* run publications on ribavirin as an emerging breakthrough in the treatment of high-risk influenza and RSV.
- July 18, 1984—Eastman Kodak makes minority equity investments in preferred stock in ICN and its subsidiary Viratek. Lehman Brothers advises. $8.4M for 5% of ICN and 10% of Viratek.
- 1984—ICN raises $61M in debt and equity securities. This includes the investment in ICN by IBM, MCA, and Eastman Kodak. Bank of America issues to ICN a $20M line of credit.
- 1984—Prudential Bache underwrites $30M in 12.5% debentures due 1999.
- March 1984—SPI buys Elder Pharmaceuticals in Bryan, Ohio, and begins dermatology business.
- 1984—ICN moves into its new corporate headquarters in Costa Mesa, California, at 3300 Hyland Avenue. ICN leases 164,000-square-foot office building from Discovision, a JV of IBM and MCA. Issues convertible preferred and pays $9.1M cash for rights to buy building at future date. Renamed ICN Plaza.
- 1984—Ted Olic joins company to direct expansion in Eastern Europe.
- May 13, 1985—Kodak forms $45M JV with antiviral pioneer ICN. Reinstates NARI to focus on antiviral, anticancer, and antiaging drugs.
- December 1985—FDA approves ribavirin for RSV. Health Canada follows.
- February 1986—Kodak agrees to fund all AIDS trials for $2M upfront payment and royalties.
- October 1986—FDA classifies ribavirin 1-AA top priority in agency review of potential AIDS treatments.
- March 6, 1986—Trials scheduled to begin at eight medical centers in the United States. Virazole testing in pre-AIDS, or ARC (AIDS-related complex), with such symptoms as swollen lymph glands, weight loss, excessive perspiration, and presence of AIDS antibodies in bloodstream.
- July 1986—Paine Webber underwrites 2M ICN common and simultaneously places $100M senior subordinated debentures at 12.875%.
- 1986—ICN raises a total of $350M in debt and equity, including six Euro convertible offerings led by Swiss Banker Jean-Francois Kurz.
- 1986—Viratek stock hits $74 per share.
- June 1986—Viratek signs 15-year agreement with US Army to fund ribavirin trials in dengue fever, lassa fever, hemorrhagic fever, and sand-fly fever.
- 1986—Biomedical goes public through DH Blair.
- January 9, 1987—ICN holds press conference at Marriott Hotel in Washington, DC, to announce preliminary data from the eight-center, 379-patient ribavirin trials on LAS and ARC patients at 600 and 800 mg.
- 1987—Edmund G. Brown Jr., Esq., elected to ICN Biomedicals Board of Directors.
- September 9, 1987—ICN buys 6.3% stake in F. Hoffmann–La Roche.
- 1987—Michel Bergerac, former chairman and CEO of Revlon, elected to ICN Board of Directors.
- January 1988—ICN boosts its investment in F. Hoffmann–La Roche to 7.3%.
- March 25, 1988—ICN sells its 8.6% stake in F. Hoffmann–La Roche for $209M.
- June 27, 1988—ICN Biomedicals Inc. lists on American Stock Exchange under symbol BIM.
- July 1988—ICN buys Mestinon, Tensilon, and Prostigmin from Roche.
- 1988—ICN discloses 25% stake in Schering AG.
- 1988—BIOMED and SPI trade on AMAX.
- 1989—Talks begin to acquire Galenika in Yugoslavia.
- April 1989—Thomas H. Lenagh elected to ICN Biomedicals Board of Directors.
- October 1989—Jean-Francois Kurz elected to ICN Biomedicals Board of Directors.
- 1989—Roger Guillemin, MD, PhD, elected to SPI Board of Directors. Dr. Guillemin is a former Nobel Prize winner in medicine.
- 1989—ICN announces that more than 60,000 infants have been treated for RSV safely with ribavirin since drug's approval.

THE EIGHTIES

WONDER DRUG

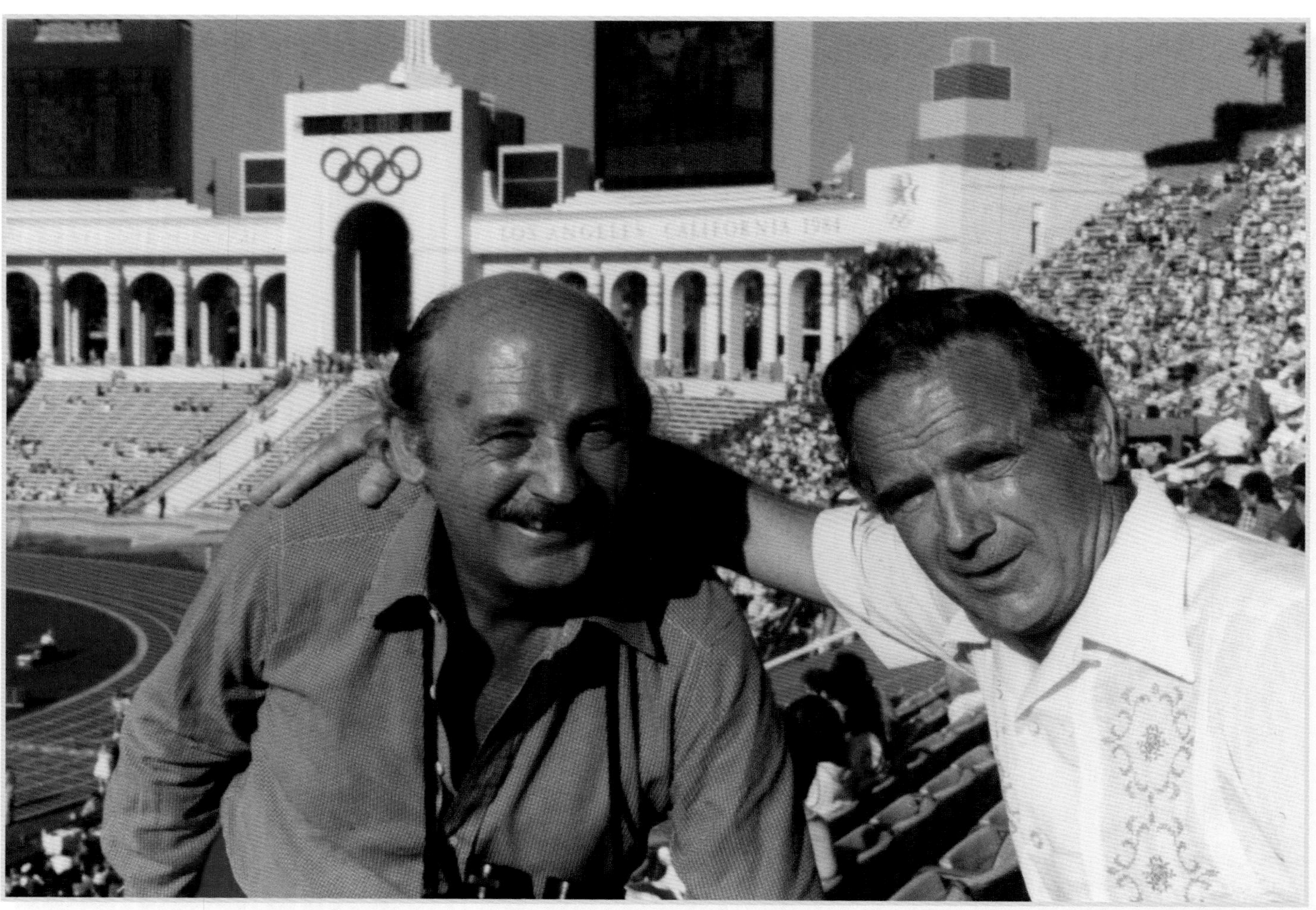

Revlon's Michel Bergerac and Milan Panic

BIOTECHNOLOGY

The turbulent '70s had ended. A new American president was in office, promising tax cuts and economic renewal. Confidence was restored, and the stock market turned up. In October 1980, a tiny start-up named Genentech sold shares for the first time, raising $35 million. It was the hottest initial public offering in more than a decade. It also marked the beginning of a new sub-sector of the drug industry called biotechnology. These were start-ups that developed protein-based therapeutics using gene expression. Initially, there were only four biotech companies. Each would follow Genentech's lead and launch its own IPO. One company, Cetus, raised more than $100 million. None of them had a single product on the market.

The public's enthusiasm for biotechnology intrigued Milan Panic and his board. In their mind, ICN was the pioneer biotech, having successfully converted nucleic acids into viable drug candidates back in the '60s.

But ICN had so much more. It had revenues, a pipeline of more than 5,000 biologically active compounds, and a potential global blockbuster in ribavirin. Genentech's revenue was a paltry $3.5 million per year, and driven by R&D partnerships, not real product sales. Their first product candidate, human insulin, was just a concept. There was widespread industry uncertainty about its pricing, manufacturing costs, margins, or whether natural human proteins could be produced efficiently, much less patented. Investors didn't seem to care. If the human body's own proteins could be made into disease-fighting agents, the potential seemed endless. Biotech was a bet on the future. It was sizzling hot, and investors wanted in.

If the human body's own proteins could be made into disease-fighting agents, the potential seemed endless.

TRADITIONAL DRUGS

Traditional drug makers were enjoying robust expansion as well. Global pharmaceutical sales had risen to more than $50 billion a year. The United States led with $14 billion, fueled by large gains in antibiotics, hormones, vitamins, and antipsychotics. Pfizer's annual R&D budget had reached a whopping $200 million, with Merck right behind at $180 million. Novel drugs were being introduced at record levels, and the pace of new discoveries showed no signs of letting up.

G.D. Searle launched a new sugar sweetener called aspartame. Squibb marketed Capoten for hypertension. Upjohn added Xanax, a tranquilizer. And SmithKline's new antiulcer drug, Tagamet, became the top-selling drug in the world. Even new drug delivery systems were hot. Controlled-release technology was extending product life cycles and patents. Adhesive patches were designed to deliver small, steady doses through the skin. The first such product was a nitroglycerine patch for angina.

Global pharmaceutical sales had risen to more than $50 billion a year. The United States led with $14 billion.

ANTIVIRALS

The dawn of antivirals was on the horizon, but the class itself was still in its infancy. Annual sales barely touched $100 million, and only a few products were approved. In fact, the FDA had just formed its first antiviral division. Nevertheless, think tanks such as Stanford Research Institute predicted huge markets ahead. More than 100 million US citizens were infected each year by various strains of the influenza virus alone, with some four to eight million hospitalized. The herpes family of viruses affected more than nine million people a year. Hepatitis was a worldwide health threat.

Alcon's idoxuridine, approved since the '60s, was the only antiviral indicated for herpes, but it was restricted to herpes simplex keratitis of the eye. DuPont's amantadine and rimantadine had been launched for influenza; however, each had limited efficacy and were accompanied by side effects. What the public needed was a broad-spectrum agent like penicillin. But nothing existed in any pipeline that even came close, except for an investigational agent called ribavirin, developed by a struggling little company in California called ICN Pharmaceuticals.

570,000 Shares

VIRATEK, INC.

Common Stock

($.10 par value)

Prior to this offering, there has been no public market for the Company's Common Stock. For information relating to the method of determining the initial public offering price, see "Underwriting." It is presently estimated that the initial public offering price will be $7.00.

THIS OFFERING INVOLVES A HIGH DEGREE OF RISK. (SEE "INTRODUCTORY STATEMENT")

THESE SECURITIES HAVE NOT BEEN APPROVED OR DISAPPROVED BY THE SECURITIES AND EXCHANGE COMMISSION NOR HAS THE COMMISSION PASSED UPON THE ACCURACY OR ADEQUACY OF THIS PROSPECTUS. ANY REPRESENTATION TO THE CONTRARY IS A CRIMINAL OFFENSE.

	Price To Public	Underwriting Discounts and Commissions(1)	Proceeds To Company(2)
Per Share	$7.00	$ 0.70	$ 6.30
Total Minimum	$3,990,000	$ 399,000	$ 3,591,000

(1) See "Underwriting" for information concerning indemnification of, other arrangements with, and substantial additional compensation and other consideration for, the Underwriters.

(2) Before deducting expenses payable by the Company estimated at $195,000 ($0.34 per share).

The shares are offered by the several Underwriters named herein when, as and if issued and accepted by the Underwriters, subject to their right to reject orders in whole or in part and subject to certain other conditions. It is expected that certificates for the shares will be ready for delivery at the offices of MacDonald, Krieger & Bowyer, Inc., 356 North Camden Drive, Beverly Hills, California 90210 on or about ...., 1981.

D. H. BLAIR & CO., INC. **MACDONALD, KRIEGER & BOWYER, INC.**

Viratek, Inc. common stock offering

VIRATEK

Whereas in the early '70s bankers were knocking down Milan Panic's door, the start of the '80s was eerily silent. ICN was just a shadow of its former self, and life had been anything but fun the past six years for its CEO. Panic had to shift from globe-trotting entrepreneur to turnaround artist, fighting fire after fire. Defying the odds, he and his downsized team of executives persevered. ICN survived and was actually nearing breakeven following five straight years of losses. The only operations remaining were Canada, Mexico, Holland, a portion of the North American business, and the original biochemical unit. United Medical Laboratories was gone.

Signing deal with Baylor College of Medicine

Since ICN's revenue peaked in 1974, 11 subsidiaries had been sold or closed. The proceeds were used entirely to pay debt. Gone were the crown jewels in Germany and Brazil, as well as much of the US and Swiss businesses. Long-term debt had been chopped from $71 million to $4.5 million, which at that point consisted mainly of mortgages and capitalized leases. Annual interest expense was reduced to under $1 million, versus a high of $7 million in 1975. Even ICN's debt-to-equity ratio, at 13:1, was nearing the industry average. In 1981, ICN posted after-tax earnings of $2 million, the first real profit since 1976. The company acquired KOR Isotopes in Cambridge, its first deal in more than eight years. Another biomedical acquisition, Schwarz Mann, followed the next year. ICN's stock, which in 1974 had dropped to $1, was back to $6.

Still, Panic and the board faced a mounting task. They had to get the pharmaceutical division growing again, raise capital, and fund ribavirin. ICN had a blockbuster on its hands, but no money. The company was so small and trivial, no bankers seemed to care. ICN's image was also tainted. Investors had been burned. And with just $40 million in annual sales, ICN could barely afford $1 million per year for R&D.

But Genentech's success inspired Panic. He just needed to find a way to get bankers excited again about ICN. Fortunately, the times were right. New boutique banking shops such as Hambrecht and Quist, Robertson Stephens, and Alex Browne & Sons were swarming the biotechs, raising hundreds of millions by using out-of-the-box vehicles such as R&D partnerships, rights offerings, and off-balance-sheet financings. Surely, the ever-creative Panic could find a tantalizing structure of his own.

One banker had an idea. While he wouldn't be able to raise institutional money on the same level as Genentech, he promised to get things started. His name was J. Morton "Morty" Davis of D.H. Blair & Co. He argued that the '80s were times of de-conglomerating. He proposed that ICN spin off ribavirin to the public in a new company—letting ICN retain the debt and function as a holding company while demonstrating at the same time that ICN's parts were greater in value than the whole. Panic could take advantage of the hot new issues market and IPO ribavirin and the NARI compounds to the public. Davis was certain that absent the burden of the parent, the new company would thrive. He advised the board to keep the share float thin and set the new company up for massive EPS growth via royalties on ribavirin. ICN's board named this company Viratek.

In late 1980, Viratek was formed, swapping all the compounds from ICN in exchange for common stock. The asset transfer included 35 domestic and foreign patents related to nucleic acid technology. The pipeline featured Compound 5825, a thiazole-C nucleoside that had shown a high level of anticancer activity and was on the National Cancer Institute's highest-priority list. Also included was 4221, or 3-Deazaguanine, which had demonstrated promising activity as an inhibitor of solid malignant tumor growth. Warner Lambert was negotiating to license it and fund phase 1 testing at M.D. Anderson and the USC Cancer Center.

But ribavirin was the star. Viratek secured complete control of the asset, including its limited foreign sales in Brazil, Mexico, and a few other countries. Investors bought in to the antiviral market opportunity at large but it was the drug's potential to deliver multiple revenue streams in influenza, herpes infections, hepatitis, viral-related childhood diseases, and various hemorrhagic fevers that sealed the deal. Ribavirin had the profile of a new penicillin. Some analysts even suggested that the drug's revenue may eventually surpass Tagamet. All ICN needed was that first FDA approval, then other indications were expected to follow.

In early 1981, Viratek went public at $7 per share. D.H. Blair sold 570,000 shares, raising $4 million. By 1982, the stock had risen to $9, fueled by the promise of aerosolized ribavirin for influenza and RSV. The pilot study in college students had worked. Moreover, the FDA had granted the US Centers for Disease Control approval to test ribavirin in injectable form to treat Lassa fever and the US Army permission to study the oral form for sand-fly fever.

Panic recruited an old friend, Robert H. Finch, to be Viratek's chairman. Finch was a former lieutenant governor of the state of California and later secretary of Health Education and Welfare under Nixon. Throughout his career, Panic would often turn to his political friends for help. Another close confidant and board member was Indiana Senator Birch Bayh, once a candidate for president. Long-time director Bob Smith took a two-year leave of absence from UCLA to be Viratek's president. Dr. Knight joined the board alongside Panic, who took no operating role. Dr. Robins and Dr. Jolley were also named as directors. Dr. Robins stayed on as director of the Cancer Research Center at Brigham Young University in Provo but was excited to be rejoining his old friends in a new quest to register and commercialize his prized discovery.

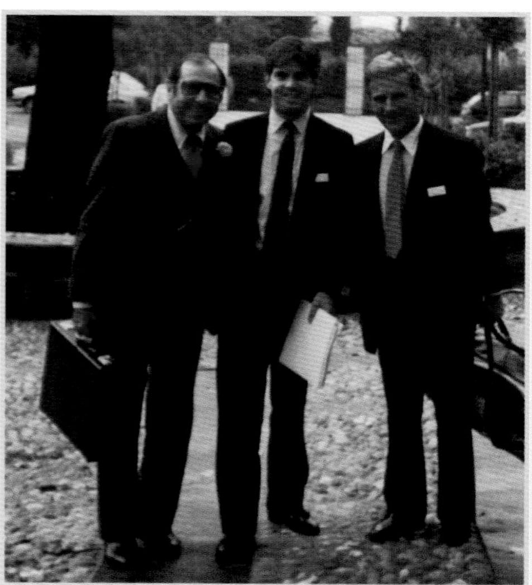

J. Morton "Morty" Davis, Mark Taylor, and Milan Panic on a road show in Europe

FLU CURE

With funding in hand, Knight's team at Baylor went to work engineering the ribavirin delivery device. It was called the SPAG, short for "small particle aerosol generator." It used compressed air to turn the lyophilized drug product into a fine mist that patients would breathe into their lungs through a face mask. Each subject received continuous treatment for 12–20 hours per day. What made it so effective was its ability to get more ribavirin to the site of infection in the respiratory tract. The inhaled mist deposited a layer of the drug on top of the infected cells where it would penetrate them and jam up viral replication.

By early '81, Knight's influenza A pilot had attracted national attention. A randomized controlled-phase 2B study in college students suffering from influenza A was under way at Texas A&M. Its positive results validated the pilot study, paving the way for pivotal multicenter studies during the '82–'83 flu season at the University of Rochester, Baylor, the University of Utah, the University of Cincinnati, and the University of Virginia. Concurrently, the University of Rochester Department of Pediatrics developed the dossier for RSV. ICN's plan was to file an NDA in 1983 for both indications, hospitalized cases of severe adult influenza and infants with RSV.

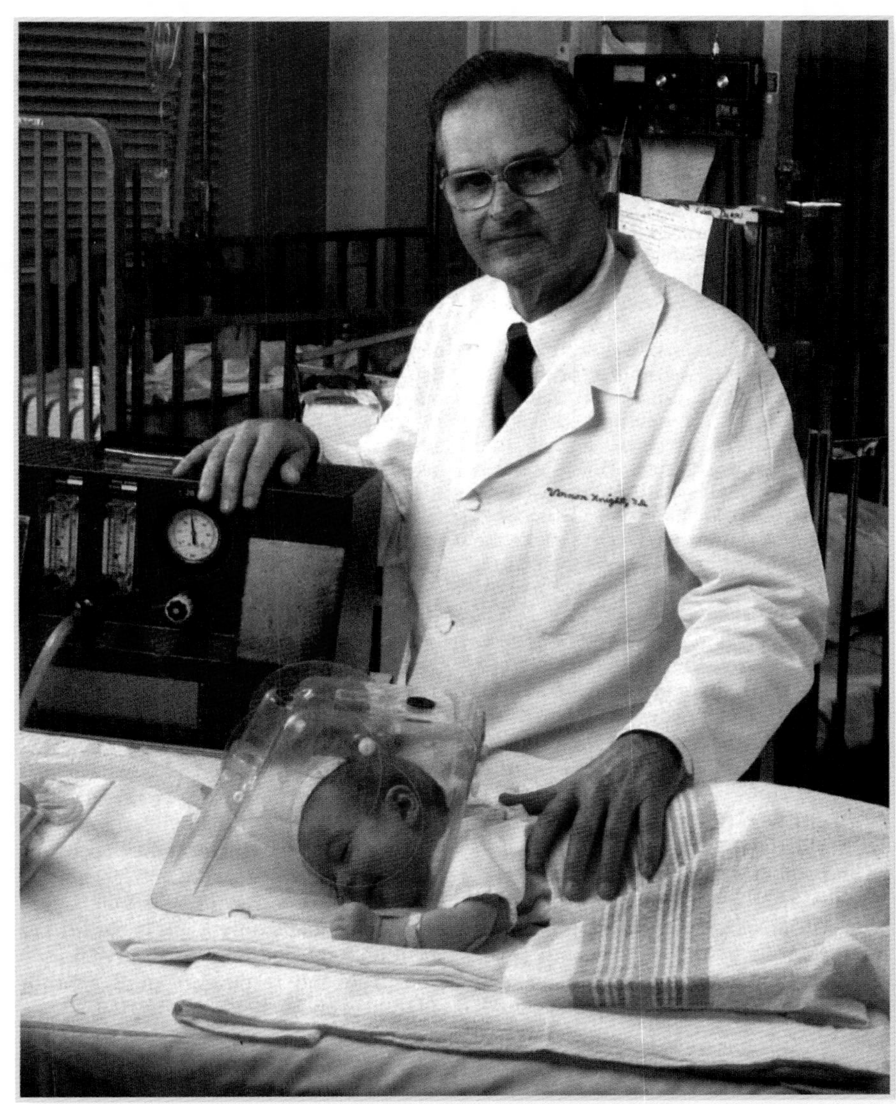

Dr. Knight featured in *Fortune* magazine, March 8, 1982

RSV

RSV was the faster direct path to approval. The clinical plan was designed to be carried out in two phases. First, Rochester studied ribavirin in healthy volunteers with experimental RSV infection that evaluated the drug's amelioration of signs and symptoms. They also investigated sensory pulmonary functions to ensure that inhaled ribavirin did not produce unwanted side effects. The drug and placebo were administered 12 hours per day for three days. The SPAG produced particles of 1.2 microns in diameter, administered at 12.5 liters per minute through the face mask. This translated to 55 mg per hour deposited in the respiratory tract. Patients received a deposited dose of 660 mg per patient per 12 hours. The ribavirin cohort drastically reduced fever and cough, with no evidence of abnormal pulmonary function. There were minimal adverse events.

The second study enrolled 33 infants with proven RSV infection who were ill enough to require at least three days of hospitalization. The subjects were randomized in a double-blind manner to receive either ribavirin or placebo by aerosol, which was administered continuously. The investigator assessed daily signs and symptoms using a severity of illness scale. Each subject underwent daily nasal washes to determine viral shedding. Seventeen infants received placebo and 16 ribavirin. Another six infants diagnosed with severe and life-threatening RSV were treated compassionately with ribavirin. The mean treatment duration was 4.9 days. Ribavirin significantly improved illness severity scores. Evaluation of various signs of illness at the beginning and end of therapy was significantly better for ribavirin. The average number of days of virus shedding in the ribavirin group was 2.9 vs. 4.3 days in the placebo group. And the quantity of virus in the nasal washes at the end of treatment was less in the ribavirin group.

The six children who had severe RSV pneumonia and were treated as compassionate cases received the aerosolized ribavirin for 7–22 days. Five completely recovered, and one died. No side effects or evidence of toxicity was evident from aerosolized ribavirin administration. Multicenter registration studies followed at Harvard Children's Hospital, the University of Toronto, the University of Glasgow, and King's College. These studies confirmed the earlier results.

Although the data on RSV were compelling, Panic, Smith, and Jolley were cautiously optimistic. It had been 12 grueling years since ribavirin was synthesized. The FDA pathway had been tough. But maybe RSV would finally be the indication that would take them over the goal line.

Maybe RSV would finally be the indication that would take them over the goal line.

FORTUNE MAGAZINE

Lee Smith, a financial writer at *Fortune*, wrote a cover feature entitled "Closing in on a Flu Cure," focused on how a little drug start-up called Viratek and its wonder drug ribavirin could turn around the ailing fortunes of its parent, once a star of Wall Street's go-go years. It was alleged to be the first time *Fortune* had devoted a cover story to an OTC company with a market cap that small. It hit the newsstands in March 1982, the first good press on ICN and Panic in 10 years. This was followed by 400 newspaper articles, ABC/NBC telecasts, and write-ups in the financial press including *Businessweek* and *US News and World Report*. Panic ordered reprints sent to more than 5,000 investors, both in the United States and in Europe. Viratek sponsored road shows in New York, London, Geneva, and Edenborough. Panic enjoyed getting back on the road to sell. A bit older at 52, he was still as lean as in his bicycle racing days and made a commanding presence. He was a born salesman.

ICN's stock rose to $9 and Viratek's to $15. In September 1983, Viratek filed an NDA for hospital use of ribaririn to treat influenza and RSV. If approved, ribavirin would be the first antiviral approved for both indications. The filing propelled Viratek to $20.75 per share and ICN to $10. The NDA was later amended, limiting the indication to just hospitalized RSV. The FDA wanted additional testing for influenza, and Panic wanted approval. The board calculated that RSV would be faster. It could get flu done in 1986. Similar filings were made in Great Britain and Canada.

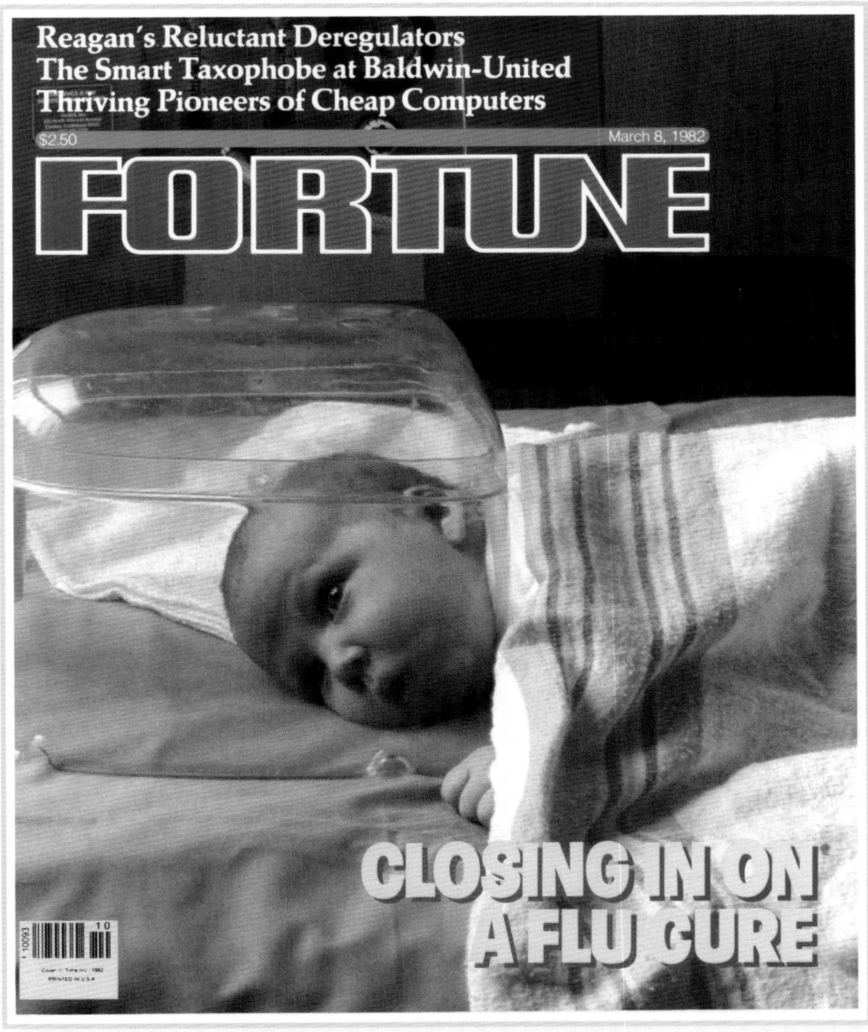

SPI

Anticipating approvals in the 1985–86 time frame presented Panic with a new problem to solve, but a good one. ICN desperately needed marketing and sales clout—and globally. The drug was nearing launch mode. It was like the problem he and the board faced in 1974. But this time things would be different. ICN would keep the asset. The Lederle debacle had been an embarrassment. When ribavirin was handed back to the company in the darkest of days of 1975, publicly it was a slap in the face. Panic vowed to never let that happen again. This time ICN would build its own sales and marketing capability. Plus, the RSV hospital market was easier to target than primary care. ICN could penetrate the market with a smaller sales force. Influenza was different, and for this Panic would have to acquire. But he had time.

Clearly, Viratek was not the right vehicle to sell ribavirin; it was just a development company. Its mission was R&D in return for royalties. Parent ICN could work, but it had debt and was not set up for pharmaceutical sales and marketing like the '70s. In fact, its recent acquisitions weren't drug companies but biochemical concerns.

The solution was to create and spin out a new pharma company, just like Viratek. The idea was to transfer all existing pharmaceutical operations to the new company and grant it a sales and marketing license for ribavirin worldwide. This would be the entity that would launch influenza and RSV. Gross margins would be in the low 60% range, not weighed down by research chemicals like at ICN. It would have no debt. Earnings would skyrocket. And the pipeline would also include ribavirin for influenza, a huge market fueled by as many as eight million hospitalized cases a year, depending on the severity of the season. Viratek had risen to $20 from $7. If priced right, this IPO could do even better. And with a higher stock price, Panic could start acquiring again. The board named this company SPI Pharmaceuticals.

260,000 Shares

SPI PHARMACEUTICALS, INC.

Common Stock

($.01 Par Value)

Prior to the date of this Prospectus, there has been no public market for the Common Stock of the Company. See "Underwriting" for the factors considered in determining the initial public offering price.

THESE SECURITIES HAVE NOT BEEN APPROVED OR DISAPPROVED BY THE SECURITIES AND EXCHANGE COMMISSION NOR HAS THE COMMISSION PASSED UPON THE ACCURACY OR ADEQUACY OF THIS PROSPECTUS. ANY REPRESENTATION TO THE CONTRARY IS A CRIMINAL OFFENSE.

	Price to Public	Underwriting Discounts and Commissions(1)	Proceeds to Company(2)
Per Share	$12.00	$ 1.02	$10.98
Total(3)	$3,120,000	$ 265,200	$2,854,800

(1) For information concerning indemnification of the several Underwriters against certain liabilities, including liabilities under the Securities Act of 1933, by the Company and the issuance of warrants to Bateman Eichler, Hill Richards, Incorporated to purchase 26,000 shares of the Company's Common Stock, see "Underwriting."

(2) Before deducting expenses payable by the Company estimated at $953,000.

(3) The Company has granted the several Underwriters a 30-day over-allotment option to purchase up to an additional 39,000 shares. If all 39,000 shares are purchased by the Underwriters, the total Price to Public will be $3,588,000, the total Underwriting Discounts and Commissions will be $304,980 and the total Proceeds to Company will be $3,283,020. See "Underwriting."

The shares of Common Stock are offered by the several Underwriters when, as and if issued by the Company and accepted by the Underwriters, subject to prior sale or withdrawal, cancellation or modification of the offer without notice, and subject to the approval of certain legal matters by counsel. Delivery of the shares to the Underwriters is expected to be made on or about October 13, 1983 in Los Angeles, California.

Bateman Eichler, Hill Richards
INCORPORATED

The date of this Prospectus is October 4, 1983

SPI Pharmaceuticals, Inc. common stock offering

Dominick Liuzzi

Viratek granted SPI a global license to develop, market, and sell ribavirin in return for a 7% royalty. On October 4, 1983, SPI became a public company issuing 260,000 shares at $12, raising $1.6 million. It traded on the OTC market as SPIP. ICN retained 90% of the stock. Pro forma revenue was $18.5 million, with operating income of $3.2 million and net profit of $1.4 million. It started off with a portfolio of 200 pharmaceutical products and operations in Montreal, Covina, Holland, and Mexico City. Panic was appointed chairman and CEO, alongside his old friend Dominick Liuzzi as president.

EASTMAN KODAK

ICN's fortunes were improving and about to get much better. In 1985, $11-billion-a-year Eastman Kodak spun out a new life sciences division whose purpose was to take the photo giant into the pharmaceutical business. Over the years, Kodak had synthesized more than 5,000 compounds outside of the photo application business, which insiders believed had potential as pharmaceuticals. For two years, Kodak had been making the rounds of drug companies looking for promising products and partners. It landed upon ICN, a company perceived to be an emerging pioneer in antiviral research. In July 1984, Kodak purchased 470,000 shares of Series A convertible preferred stock in ICN and 350,000 shares of Series A convertible preferred stock in Viratek. Total proceeds were $8.3 million: $3.4 million to ICN and $4.9 million to Viratek.

Kodak's equity stake in both companies was the first step to a joint venture. The board reinstated NARI to serve as the vehicle to synthesize both the Kodak and ICN compounds, which, if promising, would later be licensed to Viratek for development and then SPI for commercialization. In 1985, Kodak agreed to a six-year $45-million funding of NARI. Again, the focus would be antivirals and anticancer drugs. Long-time Panic colleague and board member Weldon Jolley took an executive position. Both his and Bob Smith's bets on ICN in the '60s had paid off. They each had equity and had made a few dollars but, most importantly, now had the bankroll of one of America's most famous companies to fund their dream of creating effective drugs out of nucleic acids. And they had ribavirin.

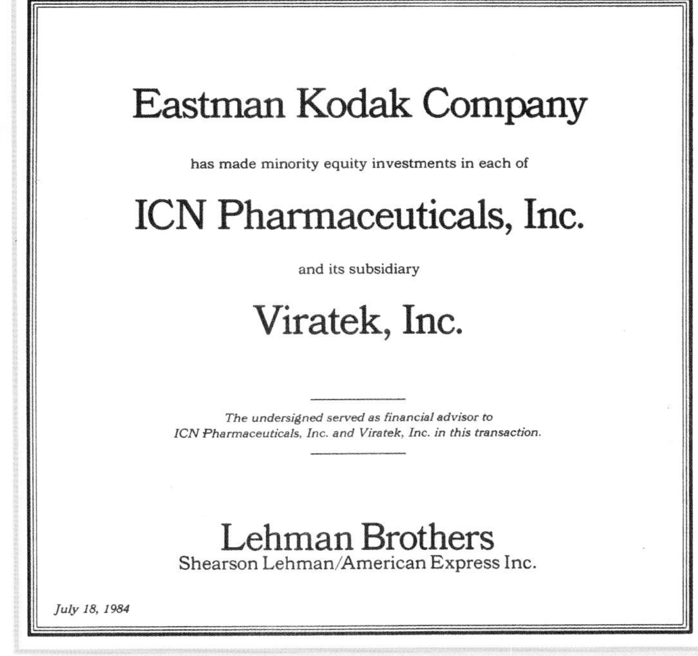
Eastman Kodak Company

has made minority equity investments in each of

ICN Pharmaceuticals, Inc.

and its subsidiary

Viratek, Inc.

The undersigned served as financial advisor to ICN Pharmaceuticals, Inc. and Viratek, Inc. in this transaction.

Lehman Brothers

Shearson Lehman/American Express Inc.

July 18, 1984

Eastman Kodak makes investment in ICN

ICN REBORN

Leveraging the rising prospects for influenza and RSV, Kodak's involvement, the high-performing Viratek and SPI spin-offs, and the much-improved outlook for ICN, Panic had credibility once again and a compelling investment story to start raising serious money. He was a deal guy, a natural business builder, and a highly capable operator. ICN started tapping the markets in '81–'83, raising $18.6 million through public offerings of its common stock and the subsidiaries. Then in November 1983 and July 1984, ICN raised another $25 million through the Kodak deals and an underwritten public offering of $30 million, 12.5% debentures due 1999. But, this would hardly fund the kind of global expansion program required to sell ribavirin for influenza. For this, ICN needed something way bigger.

It presented in response to the discovery of a new and rare virus that was rapidly becoming a global health threat. People were dying, and for some time no one in the scientific community knew why. The virus was called HIV, or AIDS.

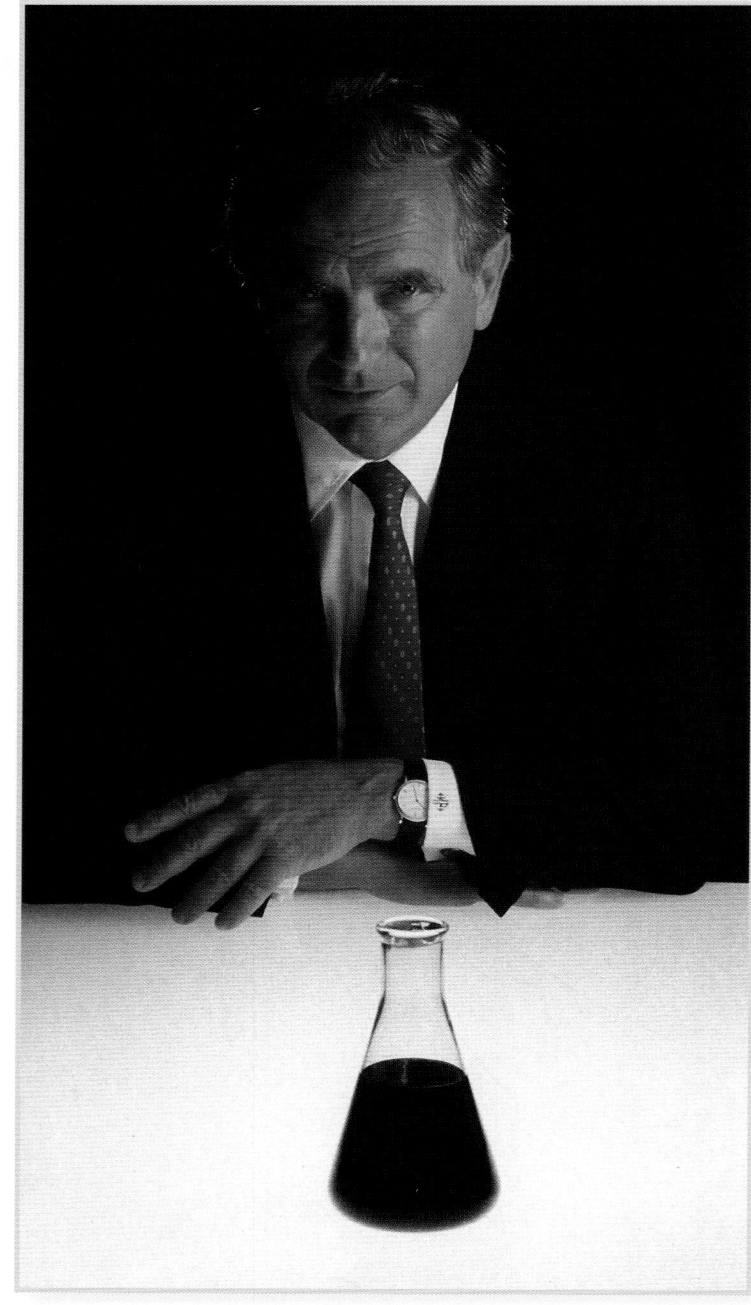

Milan Panic, 1985

AIDS

In 1981, cases of a rare lung infection called *Pneumocystis carinii* pneumonia (PCP) alleged to be associated with intravenous drug use were identified in Los Angeles. In 1982, similar cases among gay men indicated that this plague may be caused by some form of immune deficiency and that transmission could be sexual in nature. The syndrome was initially called gay-related immune deficiency or GRID. Later, the Centers for Disease Control and Prevention (CDC) used the term "AIDS" (acquired immune deficiency syndrome) for the first time.

The epidemic actually began in the mid- to late 1970s. By 1980, it had spread globally. Over this period, as many as 300,000 people were thought to be infected. Many more cases of PCP emerged. A CDC task force was formed to monitor the outbreak.

Alarming reports began to circulate that AIDS was fatal and that a majority of those infected could develop full-blown AIDS within 10 years. Others victims may develop AIDS-related complex (ARC), a subset of the disease. In 1983, doctors at the Pasteur Institute in France reported the discovery of a new retrovirus called lymphadenopathy-associated virus (or LAV), which was linked to the HTLV virus, also thought to be the cause of AIDS. These two viruses turned out to be the same; LAV and HTLV-III were later renamed HIV. By the end of the year, the number of AIDS cases in the United States had risen to more than 3,000. Fear swept the country's gay community. There seemed to be no hope for an effective treatment, much less a cure.

As the epidemic spread, mounting public frustration was redirected at the FDA. The agency was accused of dragging its feet amid increasing bureaucracy and red tape. In response, responsibility to conduct clinical trials in AIDS-related conditions was given to the National Institute of Allergy and Infectious Diseases (NIAID). This institute developed a drug selection process and an ambitious plan to develop its own protocols for all AIDS-related trials. The need for an effective antiviral that could slow the progression of HIV infection to AIDS became a national priority.

The need for an effective antiviral that could slow the progression of HIV infection to AIDS became a national priority.

RIBAVIRIN

Researchers believed ribavirin may be a promising candidate. The CDC and Harvard conducted in vitro tests demonstrating that ribavirin had activity against the HIV virus. Following that, Dr. Richard Roberts of Cornell performed pharmacokinetics studies indicating that the drug was active and nontoxic at oral dosages between 600 and 800 mg per day. Lancet reported these preliminary findings in late 1984, implying that ribavirin's antiviral effect may suppress the virus and produce clinical benefits without the significant bone marrow suppression caused by other drugs such as AZT. Suddenly, ICN found itself a leader in the AIDS race.

In October 1986, the FDA classified ribavirin as 1-AA, a top-priority classification for agency review. Accordingly, ICN began a multicenter study to evaluate the tolerance and efficacy of ribavirin. The sites included the NY Hospital–Cornell Medical Center; University of Miami/Jackson Memorial Medical Center; Los Angeles County–University of Southern California Medical Center; M.D. Anderson Hospital/Cancer Center; and the Institute for Immunological Disorders at Yale University School of Medicine. The protocol design was a double-blind, randomized, placebo-controlled trial comparing two daily doses of oral ribavirin and placebo on 164 adult men with generalized lymphadenopathy syndrome (LAS), patients thought to be at a continuing risk for developing AIDS over a two-month period. Subjects were randomized to receive ribavirin 600 mg or 800 mg. Active treatment was administered for 24 weeks, followed by a 24-week washout period.

In February 1986, ICN, Viratek, SPI, and Kodak entered into a new joint venture related to the clinical development of ribavirin for the treatment of AIDS, influenza, and herpes. Kodak paid the JV $2 million up front for rights to ribavirin for AIDS and was granted global manufacturing rights. SPI would pay the JV royalties on sales.

ICN Pharmaceuticals, Inc.

The New Frontiers of Medicine

ICN Pharmaceuticals was born at the dawn of the age of biological revolution. The discovery of the double helical structure of deoxyribonucleic acid (DNA) by Watson and Crick was only a few years old when a young Yugoslavian chemist arrived in California in 1960 with his new family and $200 in his pocket to begin his search for the American dream. Initially working as a research assistant in the laboratories of the University of Southern California and the California Institute for Biochemical Research, Milan Panic (pronounced paan-eesh) drew about him the nucleus of what was to emerge as the International Chemical and Nuclear Corporation.

Among those involved in the early days of the company's history were Max Dunn, dean of the Graduate School at University of California at Los Angeles; Dan Campbell, chairman of the Department of Immunochemistry at Caltech; UCLA Professor of Biochemistry Roberts Smith; University of Southern California and Loma Linda University Professor Weldon Jolley, and the extraordinary medicinal chemist Roland K. Robins (named 1988 Alfred Burger Award winner by the American Chemical Society.)

From salmon sperm, the company extracted DNA, then radioactively tagged its building blocks, nucleosides, and nucleotides, and made them available to scientists throughout the world for research studies — thereby making a major contribution to the unfolding of a new era of molecular biology.

ICN's first plant was built in 1960 in the City of Industry, California. In 1969, a larger facility, containing the Nucleic

Milan Panic, the founder of ICN, came to California in the sixties to study molecular biology.

Acid Research Institute (NARI), was constructed in Irvine, California. Out of this facility came an array of products used by researchers to follow the metabolic pathways of life. And out of the NARI laboratories came many promising new pharmaceutical compounds.

Unable to financially develop all of them, the NARI

ICN, an emerging antiviral leader

APPROVAL

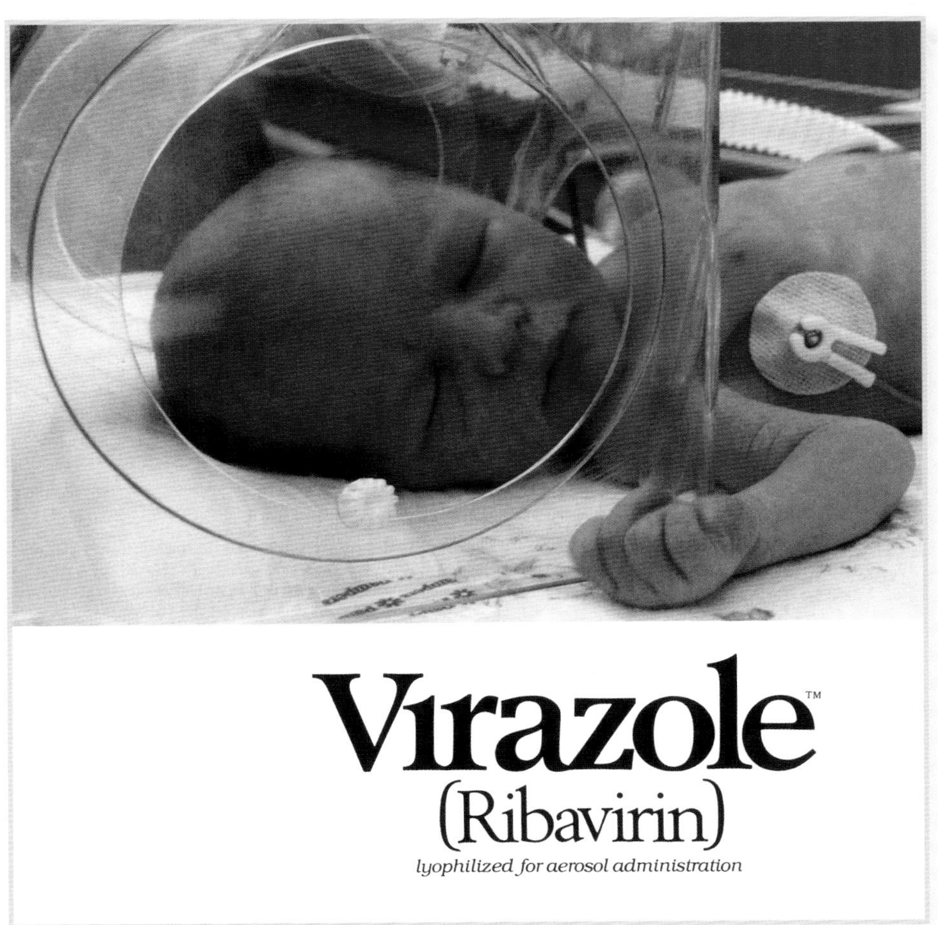

On December 31, 1985, the FDA approved Viratek's NDA for the hospital use of aerosolized ribavirin in the treatment of RSV infections in infants. Panic, Smith, and Jolley finally had their long-awaited approval. Influenza was expected later. The RSV market was small but within SPI's grasp and highly profitable. Each year, there could be as many as 200,000 infants affected with RSV, and since a hospital dosage of aerosolized ribavirin might initially cost \$60–\$100 a day, the market was easily \$40 million or more. To SPI shareholders, this meant a dollar per share of earnings. SPI launched ribavirin as Virazole late in the '85–'86 season at \$229 a vial. Their newly trained sales force detailed hospitals, hospital-based pediatricians, and infectious disease specialists. With this approval in hand, ICN was now an undisputed world leader in antiviral therapy.

December 31, 1985—FDA approves ribavirin for RSV. Health Canada follows.

BIMD opens for trading

BIMD

While everyone's attention was on ICN's drug business, Panic made sure to not neglect his founding biochemical division. ICN would spin that off as well. In July 1986, D.H. Blair underwrote an offering of 600,000 shares of ICN Biomedicals to the public, leaving 86% with ICN. The deconsolidation was now complete. ICN was the holding company, Viratek the drug development arm, SPI the sales and marketing company, and Biomed the diagnostic and research chemical division.

Before the Biomed offering, ICN had acquired Micromedic Systems from Rohm and Haas. It added radioimmunoassay reagents, instruments, and analyzers used for diagnostic testing in clinical research laboratories. Also acquired was the research products business of Miles Scientific, which contributed $5.7 million in annual revenue. Despite Biomed losing $0.44 on sales of $16 million in 1985, the IPO was successful, largely due to a favorable P&L contribution from Micromedic and ICN's credibility gained by Viratek and SPI, both of which were trading well above their offering prices. In the first half of 1986, Biomed delivered sales of $20 million and earnings of $0.29. At year end, Biomed rose to sales of $56 million. And like the biotechnology sector, there was strong investor appetite for tools, diagnostics, and life science products. The government was accelerating spending for life science research. Longtime executive Fred Andrea was tapped as CEO, with Dick Fallis and Vel Cubrilovic appointed operating VPs. Like Smith and Jolley, their bets in 1962 on tiny International Chemical & Nuclear had proved fortuitous. Now they had been rewarded with their own public company to run.

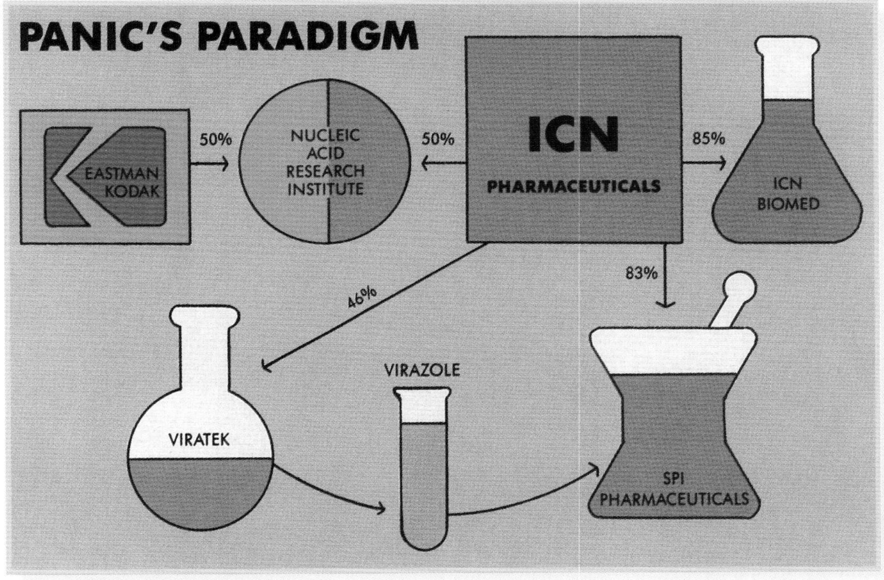

REBUILDING THE BASE

Panic sensed that 1986 and 1987 would be big years. SPI had risen to $65 million in revenue and $8 million in profit. It had successfully launched ribavirin into pediatric centers and, backed by loans from parent ICN, acquired six pharmaceutical companies at a cost of $50 million. These included Brown Pharmaceuticals, which added an oral androgen line called Testred, and a prosperous Mexican company called Grossman, acquired from Panic's friend at Revlon, Michel Bergerac. Driven by a portfolio of vitamins, penicillin, amino-glycosides, cold preps, and anti-infectives, Grossman was a leader in Mexico. Its biggest product was an injectable vitamin B complex called Bedoyecta. Vilona was also selling well. Combining Grossman with the original Servet company made the Mexican unit one of SPI's star divisions.

Canada was equally strong and had launched a new conjugated estrogen called C.E.S. Ribavirin had been approved in Canada for RSV. Holland was profitable amid a growing presence in eye care. Laboratorios Hubber, newly acquired in Spain, gave a much needed boost to Europe.

In the United States, SPI acquired Elder Pharmaceuticals of Bryan, Ohio, giving it a foothold in the fast-growing dermatology market. Elder brought leading brands such as Oxsoralen Ultra for psoriasis and skin-bleaching agents Solaquin, Trisoralem, and Eldoquin. In the health foods and nutritionals market, SPI acquired Faraday Laboratories, a potassium supplement called Kato from Legere Pharmaceuticals, and Moxie Industries, which sold a leading brand of consumer vitamins and nutritionals called Richlife.

ICN interns from the United States, Turkey, Spain, and Argentina

NEW LEADERSHIP

Back on the global expansion front, Panic started recruiting top executive talent again. In the early '80s cash-strapped ICN hired trainees out of colleges around the world using an international exchange program called AIESEC. Panic loved having young talent around him and would push each intern to the limit. Many of these aspiring recruits advanced quickly under Panic's tutelage to take on managerial responsibilities in the subsidiaries.

Larry Panitz, new chief counsel

At corporate, Larry Panitz joined from Revlon, where he was chief international counsel. Bill MacDonald was recruited to head up tax and business development. Adam Jerney was promoted to executive vice president, operations. He would later become president. Former Revlon Controller John Giordani came on board as ICN's new CFO. Paul Maier was appointed VP and controller of SPI. Knoll's Leonard Mazur was hired to run sales and marketing. Jack Scholl joined to head global communications and PR from Warner Lambert. A. Robert Abboud, president of Occidental Petroleum and former chairman of First National Bank of Chicago, was elected a board member. Michel Bergerac, Revlon chair and CEO and former president of ITT Europe, also joined the board. In 1987, David Watt assumed the post of general counsel and secretary and would become one of the company's top dealmakers.

Eying opportunities in Eastern and Central Europe, Panic recruited his boyhood friend Ted Olic to establish an office in Belgrade, Yugoslavia, their native city. Belgrade was in Serbia and still the capital of the Socialist Federal Republic of Yugoslavia (SFRY), a federation consisting of Serbia, Bosnia and Herzegovina, Croatia, Macedonia, Montenegro, Slovenia, and two provinces, Vojvodina and Kosovo. The SFRY had experienced relative stability under the authoritarian rule of long-time dictator Josip Broz Tito, but after his death in 1980, secessionist sentiment among the member states was rising amid increasing regional economic and political challenges.

Both men believed, however, that it was just a matter of time before the Balkan countries experimented with the same types of free-market reforms that were starting to be implemented in other European states. This could yield acquisition opportunities for ICN.

Olic, a former party chief under Tito, spoke 10 languages (including Czech, Polish, Serbian, Russian) and was the perfect choice in Panic's mind to flesh out opportunities from the various one-party-rule regimes. He was extremely experienced dealing with the various power brokers in each republic, as well as the Kremlin.

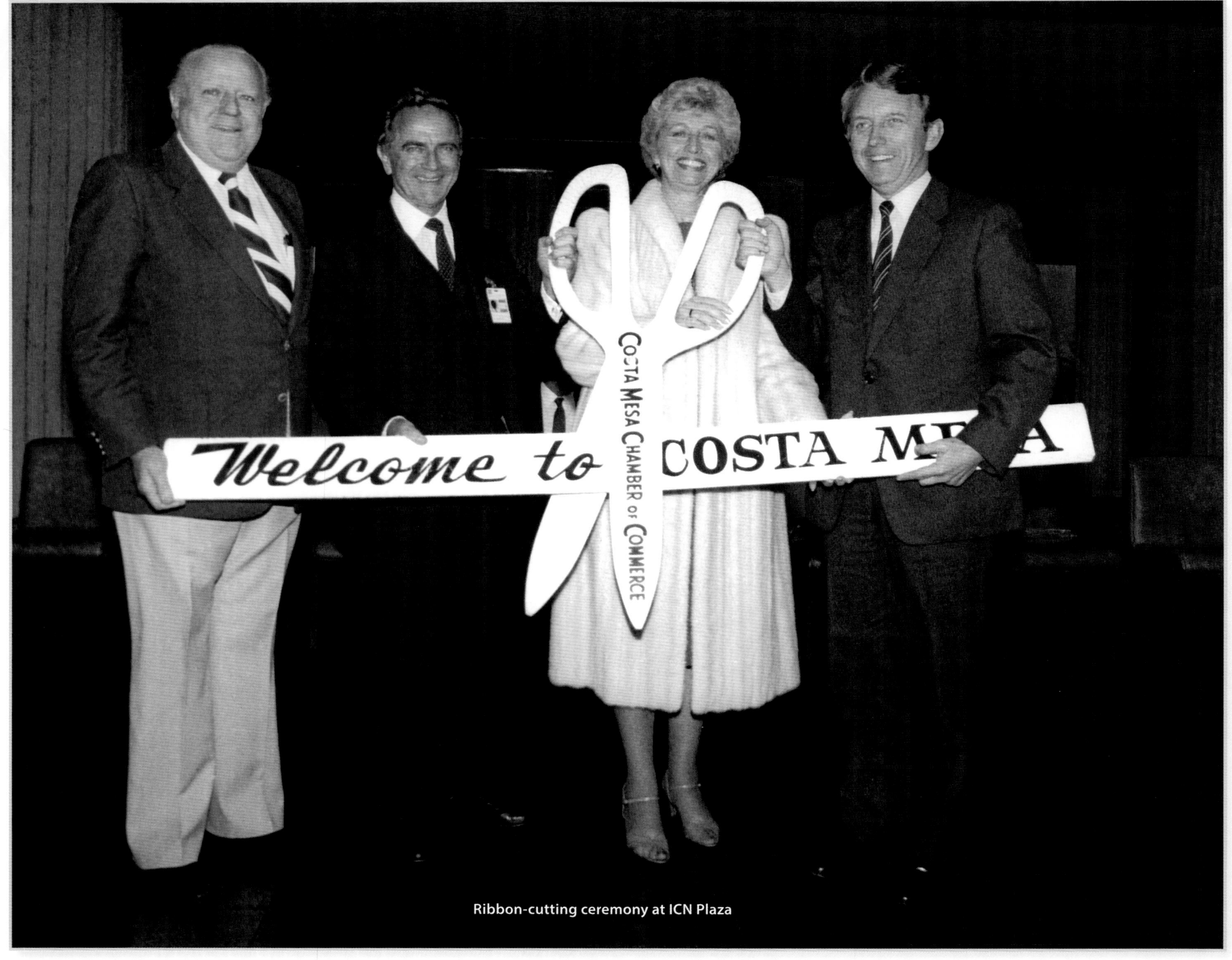

Ribbon-cutting ceremony at ICN Plaza

ICN PLAZA

Back in the United States, ICN needed a new home. Panic and Jerney had been cooped up in Covina for six years with just three offices and a conference room. Panic found a large 164,000-square-foot black marble multistory building located just off the 405 freeway in fast-growing Orange County, ICN's former home during its heyday in the early '70s. Everyone passing by would see it. Panic wanted a showcase to house his expanding international company. He named it ICN Plaza.

The building was owned jointly by MCA and IBM. Panic made a deal. He proposed a six-year lease and $9 million cash for the option to buy the building. In addition, ICN issued the previous owners 12,200 shares of 6% cumulative preferred stock, convertible into ICN at $14. Now IBM joined Eastman Kodak as top ICN shareholders. Panic beamed. Not bad for a poor little immigrant. He always looked forward. Who would remember now that ICN was just inches from bankruptcy just five years ago?

In 1986, ICN exercised the option and purchased the building outright. It would be the worldwide headquarters of ICN for the next 20 years.

He who has health has hope
and he who has hope has everything

ICN Plaza

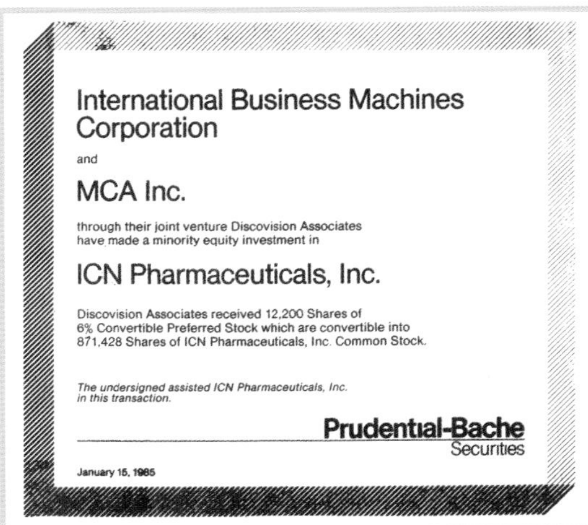

International Business Machines Corporation

and

MCA Inc.

through their joint venture Discovision Associates have made a minority equity investment in

ICN Pharmaceuticals, Inc.

Discovision Associates received 12,200 Shares of 6% Convertible Preferred Stock which are convertible into 871,428 Shares of ICN Pharmaceuticals, Inc. Common Stock.

The undersigned assisted ICN Pharmaceuticals, Inc. in this transaction.

Prudential-Bache Securities

January 15, 1985

IBM and MCA Inc. Discovision Associates make a minority equity investment in ICN Pharmaceuticals, Inc.

JEAN-FRANCOIS KURZ

Throughout his career, Panic was a regular at La Reserve Hotel located on Lake Geneva. Everyone knew him. He was colorful, a big spender, and always accompanied by family and business associates. But one night in 1984, he dined alone with a tall, elegantly dressed Swiss-German gentleman by the name of Jean-Francois Kurz. He was an innovative Swiss banker. Panic was there to engage him. He needed Kurz to help him raise $500 million to buy a big company. He figured the Swiss capital market was the place to do it.

Kurz came from a family of bankers with ties to the Swiss pharmaceutical industry. He spoke fluent German, French, Italian, and English. He was wealthy and served as mayor of Trelex, an exclusive village just outside of Geneva. Kurz was known as a somewhat unpredictable, exotic banker who constantly flirted outside the box with his financings. He would try everything, providing it made financial sense and made his bank money. His dealmaking, by no means confined to Europe, took him to India, Costa Rica, Cuba, and South America. His specialty was underwriting instruments for unconventional debtors. His deal structures often included warrants and options, which were uncharacteristic in conventional Geneva. And he was perfect for Milan Panic.

Jean-Francois Kurz

As always, Kurz came to dinner prepared with an idea. ICN was not a high-enough-rated credit to attract sizeable Swiss money, so he showed Panic a way to guarantee the principle. He proposed using some of the bond proceeds to simultaneously buy zero coupons backed by the full faith and credit of European governments that would pay the bonds' principle at maturity. ICN would then have no obligation to pay the face amount, since this would ultimately be paid by the cumulative coupon of the zero. He knew of paper guaranteed by the Republic of Italy and Kingdom of Denmark. The holder could collect interest and hold the paper to maturity, or convert into ICN, or even SPI and Biomedicals, if he or she wanted more risk and return.

In early 1986, they started by raising $19 million with a consortium of 22 banks. This marked ICN's first participation in the Swiss capital markets since the early '70s. As SPI and ICN stock rose in price that year, more financing opportunities opened. Kurz raised money for ICN in Swiss francs, Dutch guilders, and European currency units. All were convertible and paid interest between 3% and 5%. In total, ICN raised $360 million debt and equity in 1986 and $140 million more the next year, for a total of $500 million. As each financing was placed, Kurz grew more inventive. He really turned heads in 1987 when he structured and placed the first dual convertible for ICN, a Swiss franc 60-million, 3.25% bond that gave the holder the option of converting to either ICN or the Swiss pharmaceutical giant Ciba-Geigy. ICN had to acquire shares of Ciba on the open market to place in escrow for the conversions. That alone cost $35.5 million.

The management of CIBA wasn't happy and distanced themselves from Kurz and Panic. In Swiss circles, Kurz had some explaining to do. But the deal was oversubscribed, and the majority of bond holders eventually converted, a show of success for the offering. Only $6 million was left in 1991.

During those two years, Panic, Bob Smith, Larry Panitz, Bill MacDonald, and David Watt crisscrossed Europe raising money virtually every month. Basle, Geneva, Zurich, London, and Amsterdam were routine stops. The road show itself was a money-making exercise. Kurz had a system, and he and a few assistants executed it to perfection. And with a rising stock price in America, ICN offerings attracted a huge following, even among the notoriously guarded Swiss investors.

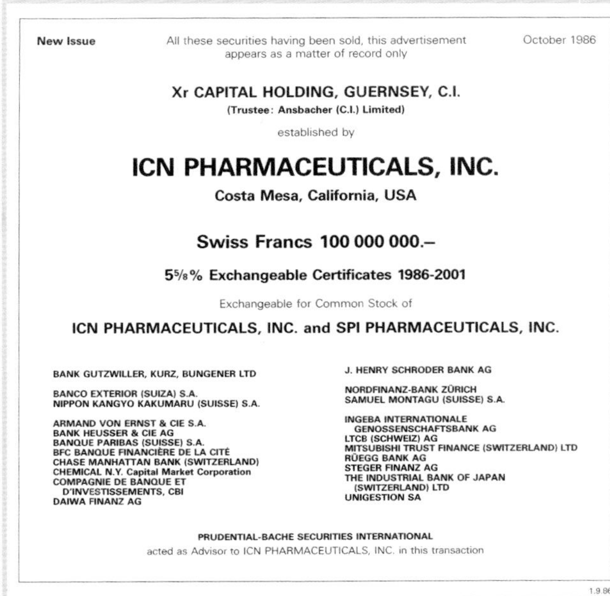

New Issue

All these securities having been sold, this advertisement appears as a matter of record only

October 1986

Xr CAPITAL HOLDING, GUERNSEY, C.I.
(Trustee: Ansbacher (C.I.) Limited)

established by

ICN PHARMACEUTICALS, INC.

Costa Mesa, California, USA

Swiss Francs 100 000 000.–

5⅝% Exchangeable Certificates 1986-2001

Exchangeable for Common Stock of

ICN PHARMACEUTICALS, INC. and SPI PHARMACEUTICALS, INC.

BANK GUTZWILLER, KURZ, BUNGENER LTD

J. HENRY SCHRODER BANK AG

BANCO EXTERIOR (SUIZA) S.A.
NIPPON KANGYO KAKUMARU (SUISSE) S.A.

NORDFINANZ-BANK ZÜRICH
SAMUEL MONTAGU (SUISSE) S.A.

ARMAND VON ERNST & CIE S.A.
BANK HEUSSER & CIE AG
BANQUE PARIBAS (SUISSE) S.A.
BFC BANQUE FINANCIÈRE DE LA CITÉ
CHASE MANHATTAN BANK (SWITZERLAND)
CHEMICAL N.Y. Capital Market Corporation
COMPAGNIE DE BANQUE ET D'INVESTISSEMENTS, CBI
DAIWA FINANZ AG

INGEBA INTERNATIONALE GENOSSENSCHAFTSBANK AG
LTCB (SCHWEIZ) AG
MITSUBISHI TRUST FINANCE (SWITZERLAND) LTD
RÜEGG BANK AG
STEGER FINANZ AG
THE INDUSTRIAL BANK OF JAPAN (SWITZERLAND) LTD
UNIGESTION SA

PRUDENTIAL-BACHE SECURITIES INTERNATIONAL
acted as Advisor to ICN PHARMACEUTICALS, INC. in this transaction

1.9.86

Swiss francs 100,000,000. – 5.625% Exchangeable Certificates 1986–2001

Bob Smith and Jean-Francois Kurz

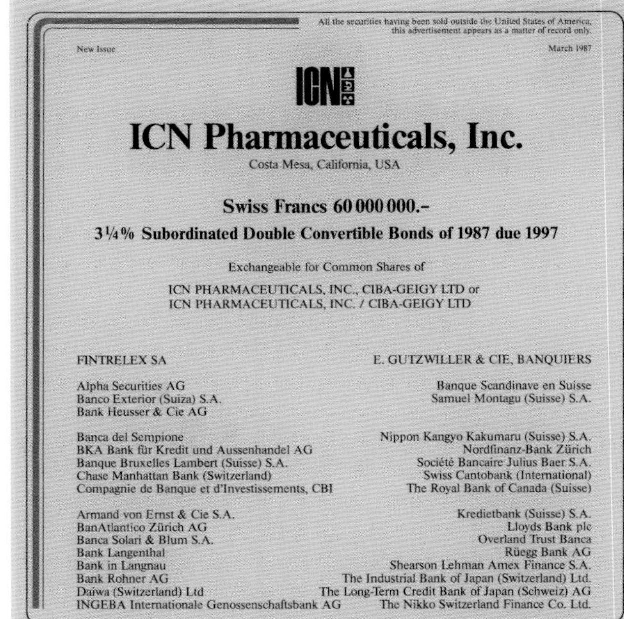

All the securities having been sold outside the United States of America, this advertisement appears as a matter of record only.

New Issue

March 1987

ICN

ICN Pharmaceuticals, Inc.

Costa Mesa, California, USA

Swiss Francs 60 000 000.-

3¼% Subordinated Double Convertible Bonds of 1987 due 1997

Exchangeable for Common Shares of

ICN PHARMACEUTICALS, INC., CIBA-GEIGY LTD or
ICN PHARMACEUTICALS, INC. / CIBA-GEIGY LTD

FINTRELEX SA

E. GUTZWILLER & CIE, BANQUIERS

Alpha Securities AG
Banco Exterior (Suiza) S.A.
Bank Heusser & Cie AG

Banque Scandinave en Suisse
Samuel Montagu (Suisse) S.A.

Banca del Sempione
BKA Bank für Kredit und Aussenhandel AG
Banque Bruxelles Lambert (Suisse) S.A.
Chase Manhattan Bank (Switzerland)
Compagnie de Banque et d'Investissements, CBI

Nippon Kangyo Kakumaru (Suisse) S.A.
Nordfinanz-Bank Zürich
Société Bancaire Julius Baer S.A.
Swiss Cantobank (International)
The Royal Bank of Canada (Suisse)

Armand von Ernst & Cie S.A.
BanAtlantico Zürich AG
Banca Solari & Blum S.A.
Bank Langenthal
Bank in Langnau
Bank Rohner AG
Daiwa (Switzerland) Ltd
INGEBA Internationale Genossenschaftsbank AG

Kredietbank (Suisse) S.A.
Lloyds Bank plc
Overland Trust Banca
Rüegg Bank AG
Shearson Lehman Amex Finance S.A.
The Industrial Bank of Japan (Switzerland) Ltd.
The Long-Term Credit Bank of Japan (Schweiz) AG
The Nikko Switzerland Finance Co. Ltd.

Swiss Francs 60,000,000. – 3.25% Subordinated Double Convertible Bonds due 1997

Above: Milan Panic at a road show in Europe

Right: ICN back on top, 1986

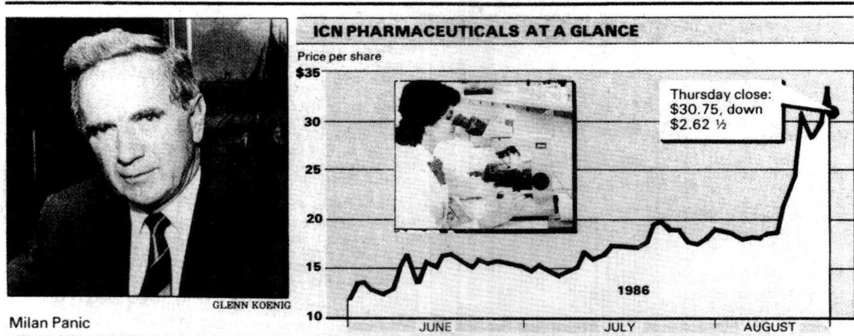

Milan Panic

ICN Returns as a Favorite of Wall Street

Drug Firm's Stock Is Soaring on Hopes for Wide Use of Virazole

By ROBERT HANLEY,
Times Staff Writer

It's been the darling of investors and a Wall Street outcast, and now it's back on top again after a deep depression in the early 1970s, when prospects dimmed amid a rising tide of red ink.

ICN Pharmaceuticals of Costa Mesa, whose stock traded for more than $36 a share during the early '70s before the drug maker fell from grace, has been on the New York Stock Exchange's most active list for more than a week. Closing Thursday at $30.75 a share, down $2.62½ on the day, the stock price has been heading toward an all-time high after dropping to as low as $1.25 a share in 1974.

ORANGE COUNTY

And ICN's Viratek Inc. and SPI Inc. subsidiaries have racked up impressive gains on Wall Street as well.

ICN stock has soared more than 60% in price since Paine Webber last week issued a report saying the company's drug Virazole has "the potential to become one of the world's largest-selling drugs." The report is believed to be the first research report on the company to be prepared by a major brokerage firm in at least a dozen years.

New-Found Attention

Despite the new-found attention, however, surprisingly little has changed at ICN: Virazole is still the drug upon which the company banks its future, and the genial Yugoslav immigrant who founded the company in 1959 is still at the helm.

It's just that, after 16 years of research, a handful of favorable write-ups in medical journals, federal approval of the drug for use as a treatment of one disease and the recent signing of a research deal with the Army, the world may finally be ready for Virazole, says ICN's founder and chairman, Milan Panic (pronounced Pan-isch).

"Being ahead of everyone doesn't always give you much of an advantage," Panic said in his thickly accented English. "We had this drug, but my God, nobody believed us. You'd go home and search your soul and think that maybe they're right."

Although ICN has always envisioned Virazole as a treatment for influenza, the deadly acquired immune deficiency syndrome seems to be the biggest reason for the company's new popularity among investors. And while ICN hasn't been shy about the AIDS connection—last year, for example, it sponsored an AIDS conference at its headquarters—Panic himself sounds like a skeptic.

"I think AIDS gets more attention than it deserves," he said. "We have no proof that our drug is effective against AIDS in humans, or else we would have filed a new drug application."

Impact of Federal Report

The whole thing got started when the federal Centers for Disease Control in Atlanta released a report in late 1984 that indicated that, at least in the test tube, Virazole may be effective against AIDS. "Under pressure of that report," said Panic, the company began testing the drug, partially with money supplied by Eastman Kodak Co., which owns 5% of ICN and 10% of Viratek.

Clinical trials of Virazole's effect on about 350 pre-AIDS patients are nearing completion at several medical centers, and the Public Health Service soon will begin independent testing of the drug in a five-year study of AIDS patients' response to Virazole and several other drugs.

But Panic insists that despite what Wall Street may be expecting, ICN won't seek FDA approval of Virazole as an AIDS drug if there isn't enough evidence to support it.

Besides, he said, the market for an influenza drug is much bigger.

Please see ICN, Page 2

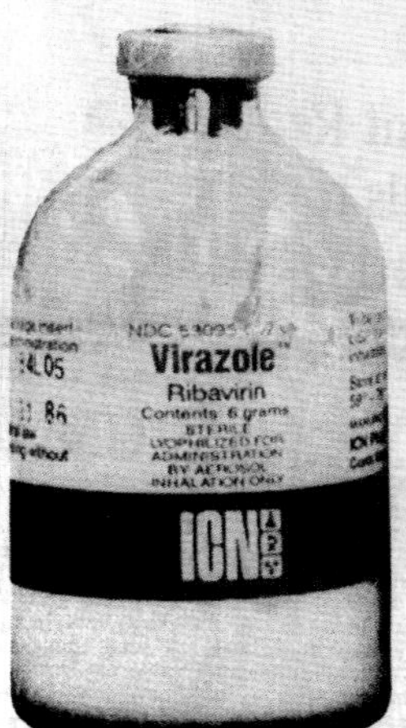

GLENN KOENIG

Virazole's prospects for AIDS treatment has made ICN stock popular with investors. Below, courtyard bears the firm's motto.

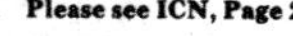

He who has health has hope
and he who has hope has everything

HOT STOCKS

Since claims about ribavirin's potential use against AIDS first surfaced in 1985 in *Lancet* and other peer-review journals, ICN's stock price moved up. Panic had found his magic again. Bankers lined up. They saw the Kurz Euro transactions and wanted in.

On July 24, 1986, Paine Webber and E.F. Hutton underwrote 2.3 million shares of ICN stock and $115 million of 12.875% sinking fund debentures, due 1998. After the financing, Paine Webber's drug analyst, Ron Nordmann, issued an ICN buy recommendation. This was the first institutional report on ICN by a top analyst since 1972.

In his report, Nordmann calculated that if 2 million patients took ribavirin for AIDS, the drug could reach $2 billion per year in revenue, more than the sales of then-leader Tagamet from SmithKline. He added that influenza may be even bigger, noting that in 1985 an estimated 107 million Americans came down with the flu. As a result, ICN shot up $12.375, or 67% of its market value, the week of the report, to close at $30.75 per share. Volume for the week was 5.3 million shares, making ICN the NYSE's eighth-most active issue.

The report unleashed a buying frenzy in Viratek and SPI stock as well. Viratek soared to $75 per share, representing a market cap of $440 million. The 493% net appreciation in Viratek's stock price was the largest percentage gain that year by the 44 stocks traded in the biotech OTC index. All eyes were glued to January 1987, the month in which the AIDS clinical study data would be released. Kodak was even rumored to buy out Viratek, which further inflated the stock.

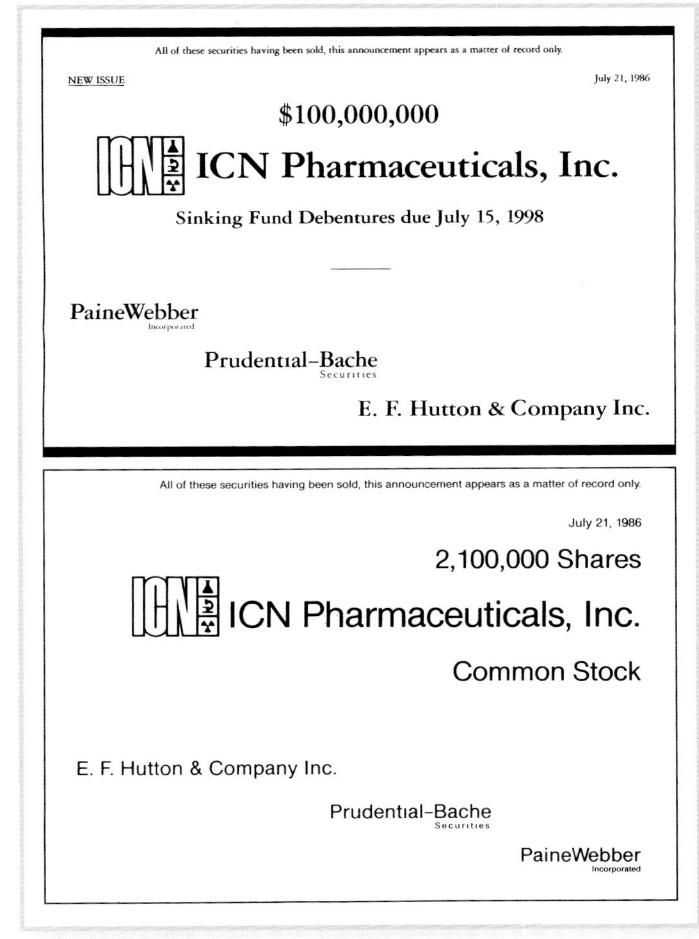

All of these securities having been sold, this announcement appears as a matter of record only.

NEW ISSUE

July 21, 1986

$100,000,000

ICN Pharmaceuticals, Inc.

Sinking Fund Debentures due July 15, 1998

PaineWebber
Incorporated

Prudential-Bache
Securities

E. F. Hutton & Company Inc.

All of these securities having been sold, this announcement appears as a matter of record only.

July 21, 1986

2,100,000 Shares

ICN Pharmaceuticals, Inc.

Common Stock

E. F. Hutton & Company Inc.

Prudential-Bache
Securities

PaineWebber
Incorporated

Paine Webber leads ICN's first major institutional financing in 15 years

Left: Milan Panic and ICN dealmaking
Businessweek, December 5, 1988

Below: Swiss press still reporting on ICN's Roche trade years later

HOSTILE TAKEOVERS HIT HIGH TECH PAGE 132

THE PLIGHT OF THE DISCOUNT BROKER PAGE 154

BusinessWeek

DECEMBER 5, 1988 — A McGRAW-HILL PUBLICATION — $2.00

People

ENTREPRENEURS

WHEN THE GOING GETS TOUGH, MILAN PANIC GOES SHOPPING

Facing federal probes, he buys into Germany's Schering

Milan Panic was even more ebullient than usual. Last May several hundred Democratic leaders and Hollywood celebrities converged on his 47-room Pasadena (Calif.) mansion for a $1,000-a-plate fund-raiser for Michael Dukakis. Former California Governors Pat and Jerry Brown were on hand. So was former Senator Birch Bayh, as well as actress Jane Seymour. And there, right beside Dukakis, stood Panic, the chairman of ICN Pharmaceuticals Inc., greeting his famous guests. For a man who fled Yugoslavia to become a capitalist, it was a moment to treasure.

Panic, 58, hasn't had many of those moments lately. Two years ago he began proclaiming that ICN's antiviral drug, ribavirin, appeared effective in combating the AIDS virus, and ICN's stock soared. But his critics say the drug's effectiveness against AIDS is totally unproven. One doctor accuses Panic of promoting ribavirin for AIDS treatment without proper government approval, and shareholders accuse him of manipulating ICN's stock by overstating the drug's potential. A federal grand jury and the Securities & Exchange Commission are investigating the charges.

Panic (pronounced "PAN-eesh") professes to be unconcerned. "ICN believes its conduct and activities in this area were honest, accurate, and carried out with dignity," he says. And the investigations certainly haven't cramped his freewheeling style. In early November he announced plans to buy up to 25% of giant West German drugmaker Schering. But industry watchers assume Panic is just trying to frighten Schering and then sell out at a premium. Their rationale: In March, a few months after buying an 8.6% stake in Swiss drug company F. Hoffmann-La Roche & Co., he was bought out for a profit estimated at up to $30 million.

ICN could use another boost like that. Last year it lost $16.6 million on sales of $121 million. But Panic insists he's not looking for greenmail. His aim, he says, is to entice Schering into some sort of cooperative venture, such as a worldwide distribution network. If that fails, however, he would consider a hostile takeover.

Preposterous? Panic says it's not: When eyeing Hoffmann-La Roche, he says, he got a "confident letter" from an unnamed financial institution to fund the deal. He says he can get one for Schering, too. Yet Schering's market value is about $1.8 billion—or 18 times ICN's. It would probably take more than $2 billion to buy it. But Schering is taking him seriously. "In our opinion it is a hostile takeover bid," says spokesman Ralf Harenberg. "It made us very angry."

Panic has a history of sudden, surprising moves. At the age of 25, en route to an international bike race where he was to compete for the Yugoslavian national team, he defected to West Germany. A year later he came to the U. S. and worked at the University of Southern California as a chemistry research assistant. He started ICN in 1960. As Panic tells the story, he founded the company with $200 and an old washing machine, which he used as a centrifuge to produce commercial DNA from salmon sperm.

OTC DRUGS. Panic gradually built ICN through a series of small acquisitions. The company now sells drugs for everything from skin cancer to manic depression, as well as a number of vitamins, over-the-counter drugs, and research chemicals. But Panic has high hopes for 18-year-old ribavirin. Although currently approved in the U. S. only for a respiratory ailment, some scientists think it might be effective against diseases ranging from the flu to herpes. In 1986 a few clinical studies showed ribavirin had promise in fighting AIDS. Although the FDA has denied approval for such use, Panic made sure investors knew about the studies. ICN's stock shot from 16 to 34 that summer.

Early in 1987, however, a doctor testified at congressional hearings that—despite the lack of FDA approval—ICN had

WILL HE RAID $1.8 BILLION SCHERING?

PHOTOGRAPH BY ALAN LEVENSON

STORMY TIMES FOR ICN'S FREEWHEELING CHIEF

MARCH, 1988

▶ As CEO of tiny ICN Pharmaceuticals, sells 8.6% stake in F. Hoffmann-La Roche & Co. only six months after acquiring it; turns estimated $30 million profit but bears out skeptics who didn't take his takeover talk seriously

SEPTEMBER

▶ Receives subpoena from Los Angeles federal grand jury investigating ICN's drug ribavirin. A doctor earlier claimed the company promoted ribavirin—approved only for respiratory infections—as an AIDS treatment

▶ Loses Eastman Kodak as venture partner; Kodak attributes pullout to its Sterling Drug acquisition, but some close to the venture say Kodak was uneasy about ICN's problems

NOVEMBER

▶ Discloses that ICN has a stake in giant Schering and plans to buy 25% of its stock; doesn't rule out a takeover

PEOPLE — BUSINESS WEEK/DECEMBER 5, 1988 **125**

M A R T I N   E B N E R   I I

Connection

Raid auf Roche: Milan Panic, ICN-Präsident.
Verteidigung organisiert: Fritz Gerber, Roche-Präsident.
Türöffner für Panic: Jean-François Kurz, Privatbankier.
Pharma-Visionär: Christoph Blocher, Ems-Besitzer.

FOTOS: ERIC BACHMANN, RDB, CLAUDE GIGER, TAGES ANZEIGER/UELI BURGMANN, EXPRESS

Wenn es unter den drei grossen Basler Chemieunternehmen eine Adresse gab, der sich Martin Ebner verbunden fühlte, war es diejenige des Pharmakonzerns Hoffmann-La Roche. In den Forschungslaboratorien von Roche – wie die Gesellschaft der Einfachheit halber genannt wird – war ein osteuropäischer Chemiker eher zufällig auf die Wirkstoffgruppe der Benzodiazepine gestossen. Ein potentes Schlafmittel, das auf dieser Basis entwickelt werden konnte, sollte dem Konzern zu weltweiter Berühmtheit verhelfen. Sein Handelsname: Valium. Die erfolgreiche Vermarktung des neuartigen Tranquilizers katapultierte Roche in die Spitzengruppe der internationalen Medikamentenhersteller.

Schon als Vontobel-Analyst hatte sich Ebner eingehend mit den Kennziffern des verschwiegenen Basler Pharmakonzerns beschäftigt. Dabei war er zur Überzeugung gelangt, dass sich hinter dieser «Substanzperle» noch weit mehr verstecken musste als das finanzielle Potential der Roche, welches der internationalen Investorenschaft ohnehin bereits bekannt war. Nach der BZ-Gründung begann Ebner vom ersten Tag an, seiner Klientel die aussichtsreichen Roche-Aktien zu empfehlen.

Im Gegensatz zu den Aktien vieler Schweizer Grossunternehmen war der Erwerb von Roche-Titeln Mitte der achtziger Jahre an keinerlei Einschränkungen gebunden, welche die Nationalität des Käufers oder die Anzahl der pro Anleger eingetragenen Aktien betraf. Der Pharmakonzern konnte sich diese liberale Regelung leisten, weil er eine sichere Mehrheit an stimmberechtigten Inhaberaktien in Basler Familienbesitz wusste. Ein «unfriendly takeover» schien a priori aus-

BILANZ 2/96 **27**

BIG FISH

By now bankers were all over Panic with merger ideas. He was a regular on Drexel Burnham Lambert's trading floor in downtown Beverly Hills for sessions with junk bond king Michael Milken. ICN had amassed a war chest of $550 million in cash and had a drug that a leading analyst predicted could sell $2 billion. Panic bid on USV from Revlon, Rorer, even Schering AG, but was thwarted each time. However, this did not dissuade him. Privately, he had his sights on much bigger game. F. Hoffmann–La Roche was undervalued; its shares had barely moved for years. Benzodiazepine (Valium) had rocketed Roche to worldwide fame, but nothing much had followed since. Valium patents had started to expire, decreasing profits. From 1975 to 1985, Roche had developed only three modestly successful drugs. By 1986, the stock was trading at historic lows.

Kurz found a way to buy a block of Roche voting shares, approximately 6.3%. Panic approved the investment, although his advisors and board members were skeptical. Roche was annualizing at $5 billion in sales, with profits of $280 million. It was the pride of Switzerland. ICN was just a paltry $100 million, with a sketchy reputation, especially in the Swiss drug kingdom of Basle still upset over the Kurz Ciba trade.

Milan Panic

But once Panic made up his mind, he wouldn't change. He had a reputation for snap judgements, but those were often his entrepreneurial instincts at work. He trusted himself. This was his deal. He'd done his homework. Besides, he'd fantasized about Roche since the '60s, always believing that the company would someday be his. Inside ICN, the secret project was code named BIG FISH.

When the trade was announced, rumors started flying. An outright takeover of Roche seemed impossible. Not only was it well beyond the reach of tiny ICN but also control of the company rested firmly with the family. Still, Panic moved ahead, upping the stake to 7.3%.

On September 22, 1988, Panic abruptly sold ICN's stake of 1,380 voting shares. Roche was not for sale and would remain in family control. ICN had purchased the shares for a total of $175 million and sold the 8.6% stake for $209 million, netting a profit of $33 million. Then in September 1988, Roche sold ICN worldwide distribution rights in perpetuity to three brands treating myasthenia gravis: Mestinon, Tensilon, and Prostigmin. The line had revenue of $20 million a year at 50% operating margins. Panic may not have achieved his ultimate objective, but the investment was profitable, and ICN did gain a hugely profitable line of products from the transaction.

It was never made clear exactly how ICN acquired the shares, only that Kurz had his hand in it. Panic's sudden sale of the shares surprised as well. Many believe he was pressured. The stock market had collapsed, and ICN could not handle a significant drop in its marketable securities portfolio. An even bigger mystery was why Roche would then follow with the Mestinon deal. Perhaps it was just another clever ICN transaction. And Panic wasn't finished, he would be back for more in the '90s. His tenure in Switzerland and dealmaking with Roche were in many ways just getting started.

THE WALL STREET JOURNAL.

FRIDAY, MARCH 25, 1988

ICN Sells Stake In Swiss Giant For $209 Million

Hoffmann-La Roche Shares Fetch $151,300; Control Firmly in Family Hands

By David J. Jefferson
Staff Reporter of The Wall Street Journal

ICN Pharmaceuticals Inc. said it sold its 8.6% stake in the voting stock of Swiss health care giant **F. Hoffmann-La Roche** & Co. for about $209 million.

A spokesman for Costa Mesa, Calif.-based ICN wouldn't identify the buyer, who paid $151,300 a share for the stock, but said the stake wasn't sold back to Hoffmann-La Roche. A spokeswoman for the U.S. unit of the Swiss company in Nutley, N.J., declined comment.

ICN's only explanation for the sale came in a terse statement from Chairman Milan Panic. "In selling our major position in the company, we understand and respect Hoffmann-La Roche's desire to remain in family control for the rest of the century," he said.

Members of the Hoffmann and La Roche families hold a controlling interest in the company. Their exact stakes aren't known, however, because Swiss laws don't require that disclosure.

In composite trading on the New York Stock Exchange, ICN shares closed at $8.25, up $1.50.

Craig Dickson, an analyst of the pharmaceutical and health-care industries with Interstate Securities Corp., Charlotte, N.C., said ICN likely sold its stake "because there wasn't anything else they could do with it. Although Wall Street never believed they could do it, the Hoffmann-La Roche stake was intended (by ICN) to be a move to acquire the company." ICN sold its stake, he said, "when it became clear they couldn't acquire the company."

Mr. Dickson estimated that ICN realized a gain of about $30 million from the sale, given the nearly $180 million it likely cost the company to acquire the stake.

ICN said it will use the proceeds to "acquire all or a part of one or more health care companies in order to expand the company's distribution capabilities, supplementing current product lines and adding compatible ones." ICN declined to identify which companies it is considering acquiring.

ICN said that partly as a result of the sale, it will reverse about $15.6 million of a $19.4 million charge for unrealized investment losses that it took in the fourth quarter ended Nov. 30. The company posted a fourth-quarter loss of $21.2 million after the charge. The $15.6 million reversal will be reflected in earnings for the first quarter ended Feb. 29, which will be released shortly, ICN said.

Separately, ICN said it received approval from the U.S. Food and Drug Administration to use its drug 8-MOP in the treatment of cutaneous T-cell lymphoma, a form of skin cancer. There are about 3,000 cases of the skin cancer reported each year in the U.S., an ICN spokesman said.

Among the other drugs that ICN and its various publicly traded units make and market is Virazole, which is being tested for use with AIDS patients.

The Wall Street Journal, **March 25, 1988**

CLINICAL HOLD

On January 5, 1987, ICN announced a press conference would be held January 9, at which time the company would release the HIV multicenter LAS data on 164 adult subjects. The stock had been dropping the previous week as short sellers spread rumors the trial was a bust. Panic and the team felt compelled to release preliminary data. He believed ICN owed the AIDS community the truth. The only approved drug, AZT, was expensive and toxic. Fifty percent of patients on it had experienced serious hematologic toxicity after one year of therapy, and 25% discontinued it entirely. AIDS sufferers were even traveling to Mexico to buy Vilona to bring back across the border.

The FDA warned against hosting the event, as it was customary for the agency to see the data first. But Panic ordered it held anyway, at the posh Marriott Hotel in Washington, DC. Bob Finch and Birch Bayh were dispatched to present the results. A live feed was linked to headquarters in Costa Mesa, providing a venue for more reporters to attend. Viratek hovered at $76, ICN at $25.25. Volume had been 10 times the normal range in the days leading up.

On January 9, ICN announced the results of controlled clinical trials testing the efficacy of ribavirin in preventing patients with LAS from progressing to AIDS. The trials enrolled 163 patients diagnosed with LAS. LAS patients were individuals who had been exposed to the AIDS virus and had enlarged lymph nodes. A significant number of LAS patients had, in the past, progressed to pre-AIDS or AIDS. The preliminary data from the trials revealed the following: none of the 52 patients who received a daily dose of 800 mg of ribavirin developed AIDS; 6 of 55 patients who received a daily dose of 600 mg developed AIDS; and 10 of 56 patients who received a placebo developed AIDS. The trials began in January 1986 at four different hospitals. The drug was well tolerated and not associated with significant side effects. The company believed that the statistically significant results indicated that ribavirin was efficacious in inhibiting the progression of LAS to AIDS in those patients treated. On January 21, 1987, Viratek filed an application with the FDA requesting a treatment IND for LAS patients using the 800-mg-per-day dose. A treatment IND allows case-by-case usage of a drug under a carefully designed protocol for treatment of certain patient groups and prior to approval by the FDA.

In a letter received April 13, 1987, the FDA informed the company it had completed its review and concluded that the data presented were not satisfactory to determine whether ribavirin provided a sufficient therapeutic benefit to HIV infected patients with LAS to justify widespread distribution of the drug under a treatment IND. Factors cited by the FDA in its letter included the number of patients with high risk of progressing to AIDS assigned to the placebo group, concentration of those high-risk patients at two of the four centers at which the trials were conducted, whether sufficient differences between treatment groups existed to support the claim for efficacy of ribavirin in LAS patients, and lack of data concerning the results of clinical trials evaluating ribavirin in the treatment of patients with ARC. ICN provided additional data and made a second request. In October, the FDA relented, and Viratek received permission to conduct additional testing.

SETBACK

The FDA clinical hold was tough for shareholders to swallow. By advertising results ahead of the FDA's review, ICN had put the agency in an awkward position with the public. The claims made ICN the target of government investigations. Panic took heat again. He was raked over the coals in the press and labeled an overzealous promoter. *The Wall Street Journal* ran a cover story chastising his tactics in holding a press conference before the FDA had seen the data. Viratek fell back to $12 a share, ICN to $6. Then, in a surprise announcement, Eastman Kodak said it would sell its 2.3% stake in ICN and a significant portion of its 9% stake in Viratek. In June '87, ICN bought back Kodak's position. Kodak opted out of NARI and returned all the compounds to Viratek. Coincidentally, at the same time it outbid Roche to buy Sterling Drug and used this transaction as the reason for discontinuing with ICN. But many speculated that the real reason Kodak sold was that it had grown tired of the aids pressure, stock volatility, and quite possibly Panic himself.

In a surprise announcement, Eastman Kodak said it would sell its 2.3% stake in ICN and a significant portion of its 9% state in Viratek.

THIS TIME IS DIFFERENT

Panic assured shareholders and employees that while the FDA rejection was a major setback, it was not 1974 again. ICN was a strong, healthy company. Sales had grown to $166 million in 1988 from $37 million in 1983. Net income was $17 million, or $1.03 per share. Gross margins were 71%. The base was growing organically at 13%. Bond market conditions resulting from the 1987 crash had enabled ICN to buy back $140 million of its high-yield debt at less than its cost, reducing annual interest expense by $6 million. The company had cash of $287 million, which could be used for additional accretive acquisitions or to retire more debt.

From a regional perspective, SPI's North America unit was selling $100 million and highly profitable. Canada and Mexico were solid contributors, each selling $20 million per year, and Europe was tracking at $35 million. The ICN family had 2,200 employees, 17 plants, and 300 products. A total of 17 companies had been acquired. Grossman in Mexico turned out to be a fabulous acquisition led by Dr. Javier Rovallo. More than 50,000 infants had been treated safely with ribavirin. And Biomed, flush with cash from its own financings, was able to step up and buy Flow Laboratories for $41 million, taking its sales to more than $100 million.

Panic was wounded but more resilient than ever. He had been through hell in the '70s, and this was far easier. Now he had cash to keep growing, a bunch of international brands, and a global footprint to expand upon.

> ICN was a strong, healthy company. Sales had grown to $166 million in 1988 from $37 million in 1983. A total of 17 companies had been acquired.

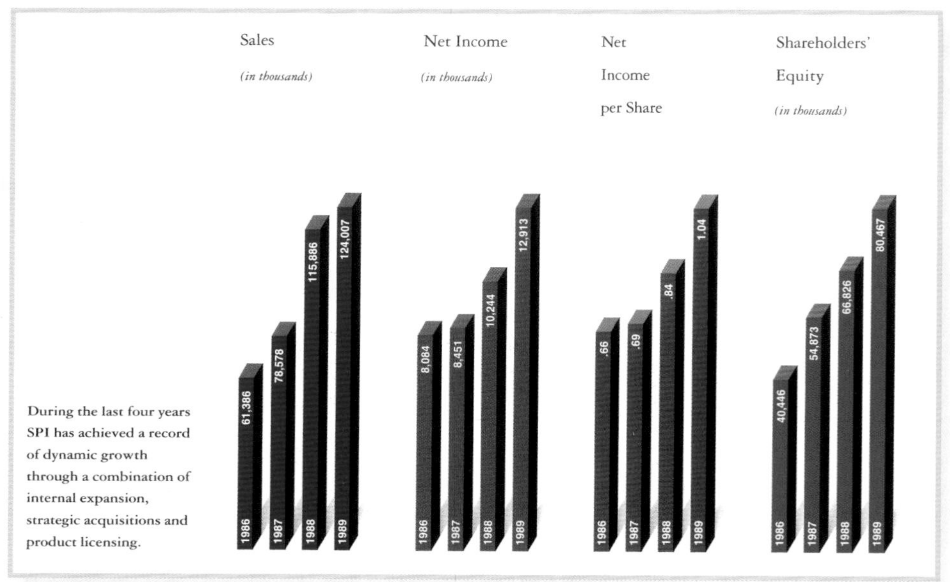

SPI growth chart, 1986–1989

SPI achieved dynamic growth through a combination of internal expansion, strategic acquisitions, and product licensing.

New Biomed board member Jerry Brown

A SILENT EPIDEMIC

Despite the FDA finally lifting its clinical hold on ribavirin, Panic and the board had had enough. They believed the data from the more than 1,265 HIV-infected patients enrolled in ribavirin clinical trials demonstrated that the drug was safe and effective against AIDS, but unfortunately the FDA did not see it that way. Five years of testing and fighting with the agency had taken its toll. In 1989, ICN terminated all development and took a $71-million write-off, which caused a loss that year of $82 million on sales of $185 million. Ironically, two years later Hungary and Ireland approved the drug for AIDS, but there would be no such luck in the United States and Canada.

However, a new opportunity for ribavirin loomed on the horizon. In the mid-1970s, Harvey J. Alter, chief of the Infectious Disease Section in the Department of Transfusion Medicine at the National Institutes of Health, discovered that the majority of post-transfusion hepatitis cases were not due to hepatitis A or B viruses but a new viral strain initially called non-A, non-B hepatitis (NANBH). In 1988, Alter confirmed the virus by verifying its presence in a panel of NANBH specimens. It was officially named hepatitis C (HCV), an RNA-induced virus. In prospective studies published the following year in the journal *Science*, it was further shown that this chronic non-A, non-B virus could develop in about 1%–5% of those multiply transfused individuals in the industrialized world. It was thought to spread primarily by blood-to-blood contact associated with intravenous drug use, poorly sterilized medical equipment, needle stick injuries in health care, and transfusions. Researchers began calling it the silent epidemic.

HCV's discovery led to significant improvements in the diagnosis and associated screening methods that would reduce the risk of blood transfusion–associated hepatitis. Still, it was estimated that in the '70s and '80s many thousands of people had contracted HCV from blood transfusions before universal screening was instituted. In the mid-'80s, the CDC estimated that the number of new HCV infections per year in the United States hovered around 180,000. The NIH estimated that as many as 10% of surgical patients who received a transfusion developed HCV after surgery. And although the hepatitis C virus was subclinical in the acute phase, its propensity to progress to chronic hepatitis, cirrhosis, and, possibly, hepatocellular carcinoma meant that an effective treatment must be sought.

In 1989, Viratek completed two phase II clinical studies at Huntington Memorial Hospital in Pasadena, California and the Veterans Administration Hospital in Taipei, investigating ribavirin's treatment effects on chronic active hepatitis, type B and type C. The results were encouraging prompting the NIH to undertake further testing. The Karolinska Institute of Sweden also initiated an oral ribavirin pilot study in patients with chronic hepatitis C virus infection.

PRIVATIZATION MODEL

Panic and Ted Olic's instincts proved fortuitous when they first began focusing on Eastern Europe for acquisitions. A wave of democratization had indeed begun. In 1989, the first free labor union was founded in Poland, leading eventually to the fall of communism in that country. The *glasnost* and *perestroika* reforms instigated by Gorbachev in 1986 in the Soviet Union had their effects on other countries, especially Poland and Hungary. Mass demonstrations against the government in East Germany led to the fall of the Berlin Wall. Authoritarian command economies were collapsing. Post-communist Europe was taking shape and, with that, the implementation of free-market reforms and privatizations of state-owned pharmaceutical companies.

Ted Olic had generated some small chemical orders for ICN but was now was on to much bigger game. Regional pharmaceutical companies were available, and for little cash. Each required fair value, but the purchase price could include a social package as well. These governments needed benefits for their workers in the form of job security, employee training and education, and health benefits.

He and Panic speculated few Western companies would take on these challenges. There was too much political and economic risk. ICN could assume these risks and gain valuable market share by being first. ICN would privatize the state-owned entities for little cash up front, establish domestic production, register and sell ICN global brands, and, in the process, become the distributor of choice to the West. With populations of 120 million in the Baltic states and another 290 million people in Russia, the revenue growth, if successful, could be staggering.

But to crack these markets, ICN had to establish GMP production, transfer accounting systems to GAAP, and deal with tremendous political and economic volatility. These state-owned companies were bureaucratic, lethargic, and overstaffed. They needed substantial capital to modernize. Fortunately, their labor forces were educated, and the companies produced quality generic products. Also, by becoming the local producer, ICN could enjoy additional protections that may pay off in times of trouble. Local producers avoided the risks of trade barriers, management earned considerable goodwill and political leverage by employing locals, and tax incentives could be gained. And in times of crisis or devaluation, local producers could often shield their margins because of low-cost production, starting with labor.

Panic knew this was a huge gamble. But he and Olic were comfortable in Eastern Europe. They knew the languages, the customs, the culture, and the communist systems. And Panic, now in business around the world for more than 30 years, was experienced. He knew what to do on the operating side. He could whip through a P&L and balance sheet in any currency. Whatever the problem, he'd likely faced it before. These markets were simply too big to ignore. This was calculated risk-taking, but with enormous payoffs if they were right.

Novi jugoslovenski premijer Milan Panić

Životopis u četiri tačke

Reč je o upornom, vrednom čoveku neverovatne energije koji je u mnogo čemu i emotivan, svojstveno njegovim korenima – kazuje dr Velimir Branković, predsednik i generalni direktor Holdinga „Galenika"

Do pre samo godinu dana ime čoveka koji ove nedelje preuzima kormilo opasno nagnutog jugoslovenskog broda, na ovim prostorima se pominjalo uglavnom među retko uspešnijim biznismenima, naučno-istraživačkim timovima biohemičara i u ne tako brojnom krugu onih koji su pomno pratili uspešne korake Srba u rasejanju.

Prvi veliki prodor u pamćenje jugoslovenske javnosti Milan Panić je napravio stavljajući potpis na

Foto: Imre Sabo

Dr Velimir Branković

Milan Panić

je odbio. On je i jedini od 25 članova izbornog štaba koji tada od novoizabranog američkog predsednika ništa nije hteo da traži. Interesantno je da je i u Karterovom i u Dukakisovom štabu vodio finansije – otkriva dr Branković.

Kao čovek koji zna kako se zarađuje novac, politika je, kažu njegovi prijatelji, bila prostor koji je za njega bila manji izazov od biznisa. Zato, smatraju oni, nije bilo nikakve poze kada je rekao:

„Mi poslovni ljudi treba da utičemo na politiku, a ne da dozvolimo da politika utiče na nas."

– Panić je kao četrnaestogodišnji dečak otišao u Drugi svetski rat – nastavlja dr Branković. – Učestvovao je u proboju Sremskog fronta. Zato nije čudno što

Galenika's Dr. Velimir Brankovic and Milan Panic

BELGRADE

Naturally, Yugoslavia was the first target. Panic and Olic were Serbs. Olic was a government insider, and Panic was a national hero. He was revered in Belgrade as a symbol of American values—capitalism, free enterprise, and political freedom. His personal story was tangible proof that democratic free-market economies worked and held promise for the Yugoslav people. Both men were familiar with Yugoslavia's largest drug company, Galenika, but weren't sure whether it could be acquired. Nor did they have any idea how it was run. It had always been owned by the state, which, after Tito's death, was now in the hands of Slobodan Milosevic, the president of Serbia. It was a socially owned Yugoslav company. Nonetheless, Olic contacted Galenika's chief, Velimir Brankovic, to see whether there was interest in a merger.

At this time, the Milosevic regime had not yet truly revealed its brutal face to the world. The Yugoslav government was then experimenting with some of the economic reforms that were being tried in other parts of Eastern Europe. Milosevic knew and admired Panic and felt that Panic could make Galenika a symbol of Western capitalism and economic success. Besides, Yugoslavia needed more friends in the West. It was about to embark on some nation building of its own and could use some world support.

"Yugoslavia looked like both a business opportunity and, just possibly, a chance to help the country of my birth at a delicate time."
—Milan Panic

Herb Lightstone and Milan Panic on a telephone call to Belgrade, 1980s

ICN Galenika

1990–2003

- May 1991—SPI acquires 75% of Galenika Pharmaceuticals in Belgrade. Joint venture renamed ICN Galenika.
- 1991—SPI reports net profit of $1.73 per share, or $30.12M, up 102% from $14.9M, or 95 cents, in 1990. Revenue grew to $364M from $140M, a gain of 158%.
- 1991—ICN included among top 50 pharmaceutical companies in the world.
- 1991—Birch E. Bayh, former US Senator from Indiana, elected to board of directors.
- 1991—Hungarian Health Ministry approves ribavirin for AIDS.
- 1991—*Lancet* reports positive findings of use of ribavirin against hepatitis C.
- October 21, 1992—SPI forms joint venture with Leningrad Industrial Chemical and Pharmaceutical Association (Oktyabr) in St. Petersburg.
- July 1995—ICN grants Schering-Plough (SGP) exclusive license to all forms of oral ribavirin to treat HCV for $23M cash up front, up to $60M in clinical trial funding, and worldwide royalties on sales. Upon achievement of certain milestones, Schering to buy $42M in ICN stock.
- December 1995—Bosnian Peace Agreement (Dayton Accords). Suspension of economic sanctions in Belgrade follow. Galenika resumes full operations and export.
- June 1997—ICN pays $145M in cash and stock for seven drugs from Roche for $90M.
- September 1997—ICN stock reaches $40 based on ribavirin/AIFN test results.
- October 1997—ICN buys 80% of Polfa Rzeszow S.A.
- October 1997—ICN buys four drugs from Roche.
- 1997—ICN Russian sales $150M from five facilities, 200 prescription products. Division employs 7,000.
- 1997—Schering files NDA on Rebetron (combination of oral ribavirin and alpha interferon) for treatment of hepatitis C.
- February 1998—ICN acquires from SmithKline the Asian, African, and Australian rights to 39 prescription and OTC products.
- March 1998—ICN acquires rights to a portfolio of 32 dermatology products sold in Argentina and Latin America from Laboratorios Pablo Cassara.
- June 1998—SGP receives FDA approval of Rebetron for alpha interferon relapsers.
- October 1998—ICN buys four products from F. Hoffmann–La Roche, Dalmadorm, fluorouracil, Librax, and Mogadon. Sales $67M. Purchase price $179M, 50% cash.
- December 1998—SGP receives FDA approval for Rebetron combination therapy, containing Rebetol (ribavirin USP capsules and Intron A [interferon alfa-2B, recombinant]) injection for patients with chronic hepatitis C.
- December 1998—SCP receives FDA approval of Rebetron for naive patients, untreated before. First-year royalties to ICN are $37M.
- 1998—Andrei Kozyrev, PhD, former minister of foreign affairs of the Russian Federation, elected to ICN Board of Directors.
- February 1999—The Federal Republic of Yugoslavia seizes control of ICN Galenika.
- April 7, 1999—Schering-Plough buys $27M of ICN stock under milestone terms of its July 1995 ribavirin licensing agreement.
- May 1999—EU awards SGP approval of Rebetron. Valid in all 15 EU states.
- October 1999—ICN re-enters Brazil via acquisition of Pharmaway Industria Farmaceutica Limitada.
- 1999—Warburg Dillon Read and Schroders Bank place $125M senior notes due 2008.
- 1999—Royalties to ICN from SGP exceed $100M.
- 2000—Kim Campbell, former prime minister, Canada, elected to ICN Board of Directors.
- 2000—Rebetron sales $1.3B.
- March 2001—Peg-Intron combo approved in EU.
- June 2001—ICN licenses levovirin to F. Hoffmann–La Roche.
- July 2001—FDA grants SGP license to market Rebetol as a separately marketed product.
- August 2001—SGP receives US approval for Peg-Intron (peginterferonalpha 2B) powder for injection for use in combination therapy with Rebetol (ribavirin USP) capsules.
- September 2001—ICN commences phase 1 trials of viramidine in Europe. Agent is a nucleoside analogue.
- November 2001—Combination of ribavirin and alpha interferon approved in Japan for HCV.
- 2001—ICN cumulative royalties on ribavirin for HCV since launch aggregate $360M.
- 2001—Milan Panic's last year as CEO and chairman. Sales $858M and net profit $64M. 54% of revenues ex-US.
- 2001—UBS leads $400M 6.5% convertible subordinated notes.
- April 2002—Ribapharm IPO (RNA). 29.9M shares, $11/share. Proceeds $276M. Market cap $1.9B. ICN sells 19.9% to public. Second-largest biotechnology offering.
- June 19, 2002—Milan Panic resigns. At time, ICN employs 11,625 people. Royalties to ICN from ribavirin for HCV that year $270M.
- December 2002—ICN becomes forty-ninth-largest pharmaceutical company in the world.
- November 2003—Board changes name to Valeant Pharmaceuticals International.

THE NINETIES

TOP 50 IN THE WORLD

ICN Galenika

GALENIKA

Founded in 1945, Galenika was established to supply a war-ravaged country with much-needed pharmaceuticals and medical supplies. Production began with antibiotics and penicillin, followed by steroids and hormonals. By the mid-'50s, Galenika was exporting pharmaceuticals to other Balkan nations and Russia. By the mid-'70s, more than 300 products were offered in topical, oral, and injectable forms. In the '80s, the company became a distributor to many top multinationals, including Pfizer, Eli Lilly, Bristol Myers Squibb, Abbott, Roche, and G.D. Searle. By 1989, annual turnover reached $189 million.

When Ted Olic first made overtures about the possibilities of ICN acquiring Galenika, he found to his surprise that the Serbian government was eying ICN in the same way. Party Chief Milosevic was an ex-banker and appreciated what wealth and profits could bring. Negotiations continued throughout 1990. Panic chaired most of the meetings. He was eager to do the deal. His team included

Ted Olic, Bill MacDonald, Adam Jerney, and David Watt. Because of the political and legal ramifications, Panic also relied on Senator Birch Bayh, his long-time personal lawyer Bernie Segal, and, from time to time, prominent California lawmaker Leo McCarthy. ICN's auditor, Coopers and Lybrand, was tasked with structuring the deal and ensuring that the new venture complied with Western accounting and legal practices.

In November, the parties agreed to terms, and ICN publicly announced the letter of intent to shareholders. ICN stock, which had languished for some time under $5 per share, started to rise, as did SPI's. The benefits were obvious. Galenika was larger than ICN. The combination would double revenues in a single stroke.

On May 1, 1991, ICN took control. SPI would be the acquiring company. The combination would be called ICN Galenika. SPI owned 75%, and Galenika Holding, a social entity created to retain all the non-core pharmaceutical assets, had the rest. Milosevic and Panic were key to the deal's closing. And for a short time, they appeared to be partners, both interested in improving conditions for the country—and in making money.

ICN Galenika was the largest privatization in Yugoslavia since World War II. The new company was valued at $360 million. In exchange for its 75% stake, SPI contributed $50 million in cash and $220 million in intangible assets, essentially four patented anticancer agents in development. The $50 million was made up of SPI stock and cash, the latter deposited into an account at Union Bank of Switzerland. Nationalism was rising among the republics. A breakup of Yugoslavia was possible. As a precaution, ICN's board insisted that the cash be kept outside of Yugoslavia so it could not be seized in the event of civil unrest.

As part of the deal, Olic designed a package that granted each Galenika employee an ownership interest in SPI. Five thousand workers received 203 shares of SPI stock. By this time, SPI stock had risen to $28, making the stock contribution worth $30 million. In addition, ICN built two apartment towers adjacent to the plant where families could live in privacy and comfort. A new bakery and kitchen were built, and three hot meals a day were served to employees, who were guaranteed job security and health benefits. Panic wanted fast, profitable growth. Management and the employees needed to be secure and happy. Galenika would serve as not only a model acquisition but also a template for future privatizations in the region. If this one worked, Panic envisioned other deals following and revenue gains in the hundreds of millions.

Galenika's transition into ICN's family was critical. Managers, lawyers, and accountants were dispatched to Belgrade to integrate the company. ICN had to reform decades of communist rule and adapt the company to Western business standards. Employees had to be trained in marketing, sales, distribution, information systems, and human resources. Coopers converted Yugoslavian accounting practices (YAP) to GAAP and filed consolidated financial statements for the first time. ICN executives were holed up for months at Belgrade's Hyatt Hotel, far from their families and the relative peace, safety, and comfort of sunny California. But it was worth it. This was groundbreaking work.

Navigating through old-line communist bureaucracies required special political skill, which couldn't easily be found among Westerners. Olic needed help, and Panic was spread too thin. His presence was required at other ICN companies and at ICN Plaza. They needed a full-time partner on the ground in the Balkans to spearhead deals—and one who could deliver. They found that person in John D. Scanlan, the former US ambassador to Yugoslavia from 1985 to 1989.

A quintessential US Foreign Service Officer, Scanlan was self-effacing, distinguished, and, above all, pragmatic in a way that sharply contrasted Panic's charismatic but sometimes overbearing Serbian style. Because Scanlon's diplomatic career was coming to an end, he joined ICN to assist Olic in directing the European expansion. He knew the languages and culture. He spoke both Serbian and Russian fluently.

He also knew the powerbrokers. He was comfortable dealing with the Communist Party *apparatchik*.

Scanlan added value from the very start. He and Olic helped Galenika secure a $22-million export order to Russian hospitals for antibiotics and analgesics. ICN had owned the company less than a year, and already Galenika would contribute more than $230 million in revenue, including $30 million to Russia.

ICN affiliates quickly obtained registrations to export to Yugoslavia. ICN Canada launched carbamazepine, and ICN Holland introduced the Unicare soft care lens. Galenika margin and revenue gains were achieved through price increases, greater purchasing power, better utilization of facilities, and workforce efficiencies. The employees were excited and motivated. Panic's Serbian roots played a big part. He was trusted. Milosevic took credit too. He wanted a better identity for Serbia, and the ICN Galenika connection was key to his own personal ambitions.

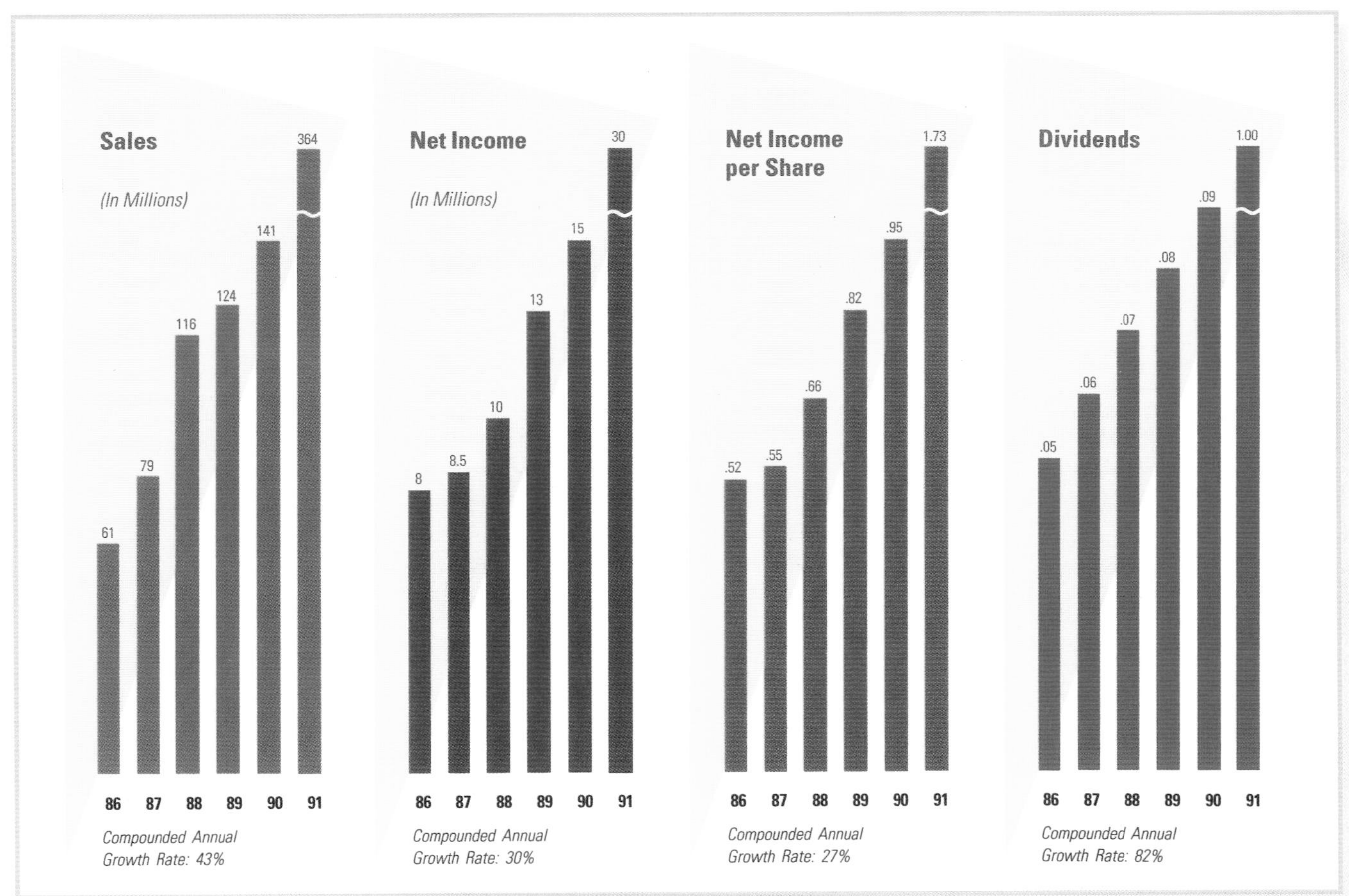

Galenika transforms SPI

TRANSFORMATION

Back home, investors cheered. The Galenika pact added $200 million in annual revenue to SPI's base. ICN put up only $50 million, all of which was deposited in a Swiss bank account for the company's use. Consolidated 1991 sales of ICN were $460 million, a record. Net income was $6 million, or $0.40. Profits before tax and minority interest were $31 million. ICN was the third-best performing stock on the NYSE that year. Panic had the company moving again.

SPI sales rose 159% to $364 million. Total employees reached 5,600, spread over plants in North and Latin America, Western Europe, Asia, and Eastern Europe. Sales of SPI's other divisions rose sharply too. The US dermatology line leaped 22%, led by a 32% increase in sales of skin bleach products. In 1991, *Forbes* listed SPI in its annual ranking of the best 200 companies in America. Since going public in 1984, SPI had grown from $24 million to $364 million.

On the R&D front, the highly prestigious medical journal *Lancet* published ribavirin's pilot results in treating hepatitis C at the Karolinska Institute. The drug was tested at 1,000–1,200 mg per day in 10 patients for 10 days. Liver enzymes dropped sharply in all 10 patients and rose again after treatment stopped. The Karolinska researchers concluded that ribavirin was a promising solution to HCV, which by now had become an emerging worldwide health threat.

Ribavirin's oral form was a key advantage. At the time, the only drug available was Schering-Plough's alpha interferon (AFN), which had to be injected. AFN spurred drops in liver enzymes but cured only 10%–20% of patients. The Karolinska scientists also recommended that ribavirin and alpha interferon be tested in combination. The drug's innovator, Schering-Plough, heard that call loud and clear. It immediately began focusing on ICN as a possible licensing or acquisition candidate. AFN/ribavirin could be a billion-dollar product.

The Karolinska researchers concluded that ribavirin was a promising solution to HCV, which had now become an emerging worldwide health threat.

RUSSIA

With Galenika done, Olic and Scanlan moved on to Russia. The former Soviet Republic, boasting a population of 290 million and a drug market estimated at $6 billion, offered tremendous potential.

Russia's market system was evolving. The beginnings of a functioning democracy were in place, and the Soviet Empire had been dismantled with minimal conflict. Russia was trying to build a market economy based on private enterprise and had for the first time a democratically elected government. Gorbachev started the evolution in the late 1980s, which was continued by Boris Yeltsin in the early '90s. Within a few years, more than 60% of the Russian economy was either in private hands or had been transferred from the state to city control.

When Panic got to Russia, he found himself negotiating for the purchase of pharmaceutical assets with Vladimir Putin, then a top aide to Anatoly Sobchak, the reformist mayor of St. Petersburg. Like Galenika, he proposed using ICN stock to compensate workers. Putin liked the idea, but Russian workers were not allowed to own shares listed on the NYSE. Instead, the plan was to deposit shares in a bank and give the workers certificates of ownership. The parties viewed this as a transfer of capitalism, a strategy that could be deployed across Russia one factory at a time.

In December 1991, SPI announced a letter of intent to enter a joint venture with Oktyabr Pharmaceutical Factories, headquartered in St. Petersburg. Founded by Peter the Great in 1714, Oktyabr was Russia's oldest pharmaceutical company. It operated five plants in St. Petersburg and sold 225 prescription/nonprescription drugs. As many as 3,300 employees were on the payroll. Oktyabr products were sold throughout the Commonwealth of Independent States and non-Commonwealth nations in other Eastern Europe countries. The product line included analgesics, vitamins, anesthetics, and cardiovascular drugs.

On October 21, 1992, SPI announced the closing and registered the new company, ICN Oktyabr, with the Russian Federation. Because of the slow transition of the Russian economy, SPI planned for a longer phase-in period than had occurred with Galenika. Building a new factory was part of the deal. Initially, ICN paid $9.8 million for its minority stake, which largely consisted of assuming Oktabyr's then-existing debt.

In March 1994, SPI began the second phase. It got a second tranche of Oktyabr shares for $43 million, payable in cash and stock. In May 1995, ICN took 75% control. The key was getting the workers to sell their shares. They had been given part of the company after the fall of communism. To exchange their ownership vouchers for SPI stock, ICN added cars, TV sets, toasters, and appliances. It was reported to be the first time Russian citizens had owned a stake in a US company.

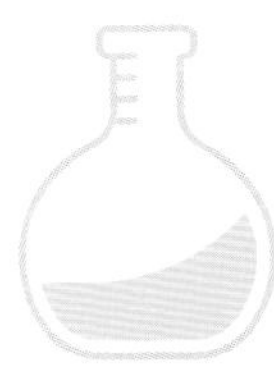

CIVIL WAR

Unfortunately in Yugoslavia, Panic's worst fears over the fate of his homeland had become reality. Galenika was working beautifully, but the political climate around it had taken a treacherous turn. Panic hoped Milosevic would pursue a reformist path in Yugoslavia, but instead the Serbian strongman unveiled a nationalist agenda. Leaders of the other republics did the same. The dismantling of Yugoslavia had begun.

By the middle of 1991, events were moving fast. On June 25, Croatia announced its independence. Slovenia followed the next day. All the republics moved to declare their own independence from the SFRY, even Macedonia.

The Milosevic regime responded with force. It tried to advance a centralized Serbian state possessing complete power and autonomy over the territories. The Yugoslav army entered Croatia and Slovenia. There was heavy fighting and bloodshed. Much to the world's horror, acts of repression and ethnic cleansing became front-page news. Serbian security forces were sent to destabilize Bosnia-Herzegovina, sparking tensions between the country's Muslim, Serb, and Croat inhabitants. The republics denounced Milosevic's actions and demanded a full, multiparty confederal state. Slovenia reformed its constitution, declaring its right to secession. Croatia expressed support for Slovenia. Bosnia and Herzegovina declared neutrality. In early 1992, the SFRY transitioned to the Federal Republic of Yugoslavia (FRY), consisting only of Serbia and Montenegro. Milosevic was president of Serbia, and the famed novelist Dobrinka Cosic was elected president of the FRY.

By the summer of 1992, the practice of ethnic cleansing, initiated first in Croatia, and then in Bosnia-Herzegovina, became widespread. Milosevic was alleged to be the perpetrator. In May 1992, world opinion was further pitted against Serbia when innocent civilians were fired upon in Sarajevo, the beautiful capital of Bosnia-Herzegovina that in 1984 had hosted the Winter Olympics. Dozens of innocent people were killed. CNN cameras on the scene projected the atrocities around the world. Because the victims were Muslims, the killing was immediately ascribed to the Bosnian Serbs, whose heavy artillery guns had encircled the city.

Milan Panic at odds with Party Chief Milosevic

SANCTIONS

Like the country, Galenika teetered on the brink. On June 1, 1992, the UN Security Council voted to impose sanctions on Serbia and Montenegro, invoking resolution 757. Nothing could be imported or exported from the FRY. This included oil, the mainstay of economic activity. The sanctions would remain in place until all the UN demands were satisfied. These demands included an end to interference in Bosnia and the disarming of all irregular Serb forces fighting there. Milosevic refused to capitulate, claiming his government was innocent.

ICN complied with the sanctions. The executive order prohibited imports and exports to Yugoslavia and the end to all cash flows to and from the country, except for humanitarian purposes. Specifically, ICN and its subsidiaries were prohibited from managing or engaging in any commercial transactions with ICN Galenika. All foreign-based managers were immediately pulled from the country.

Suppliers were required to apply for licenses before shipment of raw materials and finished goods could be made. In anticipation of shortages, Galenika increased its already high inventory levels, which increased the company's net monetary position and exposed it to further devaluations and exchange losses.

The Yugoslavian economy quickly deteriorated. Hyperinflation took over. The dinar, Yugoslavian's currency, weakened significantly against the US dollar. There were five devaluations during 1992. The exchange rate changed from 2.2 dinars per US dollar at the beginning of the year to 750 dinars per US dollar 12 months later. This forced ICN to take a $28-million foreign exchange loss in 1992. ICN and SPI stock plummeted. All Galenika export sales were lost. Shareholders feared the worst. And once again, it was all Milan Panic's fault.

aged only 44% occupancy last year, the consultant says. Schulze declined to confirm the number. But if things ever get too bad with any of the properties, he says, the Ritz-Carlton Hotel Co. could walk away from its nonrecourse loans, which give lenders no claim against the parent: "We would still have a management fee and would be very happy."

Owner Bill Johnson has plenty of management experience, but only lately with such a fancy outfit as Ritz-Carlton. A self-made man, he ventured into entrepreneurship with a Waffle House Inc. franchise back in the 1960s. Today, Johnson owns some 100 Waffle Houses, 10 Holiday Inns, and a Marriott. His greatest coup, rival hoteliers say, was purchasing the Ritz name for some $70 million in 1983. "A brilliant move," says Darryl Hartley-Leonard, president of Hyatt Hotels Corp. Only one Ritz, in Chicago, is independently managed.

DISGRUNTLED. Johnson's reputation as a shrewd operator and a masterful dealmaker garnered him numerous investors. Some say they are thrilled: "It's being managed superbly," says Allen Ostroff, senior vice-president of Prudential Realty Group, which owns 90% of the Ritz-Carlton in Laguna Niguel, Calif. He has good reason to be upbeat: Last year the hotel had a 70% occupancy rate, better than its local rivals, and average room rates topped $200 a night. "Over 90% of our outside investors are exceedingly happy," Schulze insists. "In some cases, their real estate results at the moment don't look as good, but operating results are excellent."

Many investors don't see it that way. New York's secretive Lee family, which lent Johnson some $136 million to refinance his flagship Boston property in exchange for a future ownership interest, is in negotiations to take control of the hotel, according to sources close to the situation. Koichi Lee declines to comment. Schulze confirms that "intricate discussions" are taking place but declines to elaborate. Other outside investors, stuck with underperforming properties in glutted markets, are disgruntled as well. The chain "expanded too quickly, and the properties have too much money in them at this point," says a real estate executive who works with one California Ritz investor.

To Schulze, such thinking is short-term and ill-conceived. "A hotel is built for not three years, but for 60 years," he says in hushed tones, leaning forward in his chair. "I assure you that the Ritz-Carlton Hotel Co. will be here for many, many years." That may be. But if Johnson can't figure out a way to keep his lenders happy, his role in the company's future may be vastly reduced.

By Laurel Touby in New York, with bureau reports

ALAN LEVENSON

People

ENTREPRENEURS

NO PEACE FOR MILAN PANIC

The ICN chief's fortunes are tied to war-torn Yugoslavia

PANIC: WORLD'S RICHEST SERB?

Within Yugoslavia's aspiring Serbian business community, Milan Panic is a folk hero. Not only did he escape the shackles of Communism early by defecting to the U.S. in 1955, but he also transformed himself into a millionaire pharmaceutical executive—perhaps the richest Serbian in the world. "He's a well-known and very popular name in Belgrade," says Nebojsa Vujovic, first secretary of the Yugoslavian Embassy in Washington. "He possesses a vast knowledge of the working market economy."

Too vast, in the opinion of some federal regulators and Wall Street investors. On the way to building ICN Pharmaceuticals Inc. into a $460 million international drug company, Panic (pronounced PAHN-ish) has been investigated twice by the Securities & Exchange Commission for securities-law violations. And last year, he settled a civil action brought by the U.S. Justice Dept. alleging that ICN overstated the potential of one of its compounds as an AIDS drug. Neither he nor ICN has admitted guilt in any of these cases. Some investors defend the 62-year-old Panic as an aggressive visionary. But his management has spurred numerous shareholder suits, and his own board has censured him for misuse of corporate assets (table). Panic was unavailable to be interviewed for this article.

Now, Panic has managed to wrap controversy and his Serbian heritage into a single package: The ruling Socialist party in what's left of Yugoslavia—Serbia and Montenegro—wants to draft him as the nation's Prime Minister to help stabilize the economy and stave off Western military intervention. It's unlikely he would accept—it would jeopardize his hard-won U.S. citizenship and run counter to sanctions enacted against Yu-

76 BUSINESS WEEK/JULY 6, 1992

PEOPLE

Prime Minister of the Federal Republic of Yugoslavia, Milan Panic, addresses the General Assembly of the United Nations
September 22, 1992

PRIME MINISTER

In Belgrade, however, Milosevic remained impressed with Milan Panic. He calculated that if Panic could turn around an ailing Galenika, why couldn't he do the same for the country? Besides, Panic had deep ties to Washington's political elite. Perhaps he could influence these connections to ease the sanctions on Yugoslavia.

Milosevic and Cosic invited Milan Panic to become prime minister of Yugoslavia. The move was unprecedented. An American citizen was being asked to head a foreign government under UN and US sanctions. The request, considered at the highest levels of the US government, was approved, and Panic was given the license to serve as prime minister. In effect, the Bush Administration made the conscious decision that its own foreign policy and national security interests were furthered by Panic's involvement. Panic was tasked with bringing an end to the Serbian aggression. Against the advice of nearly everyone close to him, Panic accepted the challenge. Privately, he was horrified at what was happening to the country of his birth.

On July 2, 1992, Panic took a leave of absence from ICN to begin his post as prime minister of the FRY. Adam Jerney succeeded him as president and CEO. Shareholders, shaken by ICN's dramatic reversal in fortunes, initially applauded the move. The benefits were unmistakable. A halt to the fighting would encourage the United Nations to lift international trade and economic sanctions, which had threatened Galenika's ability to operate profitably.

For nine months, Panic worked tirelessly for peace in the Balkans. At great personal risk—there were attempts made on his life—Panic did the best he could. He engaged in extensive personal diplomacy with world leaders, helped organize a peace conference, addressed the United Nations, and tried to lay the groundwork for real and sustainable democratic reforms in the country and region. However, his peacemaking was thwarted by Milosevic at every turn. Milosevic controlled the military, the media, and the bureaucracy. Panic had no chance. The two men, once partners in a noble venture, became bitter enemies. In late 1992, Panic ran unsuccessfully against Milosevic for president. After the election, he was effectively removed from his government post and forced to leave the country. By February 1993, he was back in charge at ICN Plaza, lucky to get out of the Balkans alive.

The Federal Republic of Yugoslavia (FRY) parliament in session

HEADWINDS

In 1992, before the full effect of the sanctions took hold, Galenika's revenues had risen to $326 million, yielding gross profit of $173 million and pretax income of $38 million. However, the next year sales dropped to $240 million, resulting in the company breaking even. Galenika had been awarded restricted licenses to import, but raw-material shipments shrunk to 38% of prior-year levels. Bank accounts were frozen. There were restrictions placed on the use of Galenika's cash holdings outside in Switzerland. Wage and price controls were instituted. The company had difficulty obtaining hard currency to fund operations.

Fortunately, other SPI divisions filled the gap. Ex-Galenika output rose to $186 million from $164 million the prior year. This helped weather the storm. In 1992, SPI reported $476 million in revenue, up from $364 million in 1991. Net income rose 15% to $34.3 million from $30.1 million. SPI earnings reached $1.90 from $1.69.

But in 1993 performance was down. Revenue dropped to $404 million. Earnings fell to $21.5 million and on a per-share basis to $1.03. The UN sanctions and price controls had impacted sales. The bottom line was hit with the adverse effects of hyperinflation and larger and more frequent devaluations.

Taking into context the full impact of the crisis, SPI had actually performed admirably. The base business outside of Yugoslavia grew, and Galenika did no worse than break even. Inside ICN, management was encouraged. They proved the company could operate in Eastern Europe under the worst of conditions. They overcame the challenges of hyperinflation, sanctions, raw material shortages, and the ever-present threats of nationalization from the Milosevic regime. It was time to look ahead again. The Yugoslavian conflict would soon end, and nations in the region would get back to building market economies. This would mean more companies for ICN to acquire.

Performance was down. The bottom line was hit with the adverse effects of hyperinflation and larger and more frequent devaluations.

An Important Message To All Stockholders Of ICN Pharmaceuticals, Inc.

DON'T BE CONNED BY KHAN

A controversial stockbroker called "Rafi Khan" with no pharmaceutical management experience is plotting an attempt to take over your company at your expense.

Do not sign Khan's white proxy card. Our proxy materials will be mailed to you shortly.

Remember:

KHAN LIED IN COURT

A U.S. District Court Judge found and the U.S. Court of Appeals did not reverse findings of fact that:

- KHAN WILLFULLY LIED UNDER OATH
- KHAN TRADED ON INSIDE INFORMATION
- KHAN FAILED TO MAKE MATERIAL DISCLOSURES TO THE SECURITIES AND EXCHANGE COMMISSION

KHAN HAS AN UNSTABLE EMPLOYMENT HISTORY

- 3 JOB CHANGES IN LESS THAN A YEAR

KHAN IS FACING SEVERAL LAWSUITS

Khan is the target of lawsuits by multiple parties on charges such as:

- RACKETEERING
- VIOLATION OF SECURITIES LAWS
- BREACH OF FIDUCIARY DUTY
- INSIDER TRADING
- STOCK MANIPULATION OF FUTURE COMMUNICATIONS, INC.

We do not believe that you can trust any materials or statements from Khan. He lied under oath.

DO YOU WANT A SPECULATIVE TRADER TO RUN YOUR COMPANY?

For years, Khan consistently and enthusiastically praised ICN Pharmaceuticals and its management. Now, after receiving hundreds of thousands of dollars in commissions from a recent stock offering by a subsidiary of the company, this opportunist has suddenly changed his tune, hatching a plot to take control of ICN at a critical time in the company's history.

When you receive Khan's proxy materials you will find they disclose troubling information about him and his past conduct as a short-term stock trader, and that they provide some of the strongest and most convincing reasons not to support him. Don't sign any materials from Khan. Our material will reach you shortly. We want you to understand exactly who Rafi Khan is and why we believe his actions will put the interests of public shareholders in jeopardy.

WE ARE COMMITTED TO MAXIMIZING THE VALUE OF YOUR SHARES

The board of directors and management of ICN Pharmaceuticals are unequivocally committed to maximizing the company's long-term value for all shareholders.

We look forward to the company's annual meeting on December 15, 1993, when we will provide you with a full update of our business activities and opportunities, including progress in our efforts to develop our patented drug ribavirin (Virazole) to treat chronic active hepatitis C.

In the meantime, if you have any questions about the solicitation process or need further assistance, please call our proxy solicitor, ***GEORGESON*** *& COMPANY INC.*, toll-free at 1-800-223-2064.

Thank you for your attention to this matter of grave concern for your investment.

THE BOARD OF DIRECTORS AND MANAGEMENT OF ICN PHARMACEUTICALS, INC.

The directors of ICN and the amount of ICN stock they beneficially own (including vested options) are: Norman Barker, Jr.,—1,000, Birch E. Bayh—400, Robert H. Finch—2,600, Adam Jerney—18,994, Weldon B. Jolley—112,500, Milan Panic—482,008, Roberts Smith—119,096, Richard W. Starr—22,500.

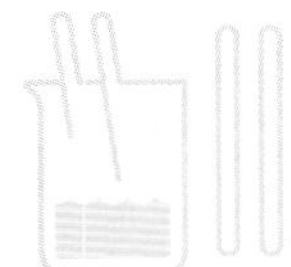

Milan Panic returns to ICN and faces a proxy fight for control of company.

ROLL-UP

ICN Shareholders, however, had a different take. The Yugoslav war had severely eroded shareholder confidence in management. Results were down, and so was shareholder value. Many complained that the companies market value should be increasing based on ribavirin's prospects for hepatitis C. And ICN's increasingly confusing structure didn't help. The holding company concept had run its course. Critics began to question whether ICN was truly executing arm's-length transactions among the subsidiaries. The parent company's debt and high interest costs were a drag on each spinout's profitability. ICN as a whole had become extremely expensive to operate.

Panic refused to give up on Eastern Europe. He asked for patience. But he could do something about simplifying ICN. Merging the subsidiaries and creating one entity again would lead to savings in annual reports, audit fees, insurance, directors, payroll admin, legal, taxes, and interest expense. Also, bankers promised that the simplification would enable a restructuring of the company's still expensive debt and provide $190 million of tax loss carryforwards. Annual interest expense would be shaved by $9 million. The restructuring would also reduce exposure to foreign translation

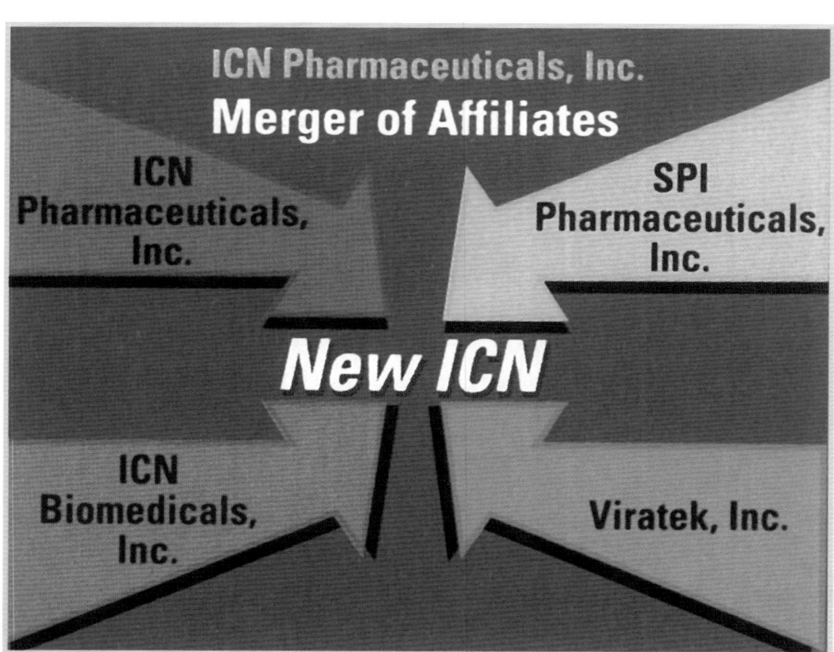

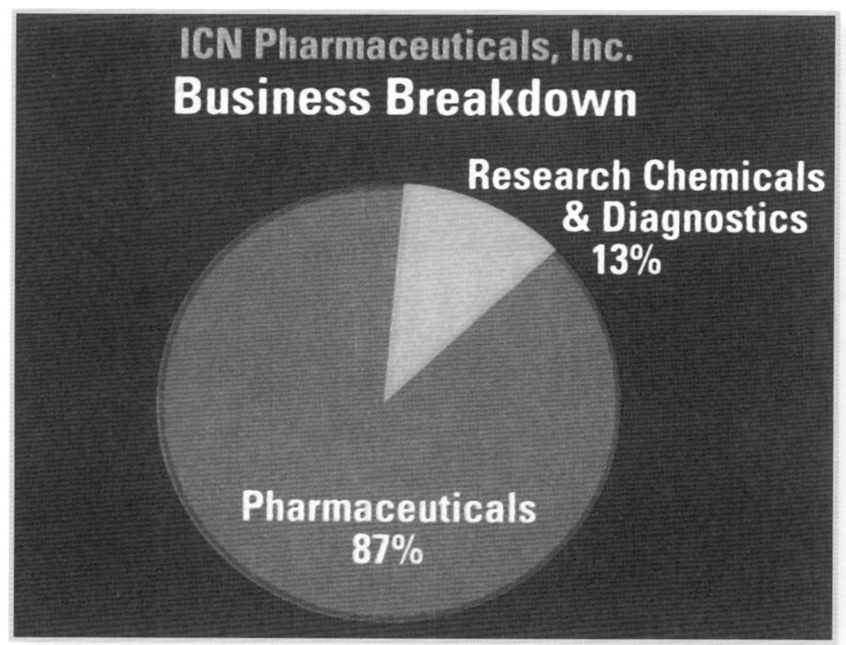

losses, which had caused considerable pain over the devaluations in Yugoslavia and the now too-frequent losses associated with the Swiss franc financings in the mid-'80s.

On November 1, 1994, the combination was consummated. SPI, Viratek, and Biomed merged back into ICN Pharmaceuticals, creating one publicly traded company again. The benefits were immediate. Reported net income that year was $37.4 million, or $1.62 per share. Panic's projections of $200 million in annual savings started to ring true. With a little luck coming from a resolution of the Balkan conflict and some good news from ribavirin, 1995 was shaping up to be a breakout year.

> 1995 was shaping up to be a breakout year.

Far left: ICN merger of affiliates

Middle: Business mix at time of combination

Right: Milan Panic explaining the roll-up

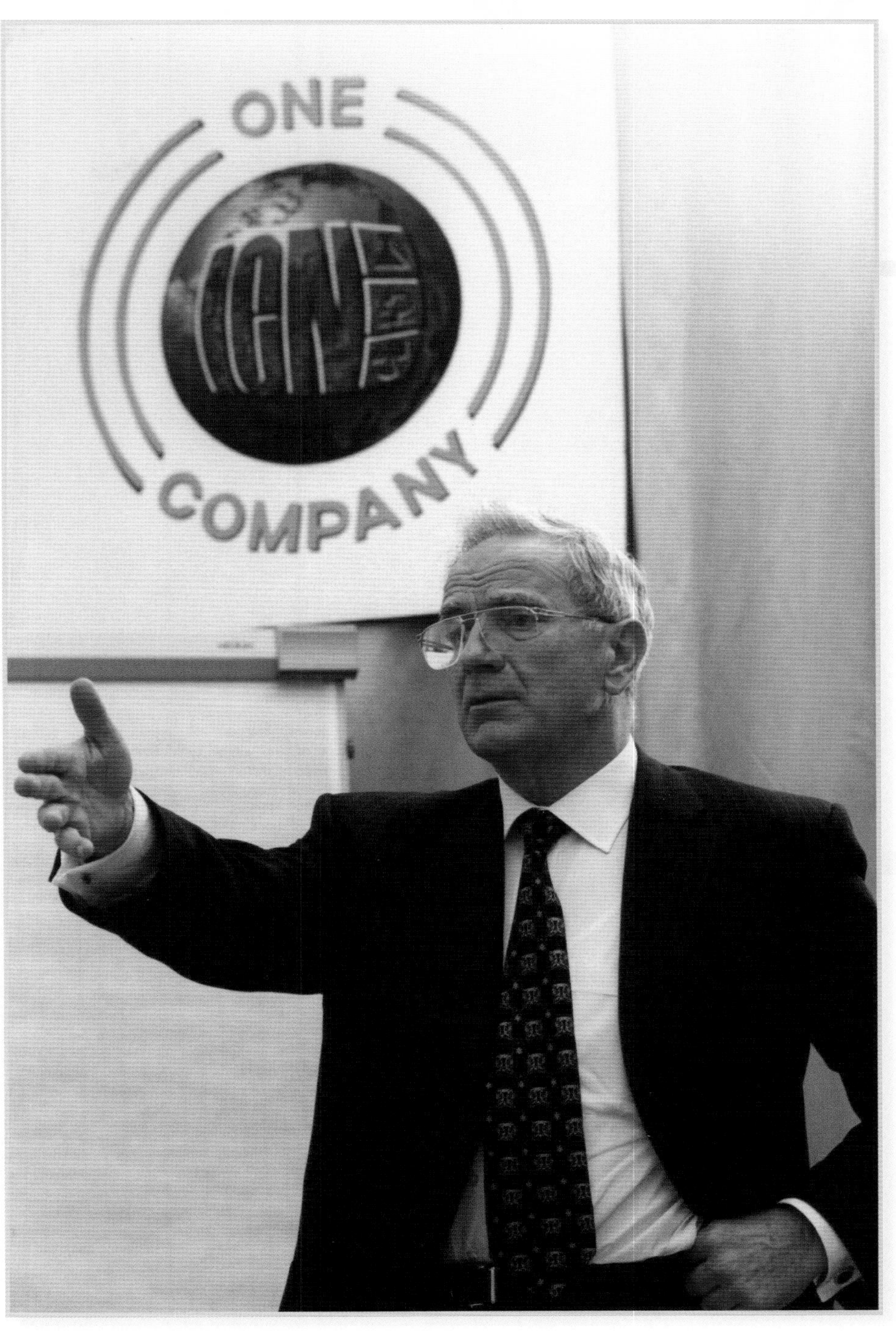

Bill MacDonald and Bob Smith

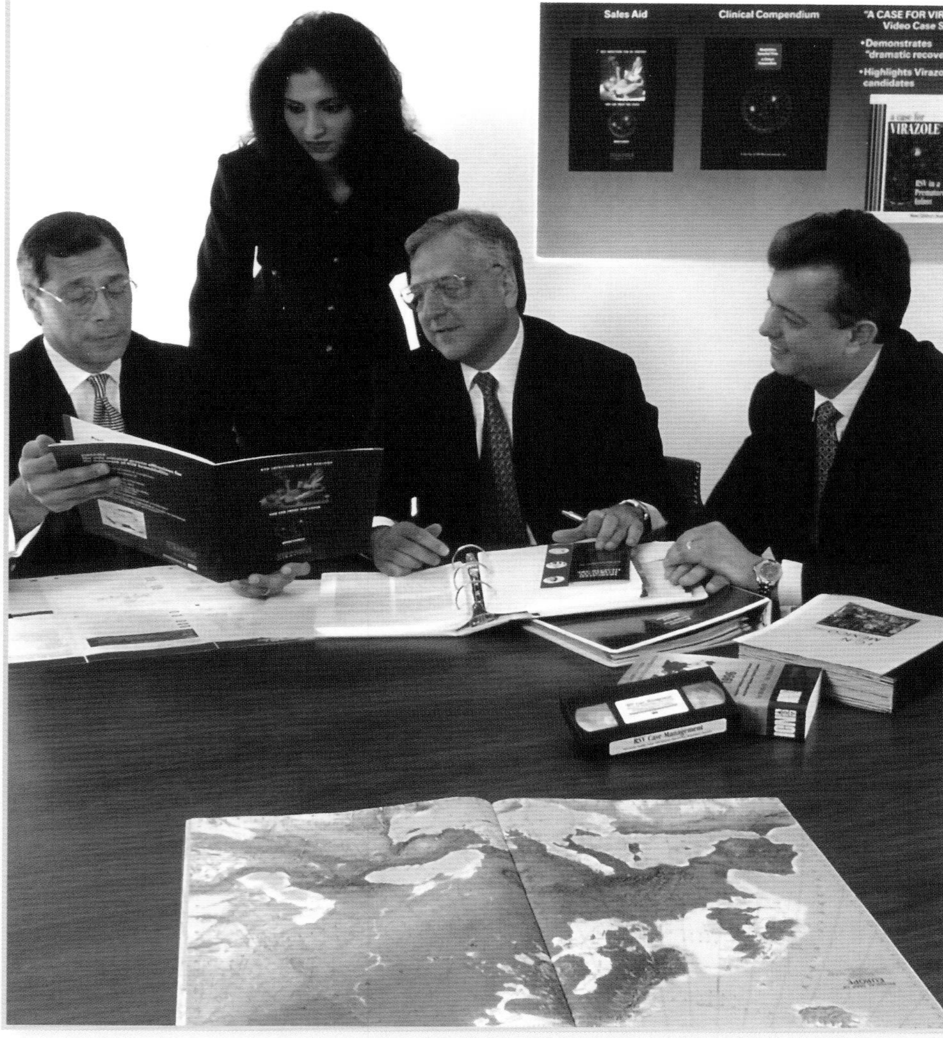

ICN executives planning for the HCV opportunity

SCHERING-PLOUGH

Schering-Plough started things moving. The drug giant licensed all oral forms of ribavirin for use in combination with alpha interferon exclusively for the treatment of HCV. ICN received an initial up-front payment of $23 million and future royalty payments on sales of the combination, including minimum royalty rates. Schering was granted exclusive marketing rights worldwide for hepatitis C, except in the EU, where ICN retained the right to co-market. In addition, Schering agreed to purchase up to $42 million in ICN stock upon the achievement of regulatory milestones.

Schering took over all regulatory and clinical development. It commenced two phase 3 trials in HCV patients who had relapsed after Intron A monotherapy. Subjects were randomized to receive subcutaneous injections of 3 million units of Intron A three times per week plus either oral ribavirin (1000–1,200 mg per day) or placebo. FDA approval was expected in 1998.

Hepatitis C had become an enormous opportunity. Twelve million people in the world's major markets were estimated to be infected, including four million in the United States. Approximately 2% of the world's population was at risk, and prevalence was growing. Shareholder enthusiasm began to rise again. ICN was finally on the verge of delivering the wonder drug it had long promised.

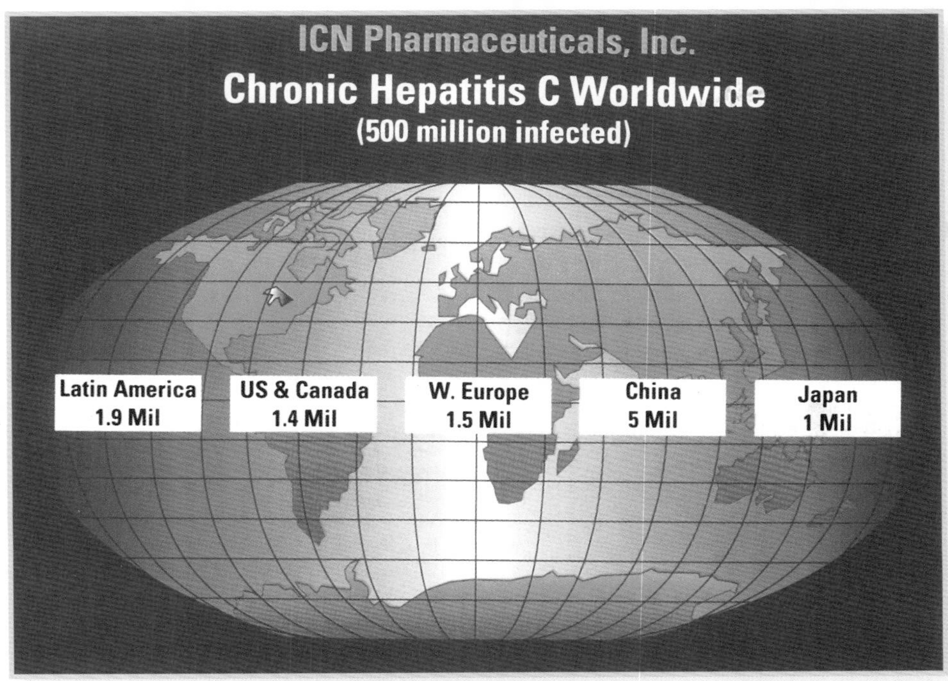

Chronic hepatitis C worldwide

July 1995—ICN grants Schering-Plough (SGP) exclusive license to all forms of oral ribavirin to treat HCV.

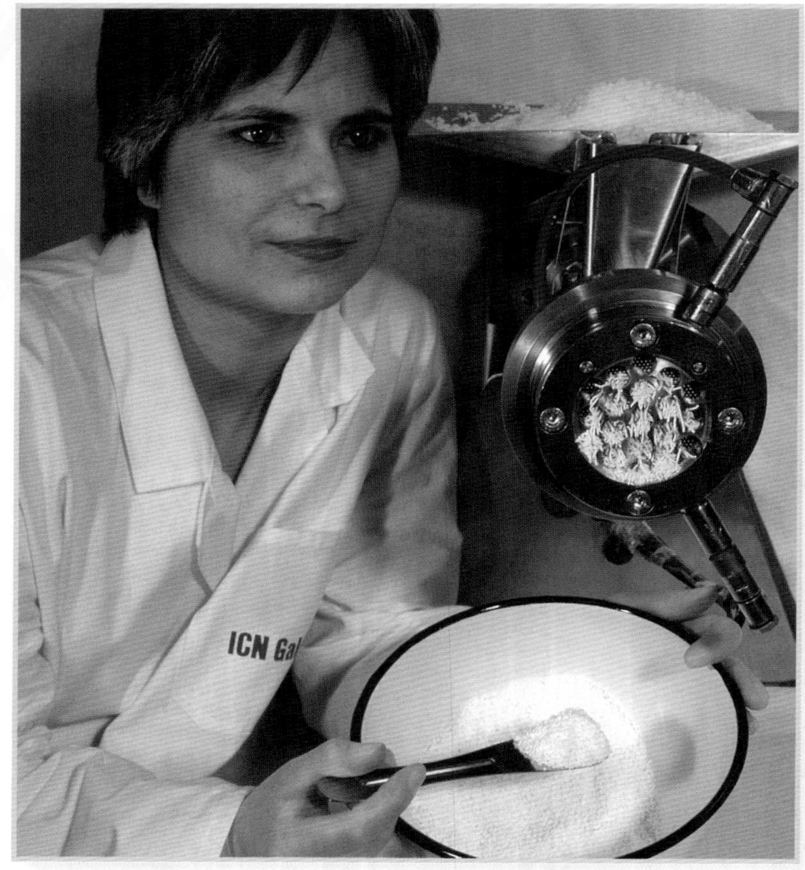

Above: ICN Galenika lab assistant

Below: ICN meeting

Milan and Sally Panic with President Bill Clinton

ONE-HALF BILLION!

The year 1995 turned out to be the single-most successful 12 months in ICN's then 35-year history. The company posted sales of $508 million, earnings of $67 million, and EPS of $2.20, up sharply from $366 million, $37 million, and $1.62 the year before. The company retired $50 million in debt, including the last of the high-yield 12.875% bonds. The Bosnian peace accords were signed, resulting in the suspension of sanctions. Galenika got back on track by launching 47 new products. ICN's share of the Yugoslav market increased to 50%, including 65% of the country's antibiotic market. Galenika also recaptured its export business, which ran as high as $46 million in the pre-sanction era. Galenika posted revenue of $235 million for 1995, up from $172 million in 1994.

The new ICN operated out of five units: North America, LATAM, Eastern Europe, Western Europe, and Asia, Australia, Africa (AAA). In North America, Virazole posted $50 million for RSV, bolstered by new guidelines from the American Academy of Pediatrics recommending its use. Dermatology sales grew, led by Oxsoralen for severe psoriasis in conjunction with ultraviolet light, and newly launched Glyquin, a combination of hydroquinone and glycolic acid for hyperpigmentation.

In Latin America, Bedoyecta had grown to $17 million per year. Sales in Canada benefited from the launch of Cesamet, an antinauseant associated with cancer chemotherapy acquired from Eli Lilly. Spain's Hubber launched the antiulcerant Nuclosina (omeprazole) and the antiosteoporosis compound Calcitonina. The biomedical business was significantly boosted by the acquisition of Siemen's dosimetry business, which added $10 million. Diagnostic sales increased, aided by ICN's purchase of Becton Dickinson's radioimmunoassay line.

1995 turned out to be the single-most successful year in ICN's then 35-year history.

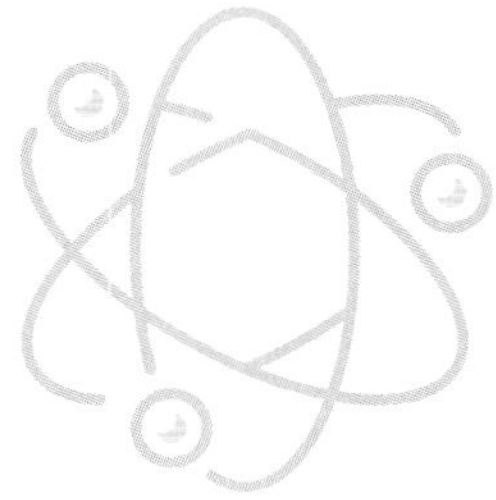

Marbiopharm deal

EASTERN EUROPE

Over the next three years, ICN experienced dramatic expansion. Sales rose from $367 million in 1994 to $614 million in 1997. Eastern Europe led the growth spurt. In 1996, this division contributed revenue of $355 million, compared to $255 million in 1995. The 39% gain resulted from Olic's aggressive acquisition program, beginning with Galenika in 1990. In Russia, the company acquired Leksredstva, adding $21 million, and Polypharm, adding $7.4 million. In Hungary, the company acquired Alkaloida, contributing $21 million. Sales at Oktyabr increased $18 million due to price and volume, and Yugoslavia recovered to $267 million based on a resumption of exports.

The Hungarian deal was especially noteworthy. Like Galenika and Oktyabr, ICN acquired a majority stake in a state-owned drug company, Alkaloida Chemical Company Ltd. ICN won the right in a competitive bidding process sponsored by the Hungarian government. ICN's initial holding was 50.02% but a few months later would increase to 75%. The Hungarian government retained 25%.

Based in northeast Hungary, Alkaloida manufactured and distributed pharmaceutical finished products and raw materials and consistently developed new products. Of the company's $66 million in annual sales, approximately 50% were derived from exports to the United States, Western Europe, Eastern Europe, and other regions. Alkaloida also exported to the former Soviet Union. Among its leading products were cardiovasculars, central nervous system compounds, antimalarials, antiasthmatics, and antiallergics. Alkaloida was also one of the largest producers of morphine and codeine derivatives. The company was fully GMP compliant and operated in an FDA-approved manufacturing unit. It employed 1,900 people, 162 in R&D.

In September 1996, ICN moved into China. It committed to invest $24 million in a joint venture with Jiangsu Provincial Wuxi Pharmaceutical Corporation (WUXI), a Chinese state-owned pharmaceutical company of which $3.6 million had been invested through June 30, 1997. China was considered the next frontier and the reason ICN added the AAA region to its family of operating divisions.

In October 1997, ICN acquired an 80% interest in Polfa Rzeszow S.A. (Polfa) from the government of Poland, a transaction connected to the government's privatization of the country's pharmaceutical industry. Polfa boasted one of the country's most modern production facilities.

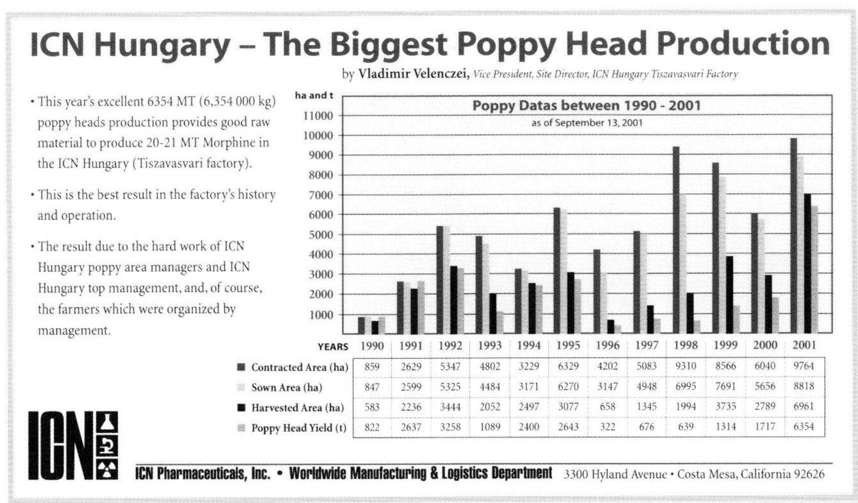

ICN Hungary – The Biggest Poppy Head Production

by **Vladimir Velenczei,** *Vice President, Site Director, ICN Hungary Tiszavasvari Factory*

- This year's excellent 6354 MT (6,354 000 kg) poppy heads production provides good raw material to produce 20-21 MT Morphine in the ICN Hungary (Tiszavasvari factory).
- This is the best result in the factory's history and operation.
- The result due to the hard work of ICN Hungary poppy area managers and ICN Hungary top management, and, of course, the farmers which were organized by management.

YEARS	1990	1991	1992	1993	1994	1995	1996	1997	1998	1999	2000	2001
Contracted Area (ha)	859	2629	5347	4802	3229	6329	4202	5083	9310	8566	6040	9764
Sown Area (ha)	847	2599	5325	4484	3171	6270	3147	4948	6995	7691	5656	8818
Harvested Area (ha)	583	2236	3444	2052	2497	3077	658	1345	1994	3735	2789	6961
Poppy Head Yield (t)	822	2637	3258	1089	2400	2643	322	676	639	1314	1717	6354

ICN Pharmaceuticals, Inc. • Worldwide Manufacturing & Logistics Department 3300 Hyland Avenue • Costa Mesa, California 92626

ICN Hungary—a global leader in morphine and derivatives

It produced and distributed a wide range of drugs from antidepressants, antifungals, and anti-infectives to pain relievers, allergy medications, cardiovascular drugs, and nutritionals.

Polfa was founded in 1950, employed 622 employees, and recorded 1997 sales of $41 million. More than 50% of output was exported to Central and Eastern Europe. ICN bought 80% of Polfa for $33.7 million.

During the Polfa tendering process, ICN competed against Hoechst and E. Merck, both willing to pay more. ICN won because it put forth a credible social package that included a minimum three-year employment guarantee for all workers and pledged capital investments of $20 million that included modernization of a new facility. Poland was a country that placed a high value on workers' rights. ICN also implemented incentive packages and bonuses, something new to Poles.

The Polfa acquisition further underscored ICN's dealmaking prowess in the region. Panic was key. His tenure as Yugoslav prime minister opened doors for the company at the highest levels of government in these countries. ICN became the partner of choice. The $33.7-million price tag for 80% of Polfa valued the company at $42 million, roughly one times sales. Companies in Western markets, and particularly the United States, fetched four to five times that multiple.

As the push into Russia continued, each new acquisition would add significant share and capacity. The purchase of shares in Leksredstva, privatized in 1992, afforded ICN an 88% stake. Located in Kursk, about 400 miles south of Moscow, Leksredstva was first to join with ICN production facilities Okytabr in St. Petersburg. Founded in 1969 as an API house, it sold 20 different finished forms of pharmaceutical products including those to treat hormone disorders, heart disease, cancer, and pain. The company also manufactured chemical and some cosmetic products at its 35,000-square-foot production facilities. Unit volume was 1.4 billion tablets annually. Company sales were $13 million in 1995 and $12 million for the first six months of 1996. Polfa employed 1,200

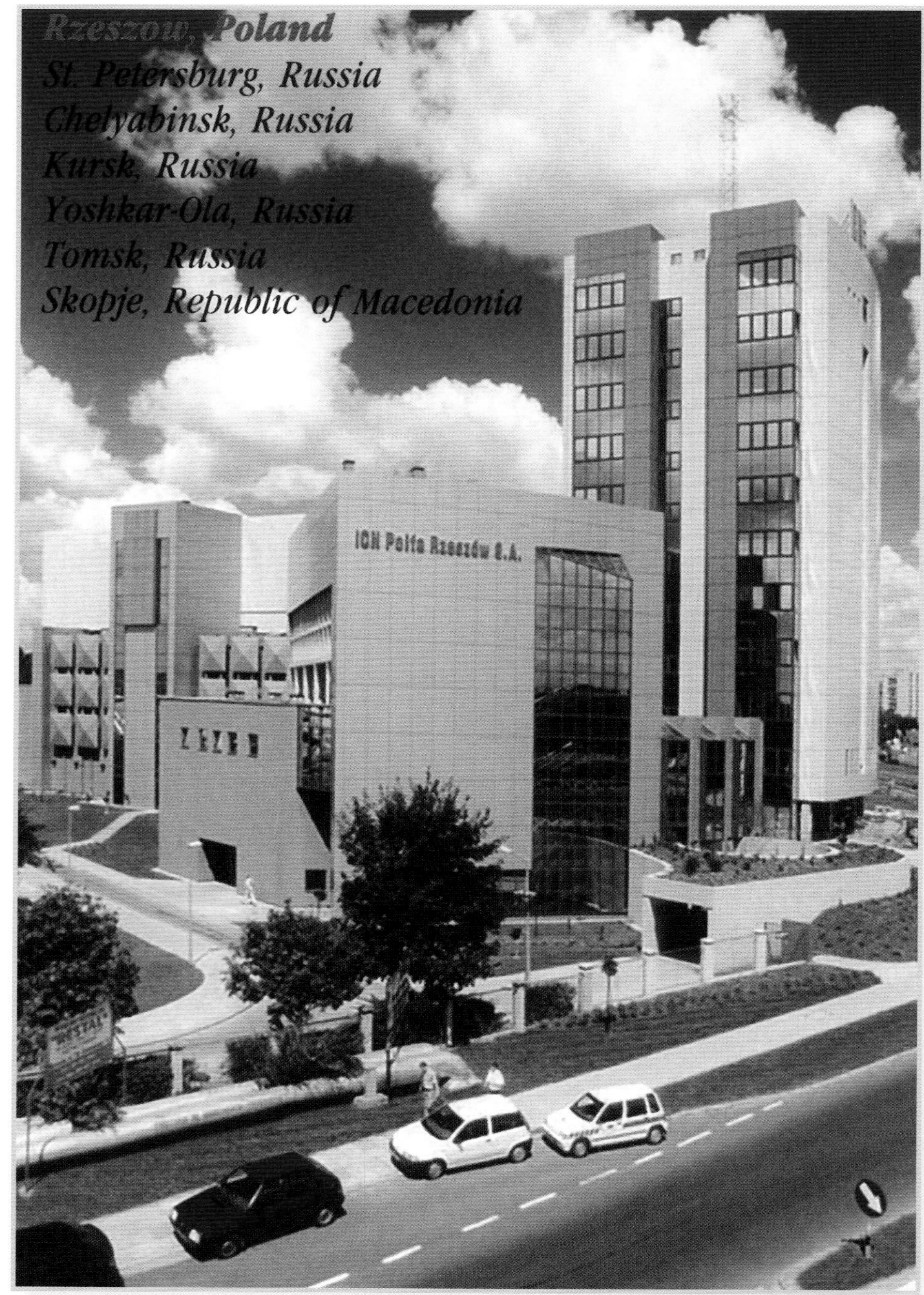

people. The company also had a JV with the German concern Fresenius to produce dialyzers used in kidney dialysis. The project, the first and only one of its kind in Russia, was expected to meet the majority of Russia's needs upon completion. Kursk was the site of the World War II battle of Kursk, the greatest tank battle in history, where on July 17, 1943, the Soviets successfully halted Hitler's Eastern Front campaign and prevented Germany from further invading the region.

Polypharm of Chelyabinsk, the third Russian company added, offered 50 different products. Located 1,000 miles east of Moscow, the company manufactured finished products in both ampoule and tablet forms, analgesics, antidepressants, tranquilizers, antibacterials, local anesthetics, vitamins, and calcium preparations. About 70% of its total production was sold through 400 distributors and wholesalers, while the remainder was sold directly to hospitals, pharmacies, and other entities. Polypharm had a 1.5% share of the domestic Russian market. Founded in 1920, Polypharm was owned by the Ministry of Health of Russia before being privatized in 1994. Sales in 1995 were $13 million, and it had 667 employees.

During 1997, ICN purchased two additional Russian companies, Marbiopharm in Yoshkar-Ola and the AO Tomsk Chemical Pharmaceutical Plant in Tomsk, Siberia. It also added a major distribution center in Moscow. Marbiopharm made and sold 74 products, posting $27 million in 1997. In October, ICN acquired a 75% interest in the AO Tomsk Chemical Pharmaceutical Plant, bringing to five the number of manufacturing facilities ICN owned in Russia. Tomsk, with 803 employees, was in Western Siberia and had a distribution network throughout Russia, as well as the Ukraine, Kazakhstan, and Uzbekistan. Tomsk sales were $37 million.

ICN Alkaloida

ICN managers in Russia

In January 1998, ICN opened its Russian headquarters in downtown Moscow, a 12-story, 100,000-square-foot building. Panic purchased it in November 1997 to support the company's expansion in Eastern and Central Europe. In September 1999, ICN acquired a chain of 88 retail pharmacies in Moscow and St. Petersburg, which represented the final phase of ICN's vertical integration of the country. With the purchase of the pharmacies, ICN operated five manufacturing facilities, four distribution centers, and 131 retail pharmacies in the country. One out of every three pills sold in Russia bore the ICN trademark.

To help provide guidance and insight into the management of the Russian and East European businesses, Andrei V. Kozyrev, former minister of foreign affairs of Russia, was elected to the board of directors. The Moscow team also benefited from the appointment of Sergei Gryzunov, former minister of press and information of Russia, and Michael Sapovsky, former first deputy of the minister of health of Russia.

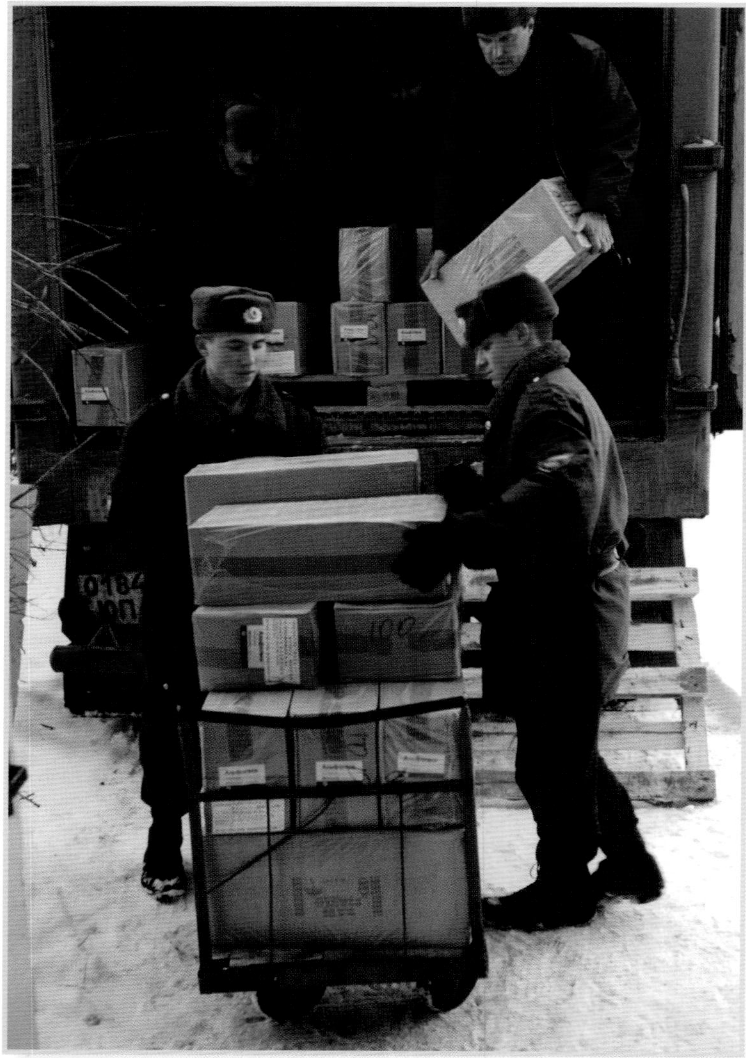

Left: Delivering products in Russia

Right and below: One out of every three pills in Russia was ICN

A CROWNING YEAR

The year 1997 was especially significant. Schering filed the ribavirin NDA for hepatitis C. Panic raised $275 million in a bond offering. Reported sales were $752 million, up 22% from $614 million in 1996. Net income was $114 million, up from $87 million. EPS was $1.69, up from $1.51. Eastern Europe sales reached $433 million, up $85 million from the prior year. ICN now had more than 15,744 employees. More than 90% of the business was pharmaceuticals, and 75% of sales were ex–United States. No single product dominated, and the portfolio had grown to more than 600 products worldwide. Analysts applauded the broad diversification, which distinguished ICN in an era when so many pharma companies dependent on a single blockbuster were being knocked off by generics.

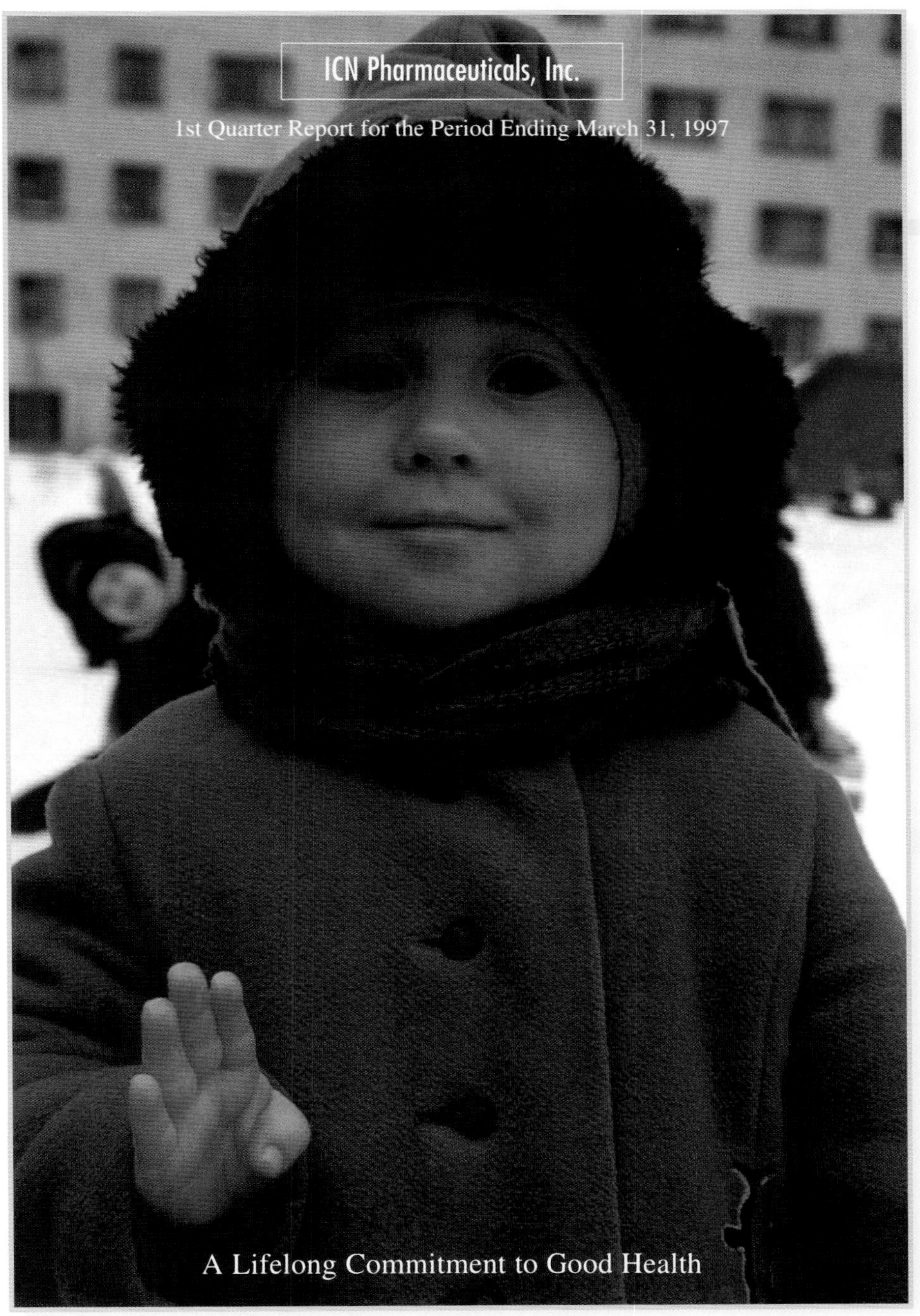

ICN Pharmaceuticals, Inc.
1st Quarter Report for the Period Ending March 31, 1997
A Lifelong Commitment to Good Health

ICN first-quarter report for the period ending March 31, 1997 showcases its growing commitment to the Russian people

The Efudex acquisition was a big boost to ICN's global dermatology portfolio.

ICN Puerto Rico Launches Efudex Cream

by **Frankie Santana,**
Vice President, Manufacturing, The Americas

Members of the various departments from the ***ICN PUERTO RICO*** *family share the moment of the first shipment of Efudex Cream out of their facility.*

Nearly 15 months ago, the first pieces of equipment for the manufacturing of Efudex Cream were received at ICN Puerto Rico. Immediately, Efudex took first priority within the many activities that were taking place at Humacao. The challenge was big. Efudex, an important product for ICN, was to be transferred to Puerto Rico in the shortest possible time frame. The fact that cream manufacturing was a new technology for the Humacao site represented even a greater challenge.

On September 18, 2001, the first Efudex shipment left Humacao towards ICN's distribution Center in Bryan, Ohio. The goal had been met! This accomplishment was the result of the effort and dedication of our groups in Puerto Rico and Costa Mesa.

The Efudex launch out of ICN PR has been a very positive learning experience for all of us. It will prepare us for even greater challenges ahead, and has placed ICN Puerto Rico closer to its vision of being a significant contributor to the ICN Corporation.

INSIDE HIGHLIGHTS

PRODUCT DEALS

ICN's acquisition program was not confined to just companies. The company had also proven itself to be a very adept acquirer of individual products. Some of its best deals had come from Roche. This continued into the late '90s. In June 1997, ICN acquired nine products from Roche for $90 million, adding sales of $52 million. A few months later, four more products were acquired from Roche, including Efudex, Librium, Levo-Dromoran, and Tensilon, all purchased for $89 million, adding another $25 million in sales. The third tranche came in 1998, a package of four drugs for $178 million generating $67 million in sales. In each deal, half of the purchase price was paid in newly structured Series C preferred shares that Roche agreed to hold for two years. In addition, ICN purchased from Roche a GMP manufacturing plant in Humacao, Puerto Rico, for $55 million. Humacao produced one of Roche's leading products, the immunosuppressant CellCept. ICN agreed to take over this manufacturing business under a long-term management contract.

The Efudex acquisition was a big boost to ICN's global dermatology portfolio. In the US, it was the leading topical for actinic keratosis; however, Roche had not promoted it for years. When ICN acquired the product, sales were $15 million. After two years of promotion by ICN's US 60-person dermatology sales force, sales grew to $50 million.

The US dermatology franchise became a star ICN division worldwide. In 1999, the US group licensed a novel photoaging cream called Kinerase that sold $10 million its first year. In March 1998, 32 dermatology products were acquired from Laboratoria Pablo Cassara in Argentina for $22 million in cash, adding $9 million. In July 2000, ICN added to its growing worldwide dermatology presence by acquiring the Swiss pharmaceutical firm Solco, based in Basel. That deal added $28 million.

In February 1998, the company acquired from SmithKline Beecham the Asian, Australian, and African rights to 39 prescription and OTC products for $45 million, consisting of cash and stock.

In Latin America, Javier Rovalo and his team had built a leading company, one of the best in Mexico. Annual sales exceeded more than $100 million. Vilona was a top antiviral, which would be advanced further by the hepatitis C opportunity. Bedoyecta was a market leading brand. Rovalo added the products in Argentina and in 1998 reunited with old Usafarma executive Carlos Picosse by acquiring his company, Pharmaway Industria Farmaceutica Limitada. Twenty years later, Panic was back in Brazil.

Former ICN executives Carlos Picosse and Antonio Cunha reunite with Milan Panic after Panic acquires Picosse's company Pharmaway Industria Farmaceutica Limitada

BLOCKBUSTER

In 1998, Schering-Plough won FDA approval for Rebetron to treat HCV relapsers. The clinical trial results showed that the Intron A and ribavirin combination resulted in a 10-fold increase in the number of patients with undetectable HCV levels compared to Intron A alone.

Rebetron's side-effect profile was excellent. The most common adverse events were flu-like symptoms, all of which resolved over time.

The product was packaged as a kit containing ribavirin capsules trademarked as Rebetol. Recommended dosing was 3 million units of SQ Intron A, three times a week, plus 1,000–1,200 mg of Rebetol twice daily.

Schering launched Rebetron in mid-'98, and the product realized rapid adoption, driven by its powerful clinical data. A few months later, the FDA approved the combination for first-line therapy.

Analysts estimated Rebetron would sell $960 million in 2000, including $685 million of Rebetol. The 25% royalty fee to ICN would yield $124 million, all pretax profit. Analysts projected that the four-year earnings gain to ICN from ribavirin may be as high as $0.08 in the first year, rising to more than $1.80 by year four. ICN stock shot up to $50 per share on the news.

In April 2001, the EU approved the combination of PEG-Intron (PEGylated interferon alpha), plus Rebetol, and in October 2001, Schering launched the Peg-Intron/Rebetol combo in the United States. It quickly became the standard of care, given its superior efficacy and improved dosing profile relative to Rebetron. In December 2001, Japan approved Rebetol and standard IFN. The Peg-Intron/Rebetol combination provided improved efficacy and dosing convenience (once weekly vs. three times weekly).

Schering launched Rebetron in mid-'98, and the product took off rapidly, driven by its powerful clinical data. A few months later, the FDA approved the combination for first-line therapy.

CARNEGIE HALL

In early 1998, ICN was flying high. Panic ordered the annual shareholders meeting be held at Carnegie Hall in New York City. It was celebration time. ICN's expanding budget reflected continued growth fueled by first-time royalties from Schering, the full-year contributions from new companies acquired in Poland and Russia, the products from Roche and SmithKline, and continued operating growth in North America, Western Europe, and Latin America. Also, ICN had just inked a distribution deal with Eli Lilly to sell its products in Russia.

ICN was on target to reach a billion in sales by 1999. Schering would buy $42 million of stock based on its obligations from the original license. ICN stock, trading around $45 per share, had more than tripled in 12 months. The market cap was $3.4 billion. Goldman Sacks and Salomon Smith Barney had issued buy recommendations. In 38 years, Panic's sponsorship from Wall Street had never been so good.

Ted Olic, Tom Stankovich, and Adam Jerney

The Moscow Times

SATURDAY, MARCH 26, 1994

SPI Takes Stake in Russian Pharmaceutical Giant

ICN's Milan Panic (flanked at left by aide Jack Scanlan, former U.S. ambassador to Yugoslavia) signing deal in St. Petersburg; mockup of stock certificate issued to Russian workers, and ICN toaster given as inducement to workers.

Anatomy of a Russian deal

ICN's Milan Panic and Jack Scanlon, former US ambassador to Yugoslavia, sign Oktyabr deal in Russia

Milan Panic and team visiting a company in Siberia

ICN managers going to Budapest

RUSSIAN CRISIS

But the euphoria was short-lived. Shareholders, basking in the glory of HCV, were suddenly hit with a financial collapse in Russia and a sharp devaluation of the ruble. ICN was exposed yet again. It had amassed an enormous portfolio of companies and products in that country. Russian sales exceeded $150 million, almost 20% of ICN's total business. The stock sold off, cutting over $1 billion in market cap.

Declining productivity, a high fixed exchange rate between the ruble and foreign currencies, and a chronic fiscal deficit sparked the crisis. The economic cost of the war in Chechnya also contributed. The Asian financial crisis, which lowered the demand for Russian oil, didn't help things either.

The inability of the government to deal effectively with its economic problems shook investor confidence and led to a run on the Central Bank. Investors sold their assets, which also put downward pressure on the ruble. This forced the Central Bank to use its foreign reserves to defend the currency, which in turn further eroded investor confidence. It was estimated that between October 1, 1997, and August 17, 1998, the Central Bank spent as much as $27 billion of its US dollar reserves to maintain the value of the ruble.

On August 17, 1998, Russia devalued the ruble, defaulted on domestic debt, and declared a moratorium on repayment of foreign debt. This created havoc in the debt and equity markets. Hyperinflation persisted, and confidence in the banking sector plummeted. By December 1999, the ruble had fallen from 6.3 to $1 to 27.5 to $1.

In 1999, ICN Russian sales fell to $92 million, a decrease of 44%. The declines in the ruble exchange rate forced the company to record translation losses of $6.7 million in 1998 and $53.8 million in 1999. As of December 31, 1999, ICN had a net monetary asset position of approximately $15.4 million, which exposed the company to further impairments. Shareholders were furious. Management's credibility was on the line again.

ICN had been through this before. The company's collections on accounts receivable were jeopardized. Before the ruble collapse, ICN Russia had a favorable experience with collections of accounts receivable from customers. But now, steps had to be taken to ensure creditworthiness and sharpen credit policies. Actions included shortening terms, suspending sales to companies with past-due balances, and instituting discounts on cash sales. The adoption of these more restrictive policies contributed to the decline of Russian sales.

Publicly, Panic went on the offensive again, but this time with Goldman Sacks at his side. He argued that the Russian market was too big and important for ICN to abandon. Instead, by digging in, ICN could gain while others lost. The company could seize market share. ICN had acquired five Russian plants for, on average, 20% of sales, or roughly 10% of the value of a US company with similiar revenue. These plants represented 20% of the domestic industry's unit volume and 7% of its dollar volume. As the crisis deepened and Russia's distributors went bankrupt, ICN could arguably acquire more distributors and ultimately control much of the country's pharmaceutical distribution network.

In the near term, Goldman predicted ICN Russia's sales would drop off dramatically in the first few quarters as demand dried up and the devaluation impacted the Russian economy. However, they argued that in time things would stabilize putting ICN back on a growth track by 2001. Goldman predicted revenue of $222 million in 2000, growing to $300 million by 2002. Moreover, they speculated that the company's margins may be more shielded than investors thought. ICN produced much of its own raw material in Russia and was already the country's low-cost manufacturer. As competitors fled, ICN could acquire and dominate share.

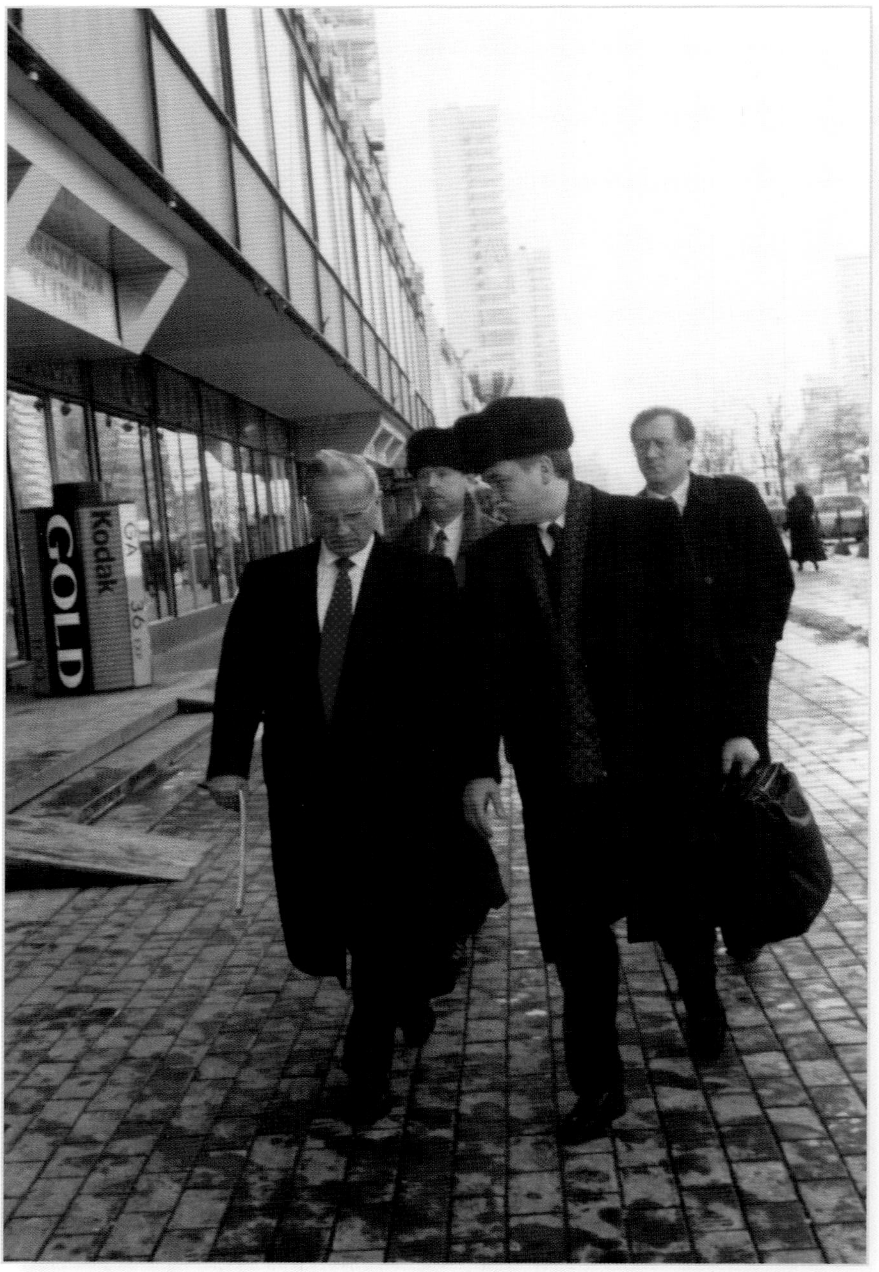

Above: ICN pharmacy

Right: Milan Panic and Sergey Gryzunov

The traditional photo-op concluding management meetings

Milan Panic Visits ICN's Yugoslav Plant After the Fall of Milosevic

Milan Panic greets ICN Yugoslavian employees

PLANT SEIZURE

Unfortunately, Russia wasn't the only issue on shareholders' minds. There was still Yugoslavia. One of the benefits of the Russian, Hungarian, and Polish expansion was reduced exposure to Yugoslavia, which again was threatening results with a new political and economic crisis. In April 1998, just before Panic's triumphant display at Carnegie Hall, the Yugoslav government devalued the dinar by 82% from 6 to \$1 to 11 to \$1. Milosevic was still in power and no friend of Milan Panic.

Even though the Dayton Accords in 1995 resulted in a lifting of sanctions, ICN continued its commitment to produce needed drugs for the people of Yugoslavia despite a deteriorating political and business environment. This required sales to the Yugoslav government, an increasingly hostile customer.

On July 15, 1998, the Yugoslav government defaulted on a \$39-million note receivable to ICN. The company was forced to record a noncash charge of \$173 million against its earnings for the quarter ending June 30, 1998. At this point, the government had ceased making all payments to ICN required under the original credit agreements.

Then in October, Milosevic struck harder. He transferred control of 25% of ICN Yugoslavia not owned by ICN from the holding company to government ownership. A few months later, he seized majority

control of ICN's Yugoslavian subsidiary, reducing ICN's ownership from 75% to 35%. The next day, Serbian police and paramilitary forces invaded ICN's subsidiary on the eve of the Kosovo peace talks in Rambouillet, France, and announced the appointment of a new government led management team.

On February 8, 1999, the US Department of State issued a statement condemning the takeover of ICN Yugoslavia, saying the Milosevic regime was attempting to avoid payment of more than \$175 million owed to ICN for medicines provided to the state health system. ICN workers rallied to protest the illegal takeover, and some were physically assaulted and jailed by Serbian police. But the damage was done. ICN Galenika was gone.

On October 9, 2000, Milosevic was overthrown. Within months, he was detained by Serbian police and transferred to The Hague to stand trial for war crimes. He would die in his cell a few years later.

REBOUND

The Yugoslavian and Russian setbacks cost ICN dearly. The company was forced to take charges of $441 million against earnings. The entire Yugoslavian operation was written off. The P&L hit was $352 million, or $4.78 per share.

In 1999, results rebounded. Product sales fell to $638 million versus $800 million, but royalties grew to $109 million versus $37 million. Net income recovered to $119 million versus a loss of $350 million, or $1.45 versus $4.78. Wall Street responded by buying $125 million of ICN's 8.75% senior notes due 2008, underwritten by Warburg Dillon Read and Schroder Bank. Russia returned to profitability in the third and fourth quarters.

Once again, all regions outside of Eastern Europe ran at record levels, up 23%. Anticipating the entry of Poland, Hungary, and the Czech Republic into the European Union, ICN transferred responsibility for those operations to Western Europe. Eastern Europe produced $9 million in operating income. ICN resumed its dominance in Russia. It had a well-known brand and a broad distribution network. By now, ICN owned and operated 131 pharmacies, mainly in Moscow and St. Petersburg. Of the 384 life essential products endorsed by the Russian government, ICN produced one-third of those in five production plants. Yugoslavia may have been lost for good, but Panic still had Russia.

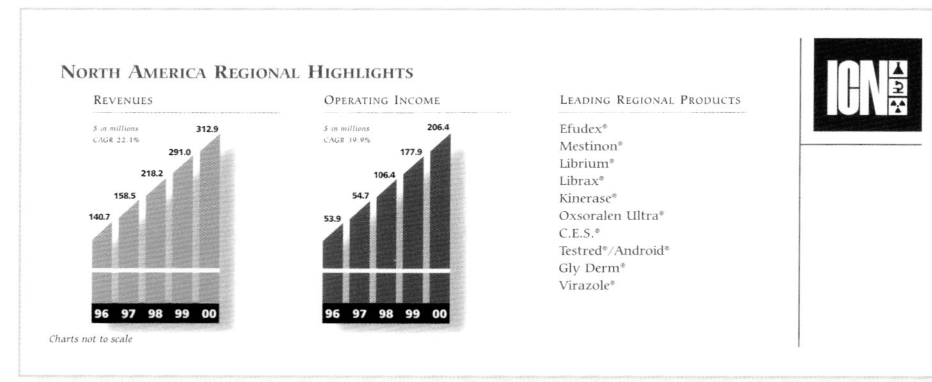

ICN North America regional highlights, 1996–2000

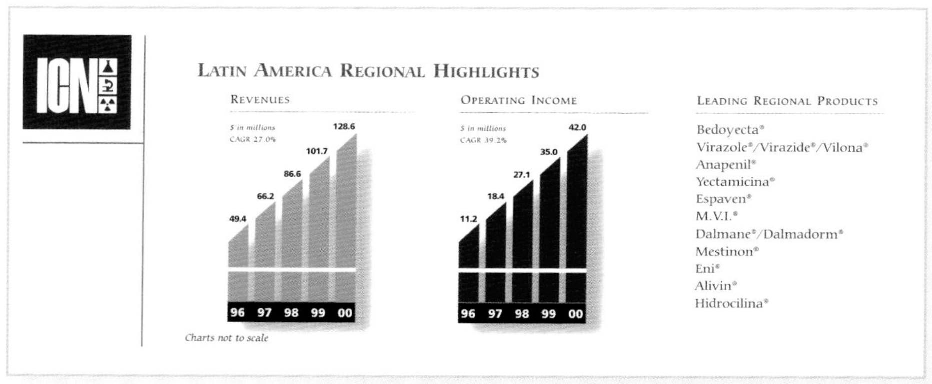

ICN Latin America regional highlights, 1996–2000

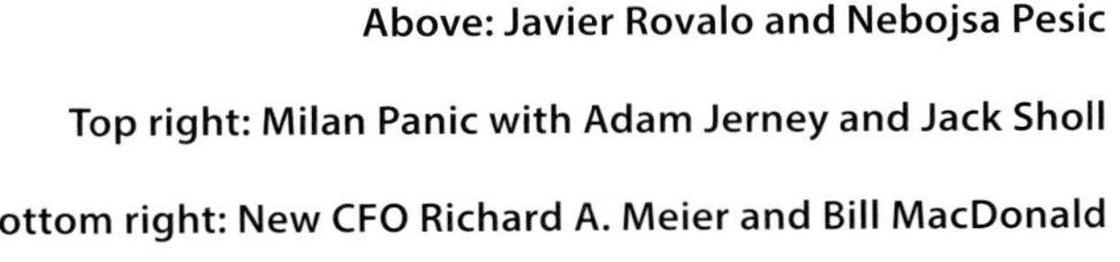

Above: Javier Rovalo and Nebojsa Pesic

Top right: Milan Panic with Adam Jerney and Jack Sholl

Bottom right: New CFO Richard A. Meier and Bill MacDonald

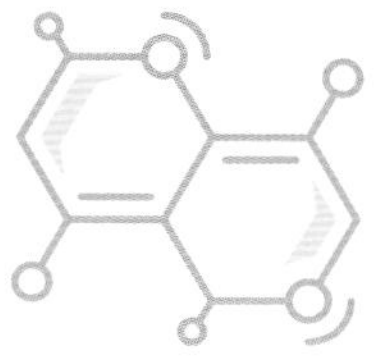

2001 five-year plan meeting

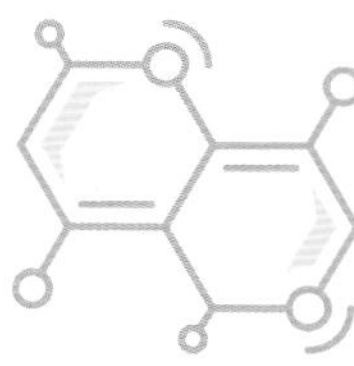

40 YEARS: AN ANTIVIRAL FRANCHISE

The year 2001 marked ICN's fortieth year in business. ICN had grown to more than 12,000 employees. The company operated in more than 100 countries, with plants in Barcelona, The Netherlands, Switzerland, Prague, Hungary, Poland, St. Petersburg, Chelabinsk, Kursk, Tomsk, Macedonia, Brazil, Mexico, Argentina, Canada, China, and the United States. Revenues had risen to $858 million, with operating income of $189 million. The company's market capitalization was $2.6 billion. Schering-Plough's sales of the Intron A/ribavirin combination exceeded $1.5 billion.

Shareholders demanded more. Analysts argued that ICN's hepatitis C royalty stream alone should justify the company's market cap. At a blended worldwide royalty rate of 25%, and ribavirin constituting 60% of total sales, royalty revenue should net $165 million, or $110 million after tax. At $21 per share, the stock was trading at only 12 times 2000 EPS estimates of $1.73 and 10 times estimated 2001 earnings of $2.15. This contrasted with a U.S. drug sector multiple of 42 and 39 times earnings, respectively. At a 20 multiple, critics argued ICN should trade at $35. That left no doubt that the company's continued exposure to the turbulence in Russia and Eastern Europe was the reason ICN was so undervalued. Something had to be done.

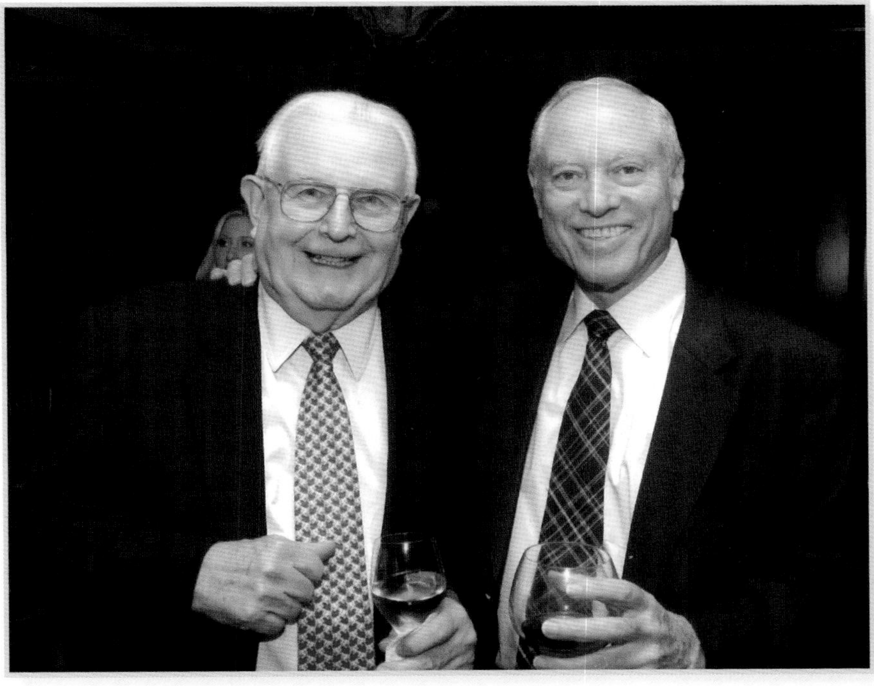

Bob Smith and Bernard Segal celebrate forty years in business

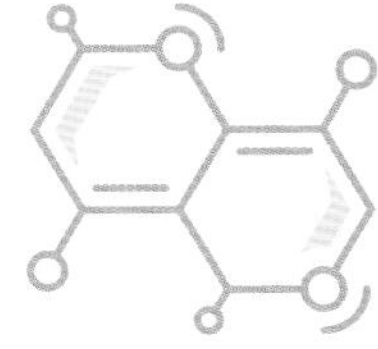

This is ICN...

Creating Value Through Performance

VALUE GROWTH INNOVATION

Financial Growth

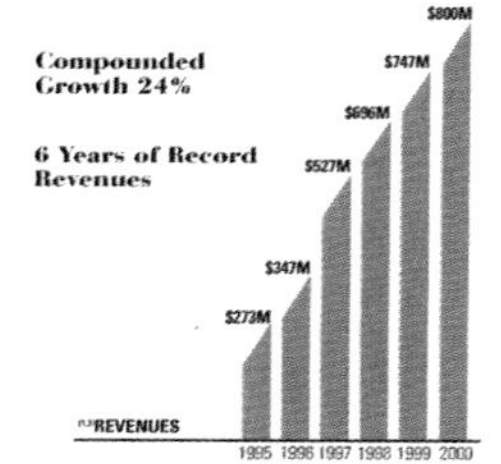

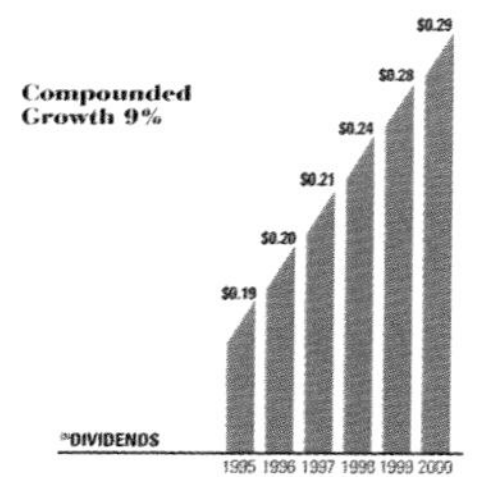

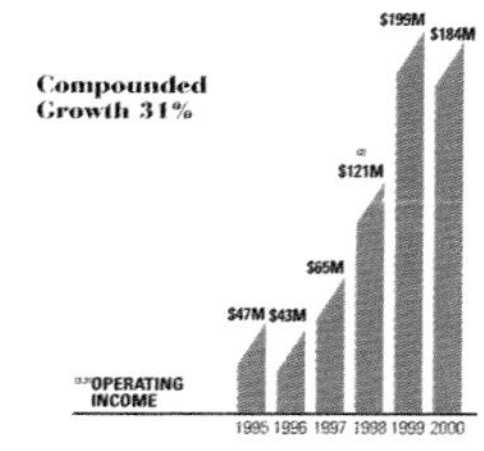

[1]Excludes Yugoslavia.

[2]Excludes Eastern European charges, including losses incurred in Yugoslavia in the second quarter of 1998, losses incurred in the third quarter of 1998, related to the Russian economic crisis, and the write-off of ICN Yugoslavia.

[3]Charts not to scale.

Proven Leadership

- **Record Performance:** Record 2000 revenues of $800 million...Another record year
- **Enhanced R&D:** Increased investment more than twofold for accelerated drug discovery
- **Increasing Royalty Stream:** 2000 Ribavirin royalties grew 42% to $155 million
- **New Hepatitis C Treatment:** EU and US approval of Rebetol® and Pegintron™ combination therapy for chronic hepatitis C
- **Restructuring Going Forward:** Significant progress in restructuring to enhance shareholder value
- **$525 million raised in convertible debenture**

Understanding Ribavirin's role in the Hepatitis C Therapies:

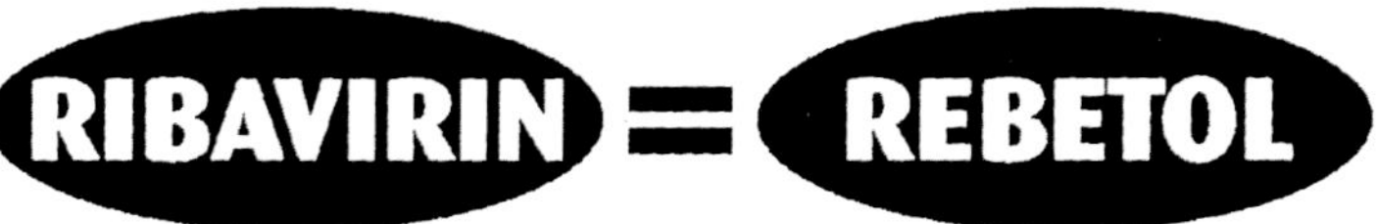

Ribavirin is marketed as Rebetol by Schering-Plough Corporation

Hepatitis C Combination Therapy

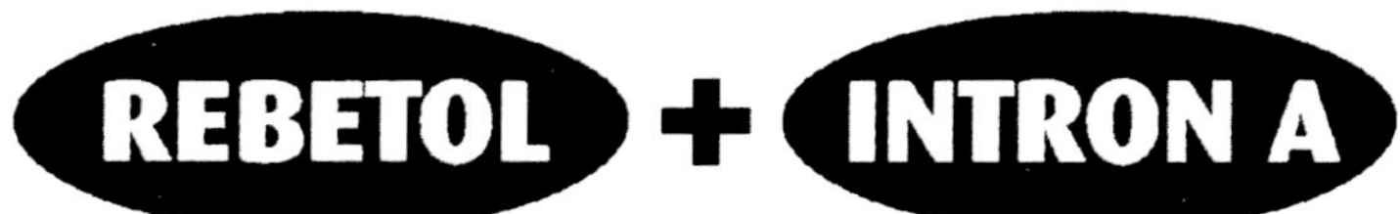

Rebetol and Intron A is marketed as Rebetron by Schering-Plough Corporation and was first approved in 1998.

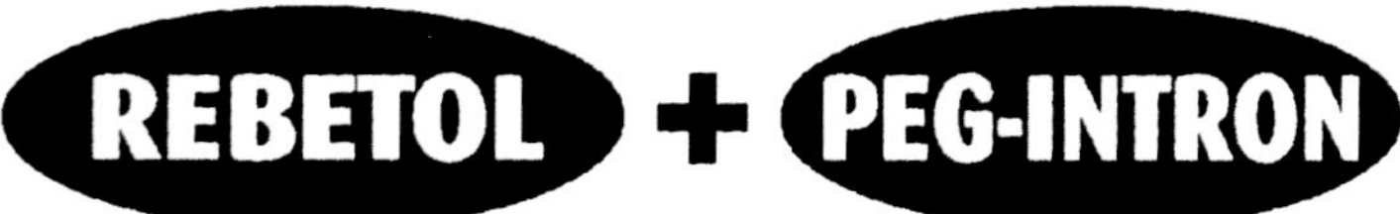

Rebetol and Peg-Intron is the new improved therapy, approved in 2001.

RIBAPHARM

Activist shareholders intesified their thesis that ICN would never reach its true value if it retained a substantial amount of its operating business in politically challenged countries. They urged the board to consider splitting the company into parts. UBS Warburg recommended that ICN spin off the ribavirin royalties and related antiviral assets into a separate company called Ribapharm. Bankers predicted that under the right market conditions such a spin-out could increase total capitalization by $1 billion. On June 15, 2000, ICN announced the plan. It would take public a new entity known as Ribapharm that would hold ICN's ribavirin and related antiviral assets. Ribapharm would be a biotechnology company and attract investors interested in a pure play in ribavirin and other promising antiviral compounds.

Ribapharm quickly took shape. ICN transferred the Schering-Plough royalties, the chemical compounds in the library, and the personnel and laboratory equipment at ICN Plaza in return for stock. The development pipeline contained two analogues of ribavirin, levovirin and viramidine, which had similar antiviral activity to ribavirin but lower anemia side effects.

Ribapharm common stock offering

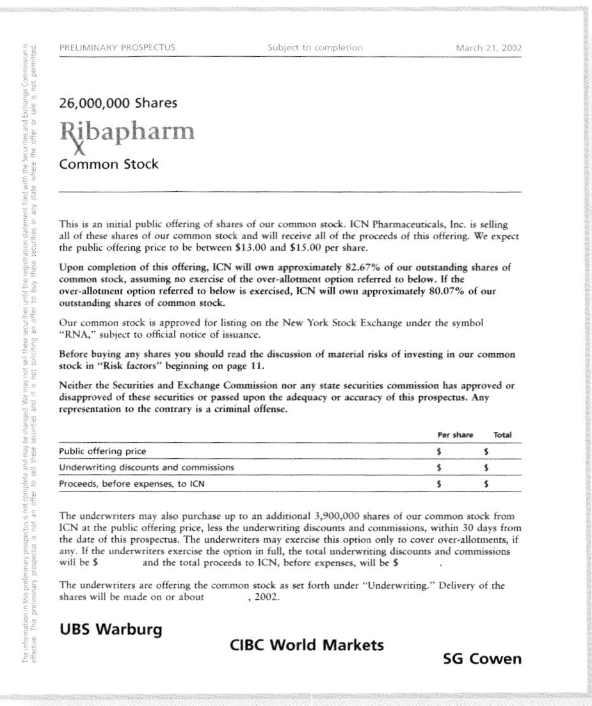

PRELIMINARY PROSPECTUS Subject to completion March 21, 2002

26,000,000 Shares

Ribapharm

Common Stock

This is an initial public offering of shares of our common stock. ICN Pharmaceuticals, Inc. is selling all of these shares of our common stock and will receive all of the proceeds of this offering. We expect the public offering price to be between $13.00 and $15.00 per share.

Upon completion of this offering, ICN will own approximately 82.67% of our outstanding shares of common stock, assuming no exercise of the over-allotment option referred to below. If the over-allotment option referred to below is exercised, ICN will own approximately 80.07% of our outstanding shares of common stock.

Our common stock is approved for listing on the New York Stock Exchange under the symbol "RNA," subject to official notice of issuance.

Before buying any shares you should read the discussion of material risks of investing in our common stock in "Risk factors" beginning on page 11.

Neither the Securities and Exchange Commission nor any state securities commission has approved or disapproved of these securities or passed upon the adequacy or accuracy of this prospectus. Any representation to the contrary is a criminal offense.

	Per share	Total
Public offering price	$	$
Underwriting discounts and commissions	$	$
Proceeds, before expenses, to ICN	$	$

The underwriters may also purchase up to an additional 3,900,000 shares of our common stock from ICN at the public offering price, less the underwriting discounts and commissions, within 30 days from the date of this prospectus. The underwriters may exercise this option only to cover over-allotments, if any. If the underwriters exercise the option in full, the total underwriting discounts and commissions will be $ and the total proceeds to ICN, before expenses, will be $.

The underwriters are offering the common stock as set forth under "Underwriting." Delivery of the shares will be made on or about , 2002.

UBS Warburg **CIBC World Markets** **SG Cowen**

The information in this preliminary prospectus is not complete and may be changed. We may not sell these securities until the registration statement filed with the Securities and Exchange Commission is effective. This preliminary prospectus is not an offer to sell these securities and it is not soliciting an offer to buy these securities in any state where the offer or sale is not permitted.

UBS agreed to serve as lead underwriter. In December 2001, bankers estimated to the board that Ribapharm's IPO value could reach $2.25 billon. UBS set the initial price range at between $13 and $15 per share.

In the late afternoon of April 11, 2002, the day before the IPO was scheduled to take place, UBS informed the board that due to market conditions and a sudden drop in the biotechnology index, the IPO would net only $10 per share, or $1.5 billion. The Dow had declined 200 points that day. The board decided to proceed anyway. The IPO went forward and was successful, raising more than $300 million in cash. Ribapharm stock increased in the aftermarket, despite unfavorable conditions. It would be the second-largest biotechnology IPO ever.

ICN executive team, 2002

Right: Ribapharm laboratory

Bottom left: Milan Panic and Ribapharm counsel Roger Loomis

Bottom right: Milan Panic discussing Ribapharm spin-off

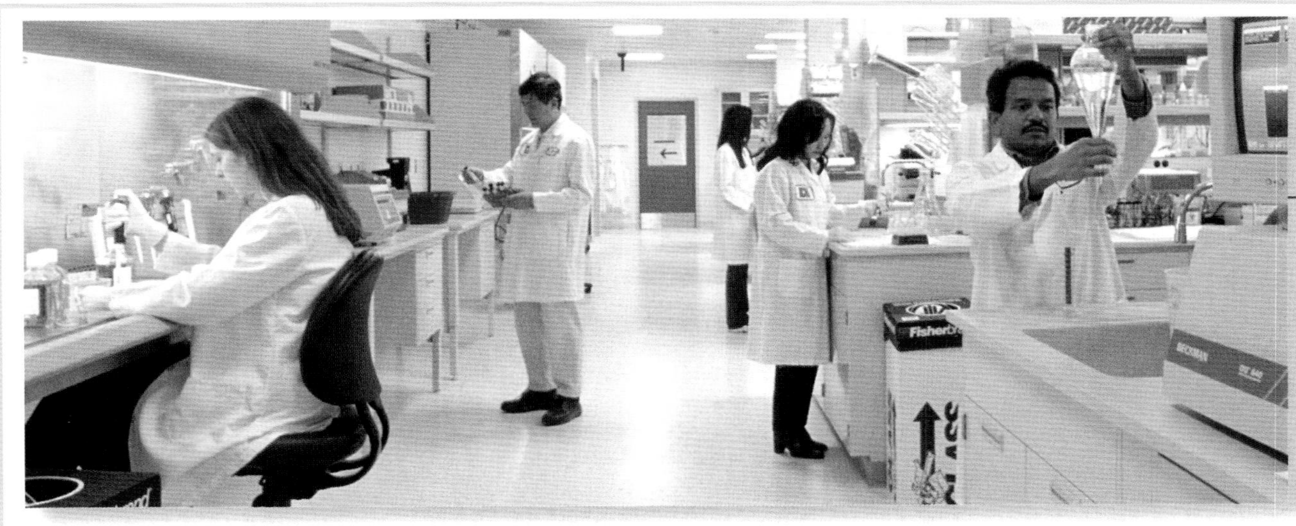

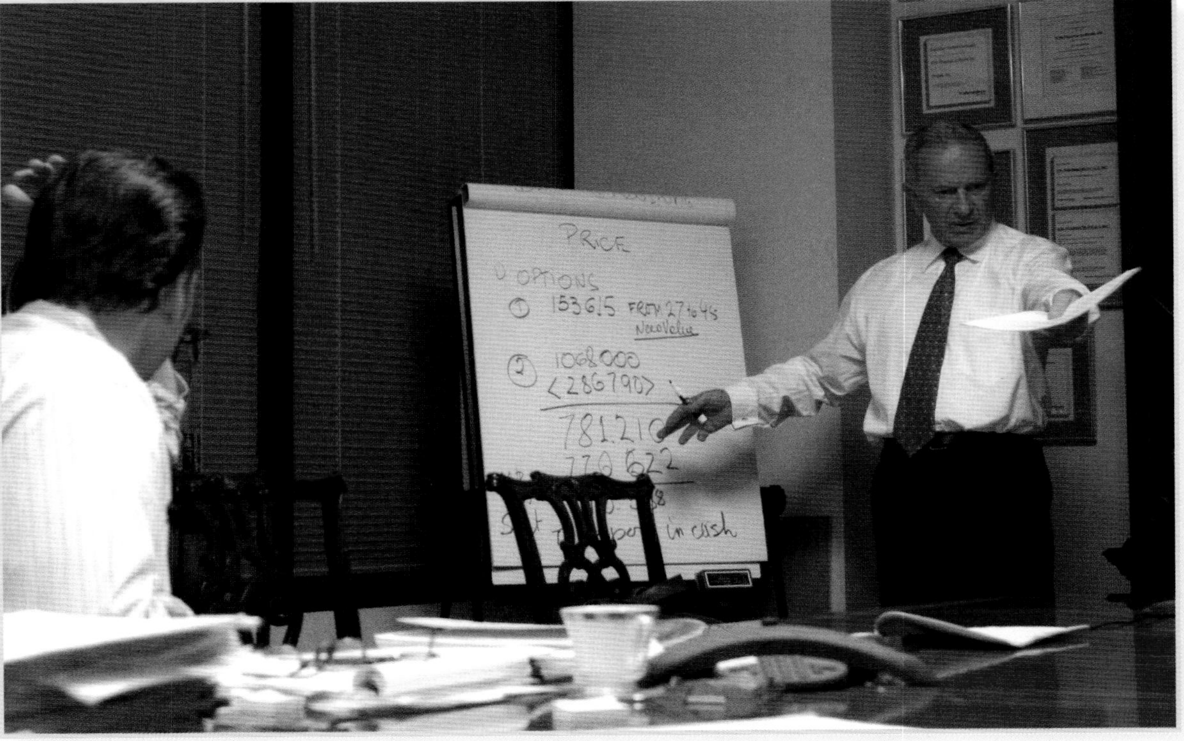

In June of 2002, a few months after Ribapharm went public, Milan Panic was forced to retire from ICN at the age of 72. He had been at the company's helm for 42 years, making him one of the longest-reigning founders/CEOs of a New York Stock Exchange pharmaceutical company.

And so ended the public company career of one of the industry's few remaining icons. Panic was an entrepreneur whose dealmaking became legendary. In retrospect, it was the man's entire body of work and specifically his achievements with ribavirin that should cement his legacy. A social, business, and political maestro, he set a bar for resilience, innovation, persistence, courage, and leadership that inspired many people. His company's drug saved lives. And to the rest of us, lucky to have some time with him, he was the ultimate boss, the true Warrior CEO!

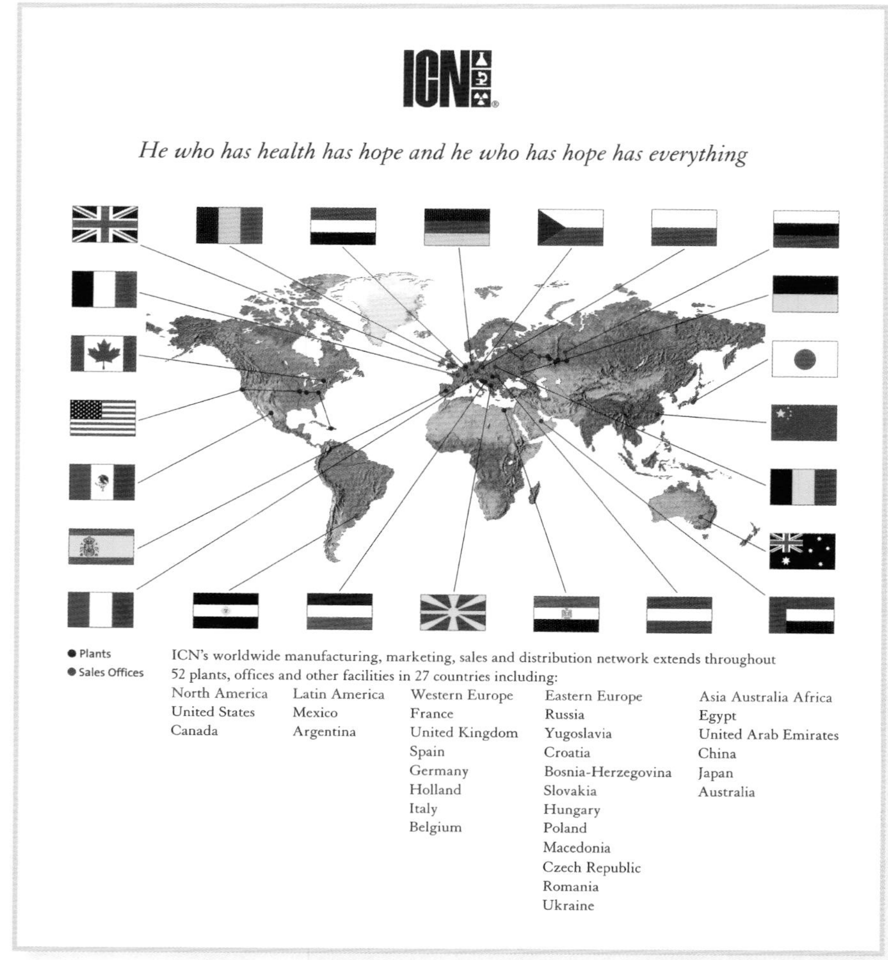

ICN
He who has health has hope and he who has hope has everything
Plants
Sales Offices
ICN's worldwide manufacturing, marketing, sales and distribution network extends throughout 52 plants, offices and other facilities in 27 countries including:
North America
United States
Canada
Latin America
Mexico
Argentina
Western Europe
France
United Kingdom
Spain
Germany
Holland
Italy
Belgium
Eastern Europe
Russia
Yugoslavia
Croatia
Bosnia-Herzegovina
Slovakia
Hungary
Poland
Macedonia
Czech Republic
Romania
Ukraine
Asia Australia Africa
Egypt
United Arab Emirates
China
Japan
Australia

ICN worldwide

In 2002 Ribavirin royalties reach $270M.
ICN becomes the forty-ninth-largest pharmaceutical company in the world.

Milan Panic and UBS banker Ben Lorello visit an ICN pharmacy in Russia

Milan Panic served at the helm of ICN for 42 years, making him one of the longest-reigning founder/CEOs of a NYSE pharmaceutical company.

In 2003 ICN sold its original biomedical business to Milan Panic for $15 million. He ran the company as MP Biomedicals for 13 years. In 2016 Panic sold the company to Valient Limited of the People's Republic of China for $150 million. He was 86 years old.

Alberto Velasquez of ICN Spain with Milan and Sally Panic in Madrid, early ‘70s

Milan Panic and Mark Taylor

MARK TAYLOR served as executive vice president of ICN during 2000–2002. He is currently cofounder and CEO of Hallux Inc., a drug developer based in Laguna Hills, California. Mr. Taylor's experience in the pharmaceutical industry spans three decades. In addition to several terms at ICN and related companies SPI and Viratek, Mr. Taylor held leadership roles at Obagi Medical and Watson Laboratories. During the period 2003–2008, Mr. Taylor was an institutional sell-side analyst covering more than 25 specialty pharmaceutical and medical device companies. Mr. Taylor resides in Newport Coast, California, with Gina, his wife of 30 years. He has three daughters who live in Seattle, Hollywood, and New York City.